Lanzarote
& Fuerteventura

DIRECTIONS

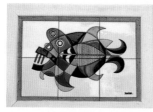

WRITTEN AND RESEARCHED BY

Emma Gregg

ROUGH
GUIDES

NEW YORK • LONDON • DELHI

www.roughguides.com

Contents

Introduction to

Lanzarote
& Fuerteventura

Ruggedly volcanic, Lanzarote and its larger southern neighbour, Fuerteventura, are blessed with a wonderfully warm climate, superb beaches and beautiful coastlines offering world-class conditions for watersports, making them a big hit with Spanish, British and German sunseekers of all ages.

▲ Caleta del Mojon Blanco

The eastern Canary Islands have been settled for centuries, but little is known of their earliest inhabitants, the pastoral Guanches, known locally as *Majos* (or *Mahos*). Lanzarote was first brought to European attention in 1312, by Lanceletto Malocello, a Genoese seafarer; ninety years later, Juan de Béthancourt, a

▼ Punta del Papagayo

Norman adventurer, claimed it – along with neighbouring Fuerteventura – for Castile, and the local rulers chose to co-operate. Béthancourt's promise of protection rang hollow, however; their strategic position in the North African Atlantic made the islands a target for Algerian, French and British pirates, who regularly raided them throughout the fifteenth and sixteenth centuries. From 1730 to 1736, and again in 1824, life on Lanzarote was torn apart by violence of a different sort when a series of cataclysmic volcanic eruptions transformed a tract of fertile terrain into the Timanfaya massif. No lives were lost, but livelihoods were irrevocably changed. Tourism, though, has turned the island's fortunes around: a Spanish territory since 1812, Lanzarote has been a busy holiday destination since the advent of affordable air travel in the 1960s.

When to visit

With over 300 days of sunshine a year, and daytime temperatures rarely wavering beyond 24°C, Lanzarote and Fuerteventura are year-round travel destinations; indeed, Lanzarote has the steadiest climate of all the Canary Islands. The **best times to visit** are March to June, when the bright, fresh days will suit the actively inclined, and September to October, when the sea is at its warmest. The busiest times coincide with school holidays: Easter, Christmas and New Year, and the summer months of July and August.

Both islands are well-established winter-sun holiday hotspots, with visitors from the UK, Germany and Spain spending weeks or even months here when the weather's cold back home. In the northern European **winter** months (Dec–Feb), the nights can be chilly and unheated swimming pools too cold for all but the very brave, but the days tend to be mild and, more often than not, sunny; even in the wettest months (Dec and Jan), Lanzarote and Fuerteventura receive less than half as much rain as London. The islands are particularly lovely in **spring** (March–June): after the winter rains, a subtle green fuzz of fresh growth covers otherwise barren-looking slopes and plains and even the *malpaís* bursts into bloom. The dry **summer** months of July and August are too hot for some – when there's a hot, dusty *calima* blowing across from the Sahara, the temperature can rise above 35°C, though, on the coast at least, there's nearly always a cooling sea breeze. **Autumn** (Sep–Nov) brings clear, mild days.

Despite several decades of full-on mass-market tourism, much of **Lanzarote** remains unspoilt. Its well-planned beach resorts are almost all low-rise, built in a style that echoes the character of its traditional rural villages, where immaculate whitewashed cottages and villas sit in Zen-like gravel gardens dotted with geraniums and cacti. The natural environment, too, is extremely well maintained – so much so that UNESCO has designated the whole island a Biosphere Reserve. This remarkable achievement is largely down to the vision of one man, the celebrated Lanzarotean artist César Manrique. An influential champion of low-impact tourism and eco-friendliness – he founded many of the island's museums and cultural centres – Manrique advocated preserving Lanzarote's culture and architectural integrity by limiting development and using local materials wherever possible. Manrique's fascinating architectural and artistic installations are essential stops on any tour of Lanzarote – the island is just 60km long and 20km wide, and easy to explore

▼ *Hotel Princesa Yaiza*, Playa Blanca

◄ Bodega La Geria, La Geria

– as are natural attractions such as geometric vineyards, secluded coves and the dramatic, black and russet volcanic landscapes.

▲ The café-bar at the Mirador del Río

Aware that they have much more to offer than sun-and-fun beach holidays, both islands are evolving rapidly. Lanzarote, in particular, is beginning to appeal to a new breed of visitor, attracted either by its swish marinas and golf courses or its flourishing rural-tourism movement, which offers a growing number of charmingly rustic and off-the-beaten-track gourmet restaurants, *bodegas* and places to stay, many in beautifully converted old cottages, village *fincas* and even caves.

While **Fuerteventura** doesn't share Lanzarote's distinctively tidy and attractive aesthetic, its best beaches outclass those of its northern neighbour, and it's a favourite destination for windsurfers and kiteboarders. Visiting Fuerteventura from Lanzarote is convenient and straightforward – it's just a twenty-minute ferry hop away from Playa Blanca in the south.

▲ Pájara, Fuerteventura

Lanzarote & Fuerteventura
AT A GLANCE

ARRECIFE

Lanzarote's capital, Arrecife, is a working city. Low-key and low-rise, it's an excellent place to get a feel for the Canary Islands' distinctive brand of contemporary urban living. It also has Lanzarote's highest concentration of quality restaurants and enjoyably brash, untouristy nightclubs and bars.

THE COASTAL RESORTS

Lanzarote and Fuerteventura's eastern and southern coasts are thinly scattered with relaxed, family-friendly beach resorts aimed at holidaymakers on package tours. The good-natured resort town of **Puerto del Carmen**, 10km south-west of Arrecife's airport, is where tourism began in Lanzarote, and

it's still popular for its abundance of unpretentious places to eat and drink. Further up the coast, the purpose-built holiday resort of **Costa Teguise** is set on a bay that's perfect for windsurfing, while fast-expanding **Playa Blanca**, in the south of the island, is arguably Lanzarote's nicest resort – it has a fantastic choice of accommodation, and the lovely sandy coves of Punta del Papagayo aren't too far away. **Corralejo**, a resort town set on the edge of beautiful, protected duneland on Fuerteventura's north-eastern coast, makes an easy day-trip from Playa Blanca. With a few more days, you could head south to explore the spectacular beaches of the **Peninsula de Jandía** – excellent for swimming, sunbathing and watersports.

Playa Dorada, Playa Blanca

TEGUISE

Up until the mid-nineteenth century this elegant inland town was Lanzarote's capital, and many fine old mansions still grace its streets. Famous for its hugely popular tourist market – held every Sunday morning – it also has a great selection of wine bars and offbeat craft and clothing shops.

▲ Volcano on the Ruta de Tremesana

by the knowledge that these volcanoes are far from extinct.

RURAL LANZAROTE

Away from the capital and the main resorts, you'll find pretty villages of whitewashed houses, cactus farms, volcanic vineyards and delightfully sleepy fishing harbours. You'll also come across interesting visitor attractions such as converted caves, rural museums and art galleries, many of them designed by César Manrique. Lanzarote's rugged interior and wild, undeveloped stretches of coast are great to explore by car, by bike or on foot. To get to know the island even better, you could stay in a *casa rural*, many of which are beautifully restored old farm cottages.

▲ Iglesia de Nuestra Señora de Guadeloupe, Teguise

TIMANFAYA

Stunningly dramatic, Lanzarote's Montañas del Fuego de Timanfaya are the island's biggest inland visitor attraction. Exploring the volcanic peaks, tunnels and craters by coach – or, even better, hiking through the Parque Nacional de Timanfaya, on the Ruta de Tremesana – you'll be awestruck by the unearthly scene left behind by the eighteenth-century eruptions that shattered this region – and chilled

▼ Farmland near Haría

Ideas

The big six

With a glorious climate and beautiful coastlines, Lanzarote and Fuerteventura are best known for their sunny, child-friendly beach resorts – and rightly so. But there's far more to the islands than sun-loungers and sand. With jaw-dropping volcanic landscapes, other-worldly botanical gardens and intriguing caves to explore, it's well worth tearing yourself away from the coast to take a trip inland by hire car, mountain bike or coach.

▼ Jameos del Agua

Transformed by César Manrique from a series of volcanic caves into a meeting place, concert hall and über-chic bar-night-club, this is a spectacular place to spend an afternoon or evening.

P.138 ▸HARÍA AND THE NORTH

▼ Jardín Botánico, La Lajita

Beautifully landscaped, Fuerteventura's stunning collection of palms, cacti and other exotics is great for a wander, particularly in spring when the flowers are in bloom.

P.155 ▸FUERTEVENTURA

▲ Montanas del Fuego de Timanfaya

Dramatic volcanoes, yawning calderas and vast fields of lava add up to an awe-inspiring spectacle in Lanzarote's greatest national park.

P.102 ▸ YAIZA AND TIMANFAYA

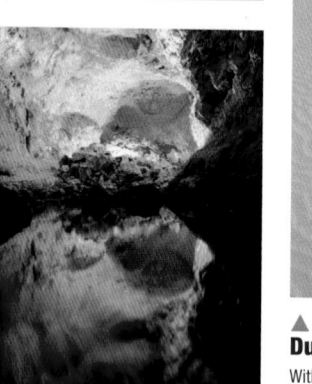

▲ Cueva de los Verdes

Tours of these lava caves in northern Lanzarote take you down winding passageways, past natural optical illusions and through impressive cathedral-like subterranean spaces.

P.139 ▸ HARÍA AND THE NORTH

▶ Fundación César Manrique

Perched on solid lava, the intriguing former home of Lanzarote's most celebrated artist, sculptor and environmentalist is now a truly inspirational art museum and gallery.

P.73 ▸ SAN BARTOLOMÉ AND TÍAS

▲ Parque Natural de las Dunas de Corralejo

With sparkling, turquoise sea, and soft dunes ranging in hue from white to palest clotted cream, this beautiful wilderness is an easy day-trip from Lanzarote.

P.151 ▸ FUERTEVENTURA

Best beaches

Both Lanzarote and Fuerteventura have an abundance of lovely beaches – and each one is different. While their west coasts tend to be wild and rocky, with swells that attract surfers from all over the world, the strands and coves on the south and east of both islands are great for swimming and sunbathing. Although both islands are volcanic, it's relatively rare to find dark sand here – palest white or deepest gold is more the norm.

▲ Playa de las Cucharas, Costa Teguise

Las Cucharas is the best place on Lanzarote to learn to windsurf; but if all you want to do is relax in the sun, you'll enjoy the safe, sandy beach and its host of bars and restaurants.

P.110 ▸ COSTA TEGUISE

▲ Playa de Mattoral, Península de Jandía

A blockbuster of a beach, with miles of shimmering sand, this is Fuerteventura's prime holiday destination, well served by comfortable resort hotels.

P.156 ▸ FUERTEVENTURA

▼ Punta del Papagayo

Well worth the dusty, bumpy trip from Playa Blanca, Lanzarote's southern sandy coves are wonderfully secluded and, at high tide, perfect for swimming.

P.86 ▸ PLAYA BLANCA

▲ Playa Grande, Puerto del Carmen

Lanzarote's most famous beach, decked out with sunloungers and backed by attractive palm trees and hibiscus, seems to get more sun than anywhere else on the island.

P.62 ▸ PUERTO DEL CARMEN

▼ Playa de Famara

This breezy beach flanked by rugged cliffs is paradise for surfers, sunbathers and walkers alike.

P.124 ▸ TEGUISE AND TINAJO

▲ Caleta del Mojón Blanco

A hidden gem on Lanzarote's wild northeast coast, this is one of a string of ravishingly beautiful white sandy coves dotted with rock pools.

P.141 ▸ HARÍA AND THE NORTH

Best views

Lanzarote and Fuerteventura have plenty of elevated spots that offer glorious panoramic views. There are wonderful vistas to be enjoyed from the islands' *miradores*, or look-out points, which can be anything from a roadside lay-by to an architect-designed viewing terrace with a restaurant or bar. But if you'd like a grandstand view of a glorious sunset, just head for any of the west-coast beaches or cliffs and watch the sun paint the sky a thousand colours as it sinks into the ocean.

▲ **Montaña Tindaya, from the La Oliva road**

Sacred to the *Mahos*, this extinct volcano is northern Fuerteventura's most majestic feature.

P.152 ▸ FUERTEVENTURA

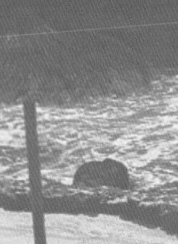

▲ **Lava flows, from the Taro de Tahíche**

César Manrique was so captivated by the dynamism of the lava fields near his home that he let the lava "flow into" its interior, incorporating it into the design and allowing large windows to frame the scene.

P.73 ▸ SAN BARTOLOMÉ AND TÍAS

► Timanfaya, from El Diablo restaurant

Settling down to a lunch that's been sizzled over a geothermal barbecue, you're sure to be impressed by the volcanic landscape surrounding you on all sides.

P.108 ▶ YAIZA AND TIMANFAYA

▼ Fuerteventura and Isla de los Lobos, from Playa Blanca

From Lanzarote's southernmost resort town, the island's near neighbours sparkle in the distance on clear days and nights.

P.83 ▶ PLAYA BLANCA

▼ Los Rostros from Femés

The village of Femés lies just beneath one of Lanzarote's highest points; from its restaurant terraces you can enjoy sweeping views of the arid southern plains and, in the distance, Montaña Roja and Playa Blanca.

P.96 ▶ YAIZA AND TIMANFAYA

▼ Isla de la Graciosa, from the Mirador del Río

Cliff-top lookout designed by César Manrique to celebrate the tremendous view from El Risco de Famara; Isla de la Graciosa appears to float like a speckled rag in the sea below.

P.140 ▶ HARÍA AND THE NORTH

Art collections and folk museums

Lanzarote's lively contemporary art scene and well-documented folk history owe much to the pioneering work of one man, César Manrique. Primarily an artist, but also a passionate defender of local traditions, he created some of the island's most interesting cultural centres, and paved the way for others. Lanzarote is regularly visited by artists and photographers who, like Manrique before them, draw their inspiration from the island's austere and twisted landscapes; their work is regularly exhibited in the island's galleries.

▼ Centro de Artesanía Molino de Antigua

The best of Fuerteventura's several rural and ethnological museums, the Centro de Artesanía Molino de Antigua has excellent displays of local crafts, and a fine cactus garden.

P.152 ▸ FUERTEVENTURA

▼ MIAC, Castillo de San José

Manrique managed the conversion of this chunky little fort into a contemporary art museum, whose small collection features important works from the twentieth-century Spanish New Avant Garde movement.

P.55 ▸ ARRECIFE

▲ Casa-Museo al Campesino

One of Manrique's earliest projects, this museum explores traditional architecture and country customs through craft workshops and folk-art exhibitions, housed in beautifully preserved farm buildings.

P.77 ▶ SAN BARTOLOMÉ AND TÍAS

▲ Museo Agrícola El Patio

This illuminating country farm museum is all about rural culture – its rhythms, hardships and rewards. In the courtyard is an old-fashioned *bodegón* where you can raise a glass to the traditions of the past.

P.122 ▶ TEGUISE AND TINAJO

▼ Museo Etnográfico Tanit, San Bartolomé

Crammed with a fascinating jumble of folk artefacts, this museum opens a window on the daily life of ordinary islanders, from the earliest settlers to the mid-twentieth century.

P.76 ▶ SAN BARTOLOMÉ AND TÍAS

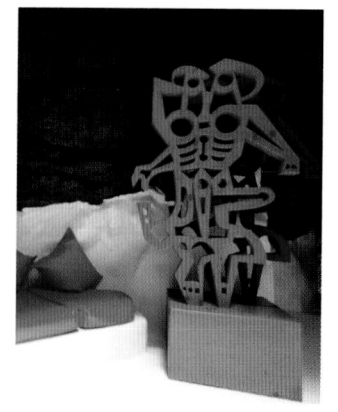

▲ Fundación César Manrique, Taro de Tahíche

Designed both as a celebration of the volcanic environment and as a witty synthesis of traditional and modern architecture, the house Manrique built is now home to his foundation, and its superb collection of contemporary art.

P.73 ▶ SAN BARTOLOMÉ AND TÍAS

Prettiest villages

Thanks in no small part to César Manrique's dedication to conserving the island's cultural heritage, Lanzarote's inland villages are charmingly traditional. Most are dotted with whitewashed cottages, their timbers painted a uniform green, brown or blue, and their chimneys topped with onion-shaped domes. The focal points of every village are its church, its plaza and its socio-cultural centre, the place where everyone goes to gossip, drink and share plates of fabulously fresh tapas.

▲ Tinajo

This understated little farming town has, in its central plaza, some ancient and impressive *dragos*, or dragon's blood trees, sacred to the aboriginal islanders.

P.122 ▸ TEGUISE AND TINAJO

▲ Guatiza

This charming rural village in the heart of Lanzarote has an impressive chapel built in the nineteenth century, when production of cochineal dye, the local speciality, was at a lucrative peak.

P.126 ▸ TEGUISE AND TINAJO

▲ Yaiza

A quiet village of neat streets with bright pots of geraniums, Yaiza perches right on the edge of Lanzarote's southern lava fields and has dramatic views of Timanfaya.

P.93 ▸ YAIZA AND TIMANFAYA

▲ Betancuria

This historic village lies in an arid valley reached by winding mountain roads. The church at its heart is the islands' only cathedral; though surprisingly small, it's tranquil and dignified.

P.153 ▸ FUERTEVENTURA

▲ Teguise

Best known for its bustling Sunday market, Lanzarote's former capital is an elegant small town featuring a fine church and old houses with beautifully carved timber doors and balconies.

P.119 ▸ TEGUISE AND TINAJO

▸ Uga

Perfectly positioned for touring Lanzarote's volcanic winelands, Uga is both pretty and delightfully down-to-earth.

P.96 ▸ YAIZA AND
          TIMANFAYA

Scenic hikes, drives and cycle tours

A great way to get a feel for the islands, and to appreciate the remarkable variety of their distinctive landscapes, is to get out and explore. Resort-based tour companies run a good variety of coach trips, which can be good as a taster, but nothing beats setting off on your own, on two wheels or four, or even on your own two feet.

▲ Parque Natural de los Volcanes and Parque Nacional de Timanfaya

The Ruta de los Volcanes coach tour is not the only way to enjoy the drama of the volcanic wilderness surrounding Timanfaya: there are superb views to be had by driving or cycling along the public roads that pass through the protected areas.

P.101 ▸ YAIZA AND TIMANFAYA

▲ Ruta de Tremesana

Walking through Lanzarote's volcanic heartlands in the company of vulcanology experts gives you an intimate appreciation of this remarkable environment where, not far off the path, the ground is often too hot to walk on.

P.104 ▸ YAIZA AND TIMANFAYA

▶ La Geria

La Geria, the most ruggedly beautiful section of Lanzarote's volcanic winelands, is fascinating to explore by coach, car or bike, dropping in at *bodegas* along the way.

P.97 ▶ YAIZA AND TIMANFAYA

▼ Yaiza to Femés

Particularly lovely in spring, when the meadows are full of wild flowers, this is a bracing walk through open countryside and over rugged hills.

P.96 ▶ YAIZA AND TIMANFAYA

▲ The LZ-1 from Arrieta to Orzola

With stunning views of the Malpaís de la Corona volcanic badlands on one side, and of sparkling ocean on the other, this is one of the island's most scenic coastal routes.

P.138 ▶ HARÍA AND THE NORTH

▲ The FV-30 from Pájara to Betancuria

With heart-pounding hairpin bends cut into sheer rock faces, and stunning views of an austere wilderness, this is Fuerteventura's most thrilling road trip – and a serious challenge for cyclists.

P.153 ▶ FUERTEVENTURA

Watersports

With nearly 500km of beautiful coastline between them, it's hardly surprising that watersports are among Lanzarote and Fuerteventura's biggest attractions. Windsurfers and surfers have been wintering here for years, and there's a growing community of kiteboarders, too. Swimmers can enjoy the islands' abundance of safe sandy beaches and fabulous hotel pools, while for sailors the upmarket Rubicón and Puerto Calero marinas are the perfect springboards for island-hopping trips to the other Canaries.

▲ Windsurfing

Reliably windy from autumn to spring, and with reasonably mild water temperatures year round, both Lanzarote and Fuerteventura are world-class windsurfing destinations.

P.112 ▶ COSTA TEGUISE
P.155 ▶ FUERTEVENTURA

▼ Snorkelling

The rocky coves and reefs of Lanzarote's eastern shores are perfect for snorkelling – even in busy resort areas, you'll see marine life just yards from the shore.

P.63 ▶ PUERTO DEL CARMEN
P.128 ▶ TEGUISE AND TINAJO

▲ Surfing

Protected by reefs of solidified lava, Lanzarote's west coast is excellent for surfing, and international championships are regularly held here.

P.125 ▸ TEGUISE AND TINAJO

▲ Sailing

Of all the boat trips available on Lanzarote, chartering a yacht – complete with expert skipper – from the swish marina at Puerto Calero has to be the best.

P.171 ▸ ESSENTIALS

▲ Swimming

Lanzarote and Fuerteventura's hundreds of resort pools are relaxing and child-friendly; many are heated, so are great for year-round swimming.

P.173 ▸ ESSENTIALS

▶ Kiteboarding

Similar to windsurfing but more strenuous – and a lot more daring – kiteboarding is the fastest-growing activity in the watersports hotspots of Lanzarote's wild northwest and Fuerteventura's Peninsula de Jandía.

P.155 ▸ FUERTEVENTURA
P.125 ▸ TEGUISE AND TINAJO

Traditional Lanzarote and Fuerteventura

Before tourism became a major source of income on Lanzarote and Fuerteventura, most of the islanders were farmers, winemakers and fishermen. Stepping outside the purpose-built holiday resort areas today, you'll discover quiet coastal villages and inland areas where the old trades are still an important part of community life. With the help of dedicated cultural conservationists, the islanders are managing to keep their traditions alive without getting stuck in the past.

▲ Windmills, Fuerteventura

Fuerteventura's *molinos* and *molinas*, once used to grind corn for *gofio*, are a distinctive feature of the breezy island landscape. Some have been preserved and are still fully functional.

P.152 ▶ FUERTEVENTURA

▲ Volcanic vineyards

Lanzarote has possibly the weirdest-looking vineyards on the planet, with C-shaped walls of broken lava protecting the vines from the punishing prevailing winds.

P.97 ▶ YAIZA AND TIMANFAYA

▲ Isla de la Graciosa

On Lanzarote's largest offshore island, life proceeds at an unhurried pace. Freshly caught fish are laid out to dry in the sun, kids play in the sandy streets, and the beaches are near-deserted.

P.142 ▸ HARÍA AND THE NORTH

▼ Folk music

The classic Canarian instrument is the five-stringed *timple*, though other guitars are almost as popular; the best time to catch a performance by a virtuoso band is during one of the islands' many fiestas.

P.169 ▸ ESSENTIALS

▲ Charco de San Ginés, Arrecife

Traditional fishing is a dying art in the islands, but wooden boats still bob on the water in the Charco de San Ginés, Arrecife's sheltered lagoon. Ringed by a waterside path, it's always been the locals' favourite spot for a *paseo* or stroll.

P.54 ▸ ARRECIFE

▼ Cactus farms

Lanzarote has a long history of organic dye production. Near Guatiza you'll see fields of *tunera* cacti, their leaves blotched with the white deposits that indicate the presence of cochineal beetles.

P.126 ▸ TEGUISE AND TINAJO

Extreme Lanzarote and Fuerteventura

If you're in the market for something to get your pulse racing, look no further. Airborne sports have – literally – taken off in a big way on both islands, while off-road biking, scuba diving and helicopter touring are good ways of getting a fresh perspective on the scenery. For the seriously fit, *Club La Santa* organizes a year-round programme of professional-standard sporting events, including the Lanzarote Ironman, one of the toughest athletic challenges in the world.

▲ Mountain biking
Both Lanzarote and Fuerteventura have plenty of wild, rocky inclines to test adventurous cyclists.

P.171 ▸ ESSENTIALS

▲ Helicopter tours

Get a whole new angle on the islands by taking a short flight over their coasts, deserts and volcanoes – you'll have the chance to look right down into the gaping calderas.

P.172 ▸ ESSENTIALS

▼ Hang-gliding

Experienced gliders with nerves of steel launch from the gusty Risco de Famara cliffs for thrilling flights along the rugged northwest coast

P.126 ▸ TEGUISE AND TINAJO

▼ Scuba diving

Both islands have a number of first-class outfits offering scuba courses, equipment hire and regular trips to local dive sites, including underwater volcanic caves.

P.172 ▸ ESSENTIALS

▲ Lanzarote Ironman

Strictly for the dedicated, this triathlon is the ultimate all-day endurance test – a 3.8-kilometre swim, 180-kilometre bike race and 42.2-kilometre run, with barely enough time to catch your breath between each gruelling leg.

P.171 ▸ ESSENTIALS

Kids' Lanzarote and Fuerteventura

With reliable weather, lovely beaches and swimming pools, and clued-up hotels and restaurants, Lanzarote and Fuerteventura have all the ingredients of a great family holiday. Independent-minded families can enjoy the freedom of their own private villa or apartment, but the easiest and most popular plan is to book into one of the many resort complexes, whose facilities more often than not include fun stuff such as playgrounds, activity clubs and mini-discos.

▼ Playa Dorada, Playa Blanca

Easy to get to, with soft, pale sand and safe, shallow water, this beach is just right for swimming and sandcastle-making, and there are ice-cream shops nearby.

P.85 ▶ PLAYA BLANCA

▶ Baku Water Park, Corralejo

The newest and best of the islands' water-park complexes, Baku's slides, tubes, pools and games are a big hit with children and teenagers.

P.150 ▸ COSTA TEGUISE

▼ Oasis Park La Lajita

Kids will love meeting the well-kept inmates – from marmosets and flamingoes to hippos and giraffes – at this attractive animal park. There are crocodiles to stroke, snakes to drape around your neck and hilarious performing sea lions.

P.154 ▸ FUERTEVENTURA

▼ Camel rides, Parque Nacional de Timanfaya

Animal-lovers of all ages can take a short ride on the back of an even-tempered "ship of the desert" in the foothills of Lanzarote's Montañas del Fuego.

P.104 YAIZA AND TIMANFAYA

▼ Kids' clubs

Most resort hotels organize daily kids' club sessions with art workshops, shows and games, often held in a dedicated complex; some of these, such as Kikoland in Playa Blanca, also have good sports facilities.

P.87 ▸ PLAYA BLANCA

Shopping and markets

The shopping scene on Lanzarote and Fuerteventura is not going to rock your world, but Lanzarote has several lively craft markets, and all the major centres have shops selling clothing, jewellery and souvenirs. Both islands are good for funky, youthful surf gear, and you can sometimes find cheap electronic gadgets in the resort towns, but the best buys are local produce such as goat's cheese, handmade lace, or *malvasía* wine, drawn straight from the barrel.

▲ Mercadillo de Teguise

Lanzarote's most famous weekly market is a bustling social event with some great little craft stalls plus a liberal spread of tat, including cheap clothing, junk jewellery and fun, gimmicky gifts.

P.22 ▶ TEGUISE AND TINAJO

▼ Winery shops

Even if you don't take a winery tour, a visit to Lanzarote's *bodegas* to buy direct from the producers is an outing in itself. Prices are very competitive, and you can taste the various vintages before you buy.

P.78 ▶ SAN BARTOLOMÉ AND TÍAS
P.98 ▶ YAIZA AND TIMANFAYA

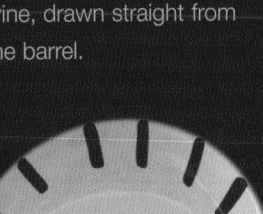

▲ Fundación César Manrique boutiques

The gallery shop at the Taro de Tahíche stocks desirable objects and books featuring César Manrique's work; there are additional branches in Arrecife, Puerto del Carmen, Teguise and the airport.

P.73 ▶ SAN BARTOLOMÉ AND TÍAS

▲ Marina Rubicón

Playa Blanca's smart new marina has a contemporary art gallery and a fine selection of independent boutiques selling designer fashions and interesting gifts.

P.85 ▶ PLAYA BLANCA

▼ Mercadillo de Haría

A gentle, low-key affair held on Saturdays, this is a good place to look for local lace, plants, bread, goat's cheese and cactus jam.

P.135 ▶ HARÍA AND THE NORTH

◀ Mercadillo de Pueblo Marinero, Costa Teguise

Held on Friday evenings, this little market is always busy with browsers nosing around the jewellery and craft stalls before heading for the nearby bars for a beer or two.

P.114 ▶ COSTA TEGUISE

Fiestas

Traditional festivals in the Canary Islands bring a riot of colour to the fabric of local life. As well as marking the highlights of the Catholic calendar with great gusto, every town and village has an annual fiesta to honour its patron saint, typically with religious processions and fireworks, or with a *romería*, or pilgrimage. There's also much music, dancing, drinking and general revelry, with visitors more than welcome to join in.

▲ Carnaval pageants

Though lower key than Tenerife's world-famous Carnaval, Lanzarote and Fuerteventura's February pageants are always glitzy affairs, featuring marching bands, drag artists and lively satirical singers.

P.169 ▶ ESSENTIALS

▲ Lucha Canaria

Patronal fiesta programmes often feature traditional wrestling bouts – unique to the Canaries, these impressive displays of machismo draw big crowds.

P.174 ▶ ESSENTIALS

◀ Fiesta del Nuestra Señora del Carmen

There's plenty of spirited music and dancing in Teguise's central plaza when the historic town celebrates its patronal fiesta on July 16.

P.123 TEGUISE AND TINAJO

▼ Romería de los Dolores

This Catholic pilgrimage brings walkers in peasant costume from all over Lanzarote to Mancha Blanca, where they give thanks for the halting of the lava flows that once threatened to devour the town.

P.100 ▸ TEGUISE AND TINAJO

▼ Cabalgata de los Reyes Magos

On the feast of Epiphany, three costumed "kings" ride through the streets of each town on camels, throwing sweets to the crowd, to commemorate the arrival of the Three Wise Men in Bethlehem.

P.169 ▸ ESSENTIALS

▼ Entierro de la Sardina

On Shrove Tuesday, a giant model of a dead fish, symbolizing the Lenten fast, is paraded through Arrecife by irreverent Carnaval "mourners" and then set on fire with great jollity.

P.55 ▸ ARRECIFE

Sculptures and mobiles

The abundance of public art and sculpture on Lanzarote is one of the many manifestations of César Manrique's lasting creative influence; indeed, much of the best work is by Manrique himself. Particularly distinctive and intriguing are his *juguetes del viento*, or wind toys, elaborate mechanical sculptures designed to swing, rotate or gyrate like post-modern windmills. Many of these adorn roundabouts – fun, but a little distracting when you're trying to negotiate the island's notoriously confusing intersections.

▲ Monumento al Campesino

Manrique created this tall, cubist conglomeration of white-painted vessels as a tribute to Lanzarote's peasant heritage and to the determination and creative ingenuity of the people who shaped the island's past.

P.77 ▶ SAN BARTOLOMÉ AND TÍAS

▼ Energía de la Pirámide, Taro de Tahíche

This *juguete del viento* outside Manrique's former home is one of the artist's later works; it stands on the edge of a lava field where figs and vines grow.

P.73 ▶ SAN BARTOLOMÉ AND TÍAS

▲ Juguete del Viento, Montaña Blanca roundabout

This colourful *juguete del viento* sits at the foot of Montaña Blanca, but is not as well known as Manrique's other mobiles – it's on a relatively quiet road between San Bartolomé and Tías.

P.79 ▸ SAN BARTOLOMÉ AND TÍAS

▲ Veleta, Arrieta roundabout

This *juguete del viento* has been nicknamed "the Madonna sculpture" because of its cone-shaped appendages.

P.135 ▸ HARÍA AND THE NORTH

▼ Jameos del Agua sign

Easily mistaken for a lobster, Manrique's sign for the Jameos del Agua actually depicts a *jameito*, the species of blind crustacean that inhabits the subterranean lake inside the caves.

P.38 ▸ HARÍA AND THE NORTH

▼ Juguete del Viento, Tahíche roundabout

One of the largest and most conspicuous of the *juguetes del viento*, this sculpture, nicknamed "the egg whisk" for obvious reasons, stands near the spot where Manrique died in a road accident.

P.73 ▸ SAN BARTOLOMÉ AND TÍAS

Eccentric Lanzarote

Maybe it's the surreal landscapes and sculptural vegetation, but there's something about Lanzarote that seems to appeal to the quirkiness in people. A few of the island's wonderful oddities are highly conspicuous – you can't miss the roundabout wind mobiles and the carnival drag queens. Even more intriguingly, there are recherché eccentricities galore in the island's cultural centres and public gardens.

▲ Jardín del Cactus

This beautifully designed collection of cacti includes hundreds of exotic specimens, from the gigantic and prickly to the tiny and feathery.

P.127 ▶ TEGUISE AND TINAJO

▲ Geothermal tricks, Montañas del Fuego de Timanfaya

The national-park staff delight in showing visitors just how hot a dormant volcano can be by pouring water into a gap in the rock – and then standing well back.

P.102 ▶ YAIZA AND TIMANFAYA

◀ Majo-style clay figures

The artisans at the Casa-Museo del Campesino have a nice line in souvenirs inspired by aboriginal fertility figures, which seem to go down particularly well with the islands' naturist visitors.

P.77 ▸ SAN BARTOLOMÉ AND TÍAS

▼ Found-object art

Manrique's installations feature quirky sculptures made from recycled materials, a trend that many of the island's artists have since picked up; there are often good examples for sale in Teguise's gallery shops.

P.129 ▸TEGUISE AND TINAJO

▲ Señores y señoras

Visitors wishing to powder their noses while exploring the island's cultural centres are in little danger of choosing the wrong door; the signs, like these at the Taro de Tahíche, tend to be helpfully graphic.

P.73 ▸ SAN BARTOLOMÉ AND TÍAS

◀ Whale skeleton, Puerto Calero

The swish marina in Puerto Calero has an impressive new mascot: the massive skeleton of a Bryde's whale, which adorns the entrance to the Museo de Cetáceos de Canarias.

P.99 ▸ YAIZA AND TIMANFAYA

Light bites

Like the mainland Spanish, the Canarians like nothing better than to relax over a drink, sharing little plates of tasty delicacies. Tradition dictates that it would be simply wrong to order a beer or a glass of wine without an *enyesque* – something to nibble on. The more traditional of the islands' tapas bars and bar-restaurants are great places to try local specialities such as *papas arrugadas* (salty new potatoes) with *mojo verde* (garlic and coriander dip).

▲ Casa-Museo del Campesino

Traditional in every detail, with jaunty folk songs playing in the background, the Campesino museum's ground-floor tapas bar is perfect for a light lunch.

P.81 ▶ SAN BARTOLOMÉ AND TÍAS

▲ La Saranda, Mácher

Brush up on your Spanish if you want to keep up when your waiter rattles off the specials of the day at this rustic eatery where, late on Fridays, you'll be serenaded by a first-class *timple* trio.

P.82 ▶ SAN BARTOLOMÉ AND TÍAS

▼ Café del Mar, Marina Rubicón

A new venture from the people who have been spinning cool jazz and chillout music on Ibiza for over 25 years, this mellow wharfside venue is the perfect spot for late-night drinks and snacks.

P.92 ▸ PLAYA BLANCA

▲ Café la Ola, Puerto del Carmen

This hip all-day, late-night coastal bar serves drinks and Asian-fusion food in a space decorated like a fantasy Thai temple, with a gorgeous outdoor pool deck.

P.69 ▸ PUERTO DEL CARMEN

◀ Casa Isaítas, Pájara

Using locally sourced organic ingredients, this delightful *casa rural* serves delicious modern classics such as rocket salad, and sausages in wine.

P.159 ▸ FUERTEVEN-TURA

Bodegas

There's no better way to enjoy Lanzarote's speciality wines than to settle down in a rural *bodega*, or wine bar, where the person who pours you a glass of chilled white *malvasía* and cuts up some local cheese and homemade bread to go with it may well be the master winemaker himself. There are also some excellent urban *bodegas* in Arrecife and Teguise, where you can sample good food and fine wine from all over Spain, in highly convivial surroundings.

▲ Palacio del Marquéz, Teguise

The oldest mansion in the Canaries is home to a wine connoisseur with a remarkable collection of vintages. The patio wine bar is one of the Lanzarote's loveliest places for lunch on a sunny day.

P.132 ▶ TEGUISE AND TINAJO

▼ Bodega El Chupadero, La Geria

Fabulous, funky little *bodega*, with a particularly rich and tasty moscatel. The terrace has amazing views of the surreal volcanic vineyards and glimpses of the faraway sea.

P.107 ▶ YAIZA AND TIMANFAYA

▼ Bodega Santiago de Yaiza, Yaiza

Far more than just a wine-and-tapas place, this understated gourmet restaurant also serves interesting dishes such as beef with peaches, and chicken breast with apple.

P.107 ▶ YAIZA AND TIMANFAYA

▼ Bodega de Uga, Uga

Soak up the atmosphere, and some excellent local and Spanish vintages, at this intimate boutique winery, which also serves huge, delicious plates of olives, cured meat and marinated vegetables.

P.107 ▶ YAIZA AND TIMANFAYA

▲ Bodega Santa Bárbara, Teguise

The tiny, cool, leafy patio of this charming little wine bar is the perfect refuge from the crowds thronging Teguise's popular market on a hot Sunday morning.

P.130 ▶ TEGUISE AND TINAJO

Dining in style

The choice of everyday international-style eateries on Lanzarote and Fuerteventura is enormous, but if you're looking for excellence, you have to know where to go. The following rank among the island's best, most glamorous international restaurants: all pride themselves on their discreet, knowledgeable service and their imaginative gourmet cooking.

▲ La Graciosa at Gran Meliá Salinas, Costa Teguise

With the kind of old-fashioned elegance and attentive service that make it a great choice for anniversaries and other special occasions, this top-end hotel restaurant specializes in classic dishes such as lobster and finest sirloin.

P.116 ▸ COSTA TEGUISE

▲ Hotel Gran Meliá Volcán, Playa Blanca

This luxury resort hotel has several dining rooms, each with a different culinary speciality; while all are very good, the Spanish and Mediterranean-style cooking here is outstanding.

P.88 ▸ PLAYA BLANCA

▲ LagOmar, Nazaret

A *haute-cuisine* restaurant and occasional bar-nightclub with one of the most dramatic settings on the islands; it's tucked under a sheer rock-face in the grounds of a house built for Omar Sharif.

P.131 ▶ TEGUISE AND TINAJO

▼ Castillo de San José, Arrecife

Avant-garde when César Manrique created it in the 1970s, and a design classic today, the sleek glass-walled restaurant at MIAC is the place where Arrecife's movers and shakers meet for power lunches.

P.58 ▶ ARRECIFE

▲ Agua Viva, Playa Honda

A little hard to find but well worth seeking out, this delightful place serves superb French-style cuisine accompanied by the finest sauces to come out of any kitchen on the islands.

P.81 ▶ SAN BARTOLOMÉ AND TÍAS

Rural restaurants

Rural gourmet eating is Lanzarote and Fuerteventura's best-kept secret. You'll struggle to find any restaurants that serve delicious country-style food in the resort areas, but inland there are some real gems, many of them in beautifully converted *fincas*.

These characterful restaurants serve the freshest local meat, fish and vegetables, and, in many cases, island specialities such as roast kid, grilled rabbit, *sancocho* and ice cream made from *gofio*.

▲ Don Antonio, Vega de Río de Palmas

Well off the beaten track but worth the journey, this charmingly rustic village restaurant serves Canarian cooking with a sophisticated twist.

P.160 ▸ FUERTEVENTURA

▲ Taberna Strelitzia, Tiagua

A lovely, romantic country inn, which feels like a little pocket of Provence transplanted to rural Lanzarote, with a menu of superb French cuisine complemented by excellent wine from the cellar.

P.132 ▸ TEGUISE AND TINAJO

► El Risco, La Caleta de Famara

This friendly family restaurant overlooking the sea in the village of Famara is worth visiting for the César Manrique originals on the walls as much as for the fine views and good, unpretentious food.

P.130 ▶ TEGUISE AND TINAJO

◄ Mesón Tiagua, Tiagua

Behind the understated exterior, this cosy gourmet restaurant boasts a genius of a chef who specializes in original and deliciously creative blends of spices.

P.131 ▶ TEGUISE AND TINAJO

▼ La Era, Yaiza

The very best place on Lanzarote to sample gourmet *cocina conejera* (local cooking), *La Era* is a dignified rural restaurant with a fine pedigree – Manrique had a hand in the restoration of its buildings.

P.109 ▶ YAIZA AND TIMANFAYA

▲ Caserío de Mozaga, Mozaga

In an elegant old *finca* with an intimate atmosphere, this fine-dining venue has friendly, discreet service and impeccable Canarian and French-style cooking; it's a perfect choice for a special occasion.

P.81 ▶ SAN BARTOLOMÉ AND TÍAS

Rural retreats

The islands' best *casas rurales* are as secluded as their finest rural restaurants, and just as charming. Hunt around and you'll find beautiful, original places to stay – in converted country mansions, historic farm buildings, wineries and even caves. All are located away from the busy resorts, in countryside that is picturesque, peaceful, or both, and most benefit from having their own lovely private pool.

▲ Caserío de Mozaga, Mozaga

There's a warm welcome in this quiet, elegant country-house hotel; staying here feels like visiting the family home of some well-off friends who have lived on the island for generations.

P.79 ▸ SAN BARTOLOMÉ AND TÍAS

▲ Casona de Yaiza, Yaiza

This former country manor house, its spacious suites individually decorated with Baroque-style murals and ceiling paintings, is a wonderfully romantic place to stay.

P.106 ▸ YAIZA AND TIMANFAYA

◀ Refugios de las Cuevas, La Asomada

Three small but beautiful and original apartments set in a secluded rocky valley a short, bumpy drive from the coast, with rooms built around – and in – natural caves.

P.80 ▶ SAN BARTOLOMÉ AND TÍAS

▼ Mahoh, Villaverde

With rough stone walls and luxurious four-poster beds, this country hotel is the ultimate in rugged rustic chic; it has a decent restaurant, too.

P.158 ▶ FUERTEVENTURA

▶ Casa Tomarén, El Islote

An enchanting option, with spacious accommodation in carefully converted farm buildings, furnished in funky East-meets-West style, and one of the most beautiful pools of any of the islands' *casas rurales*.

P.80 ▶ SAN BARTOLOMÉ AND TÍAS

Places

Arrecife

The compact city of Arrecife, strategically situated on Lanzarote's sheltered eastern shore, is the island's capital, and home and workplace to a large proportion of its permanent residents. Despite this, it never really gets beyond third gear when it comes to pace, passion or pizzazz, and is subsequently overlooked by many visitors. It does, nonetheless, have character – its tightly packed apartment blocks and narrow backstreets give it an appealing urban edge that sets it apart from the inland villages, and its busy grocery shops and *tascas* infuse it with the kind of authentic flavour that's scarce in the beach resorts.

Arrecife took over from the inland village of Teguise as capital of Lanzarote in 1852, when maritime traffic was big business and it made sense to develop the port. Sheltered by the reefs that give Arrecife its name, the city was an important stopover for nineteenth-century traders and adventurers. These days, the main focus is its low-key central commercial district, which has a great selection of restaurants and down-to-earth drinking dens, and the broad promenade that stretches along the seafront and around the picturesque El Charco de San Ginés. Arrecife's artistic connections are notable, too, thanks to the creative enterprise of celebrated Lanzarotean artist

César Manrique, who was born in the capital, and founded its contemporary art museum.

The central seafront

Arrecife's main draw is its **promenade**, a pleasant 1-kilometre walkway that traces

▼ PUENTE DE LAS BOLAS

Arrival and information

If you're arriving in Arrecife **by car** you may have trouble finding a parking space in the centre. The easiest (but most expensive) option is the underground car park near the seafront tower block housing the *Arrecife Gran Hotel*.

    Buses (*guaguas*) from all over the island terminate at Arrecife's bus station on Vía Medular, just north of the centre. From here it's a fifteen-minute walk to the seafront, where the **tourist office** on C/Blas Cabrera Felipe (☎928 81 17 62, @info@turismolanzarote.com; Mon–Fri 8am–2pm, till 3pm in winter) has good maps of the city and the island, plus information about Lanzarote's government-owned attractions. The bandstand on the seafront opposite the post office sometimes operates as a tourist office, too.

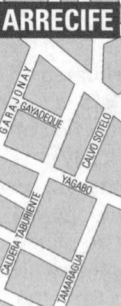

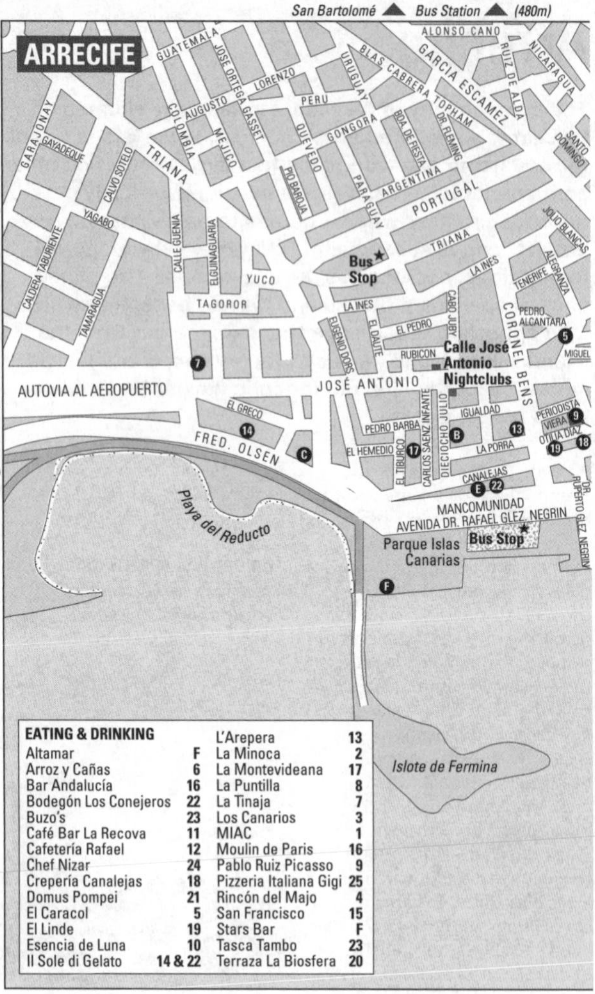
San Bartolomé ▲ Bus Station ▲ (480m)
20, ▲ Airport & Puerto del Carmen
ARRECIFE
AUTOVIA AL AEROPUERTO
FRED. OLSEN
JOSÉ ANTONIO
CORONEL BENS
TRIANA
PORTUGAL
ARGENTINA
GARCIA ESCAMEZ
BLAS CABRERA TOPHAM
ALONSO CANO
Bus Stop
Calle José Antonio Nightclubs
MANCOMUNIDAD
AVENIDA DR. RAFAEL GLEZ. NEGRIN
Parque Islas Canarias
Bus Stop
Playa del Reducto
Islote de Fermina
EATING & DRINKING
Altamar F
Arroz y Cañas 6
Bar Andalucía 16
Bodegón Los Conejeros 22
Buzo's 23
Café Bar La Recova 11
Cafetería Rafael 12
Chef Nizar 24
Crepería Canalejas 18
Domus Pompei 21
El Caracol 5
El Linde 19
Esencia de Luna 10
Il Sole di Gelato 14 & 22
L'Arepera 13
La Minoca 2
La Montevideana 17
La Puntilla 8
La Tinaja 7
Los Canarios 3
MIAC 1
Moulin de Paris 16
Pablo Ruiz Picasso 9
Pizzeria Italiana Gigi 25
Rincón del Majo 4
San Francisco 15
Stars Bar F
Tasca Tambo 23
Terraza La Biosfera 20

the shoreline from Playa del Reducto to El Charco de San Ginés, and is lined with palm-shaded gardens and kiosk-type cafés. A small **craft market** is held here in the Parque José Ramírez Cerdá, near the bandstand, on Wednesday mornings (9am–3pm). Looming over the promenade's western end is the *Arrecife Gran Hotel*, a source of much controversy when it was first built in the 1960s: as the island's only tower block, it became a symbol of everything that passionate traditionalists such as César Manrique (see p.73) wished to avoid, and a major impetus behind the shaping of the island's unique heritage programme. Manrique also

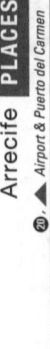

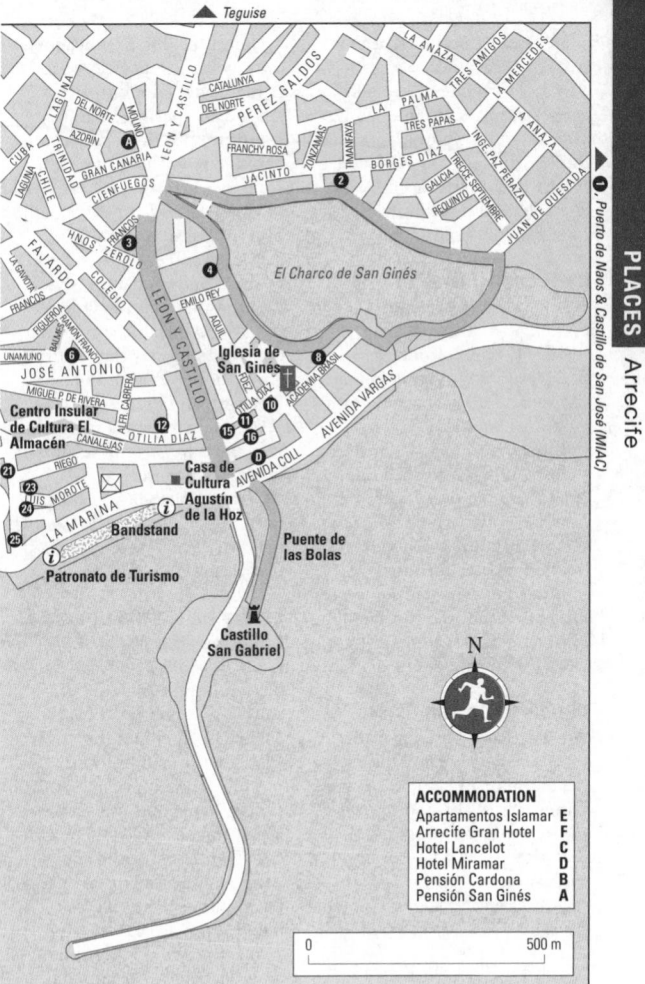

▲ Teguise

▲ ❶ Puerto de Naos & Castillo de San José (MIAC)

El Charco de San Ginés

Iglesia de San Ginés

Centro Insular de Cultura El Almacén

Casa de Cultura Agustín de la Hoz

Bandstand

Patronato de Turismo

Puente de las Bolas

Castillo San Gabriel

N

ACCOMMODATION

Apartamentos Islamar	E
Arrecife Gran Hotel	F
Hotel Lancelot	C
Hotel Miramar	D
Pensión Cardona	B
Pensión San Ginés	A

0   500 m

had designs for the **Islote de Fermina**, an islet connected to the seafront by a causeway near the tower: currently derelict, it was to be a public park, with swimming pools and gardens. The island government, mindful that their capital could do with some updating here and there, have turned their attention instead to a number of other regeneration projects, including a new dock for cruise liners in the Puerto Naos quarter.

Arcing west from the *Arrecife Gran Hotel* is the city's small, attractive beach, **Playa del Reducto**, with safe, shallow water and pale sand shaded by palm trees. Despite being conveniently close to the centre, it's rarely crowded.

The area around the harbour still bears reminders of the city's past as a coastal defence, such as the landmark **Puente de las Bolas,** or Cannonball Bridge, and the **Castillo de San Gabriel**, which now houses a small archeological museum (closed for long-running renovations).

Calle León y Castillo

At the heart of Arrecife's commercial district is Calle León y Castillo, a modest pedestrianized street lined with shops and informal eateries. It's a curious jumble: 1950s-style outfitters with high-stacked teak shelves and glass-fronted display cases share the street with the funkiest of twenty-first-century surf-gear shops. It may not be the best area for souvenir hunting, but there are some great little boutiques and just enough big-name brands to make for a truly varied shopping experience.

El Charco de San Ginés

A particularly pleasant place to while away a lunchtime is the shore of El Charco de San Ginés, the tidal lagoon just east of the shopping district, where a few places set tables out beside the water.

Dotted with brightly painted fishermen's boats, and with a backdrop of distant volcanoes, the lagoon is especially scenic at high tide. The footpath around the perimeter is a favourite spot for a *paseo*; you could extend this to visit the attractive **Iglesia de San Ginés** in Plaza de las Palmas, a couple of minutes' walk away. Built in the seventeenth century in the island's signature style (whitewashed facades edged with dark volcanic stone), it contains religious statues from Cuba, home to a number of Lanzarotean families since economic emigrants made their way there in the eighteenth and nineteenth centuries.

César Manrique was born near El Charco, in a house that is now a down-to-earth *comedor* restaurant, *Casa Ginory*.

Centro Insular de Cultura El Almacén

C/José Betancort 33 ☎ 928 81 01 21. This cultural centre, in an old storehouse converted by César Manrique, includes the Galería El Aljibe, an exhibition space used for contemporary art shows. Manrique was passionate about nurturing local creative talent, and he devised the centre as a platform for island-based painters and sculptors. There's also a pleasant bar-restaurant (see p.59), named after Manrique's friend and contemporary, Pablo Picasso.

Casa de Cultura Agustín de la Hoz

Avda Marina 7 ☎ 928 80 28 84. Mon–Fri 10am–1pm & 5–8pm.Built in the nineteenth century, this former town hall is now a cultural centre, hosting free public exhibitions ranging from photorealistic portraits by contemporary Canarian painters to video instal-lations on global biodiversity.

▼ EL CHARCO DE SAN GINÉS

▲ CASTILLO DE SAN JOSÉ

Castillo de San José and the Museo Internacional de Arte Contemporaneo (MIAC)

Castillo de San José, Ctra de Puerto Naos ☎928 81 23 21, ⊛www .cabildodelanzarote.com/cact. Daily 11am–9pm; free.Completed in 1779, the Castillo de San José was ostensibly planned as a defence against pirates. In truth, however, there wasn't much of a port to defend at the time, and the guiding strategy behind the construction was the provision of much-needed employment in the aftermath of the volcanic eruptions that devastated the island between 1730 and 1736.

The castle, a rather squat, glowering basalt fortress, was saved from ruin by César Manrique, who set about transforming it into a modern-art museum, the Museo Internacional de Arte Contemporaneo (MIAC), which opened to the public in the mid-1970s. There's one principal exhibition

Fiestas in Arrecife

Arrecife is an excellent place to be during one of the island's major fiestas. At **carnival** time (the fortnight leading up to Shrove Tuesday), it's the hub of the action, with pageants, costumed parades and drag shows to enjoy. The climax is the bizarre ritual of **El Entierro de la Sardina** (The Funeral of the Sardine – though Cremation of the Giant Fish would be more apt a name), where merry "mourners" parade an effigy of a dead sardine through the streets before setting it alight.

At **Corpus Christi**, in June, parishioners traditionally decorate the streets with elaborately patterned carpets of coloured salt, a local twist on the petal-carpet tradition of other Hispanic territories; flowers are in rather short supply on Lanzarote. In recent years, enthusiasts have been fighting to prevent this tradition from dying out as secularization gains a foothold among the islanders.

Quite definitely alive and kicking is the celebration of the **Fiesta de San Ginés**, which keeps Lanzarote in party mood throughout August. San Ginés is Arrecife's patron saint, and the city celebrates with a funfair and various events, particularly on the patronal festival day, August 25. It's well worth cheering on the El Charco boat race, a madcap tradition in which competitors paddle tiny tubs across the lagoon using only their hands.

space on the entry level, plus two smaller adjoining rooms and, downstairs, a space for temporary displays. The small but satisfying permanent collection of paintings, sculptures and assemblages includes important works from the twentieth-century Spanish New Avant Garde movement, including pieces by Antóni Tápies, Manolo Millares and Manrique himself – but most visitors are far more interested in the incredible Manrique-designed restaurant downstairs (see p.58) than the art.

Hotels

Arrecife Gran Hotel

Parque Islas Canarias ☎928 80 00 00, ⊛www.arrecifehoteles.com. Lanzarote's only tower block, seventeen storeys high, now houses Arrecife's only five-star hotel. It's the city's smart-est address, with vast, elegant, marble-clad public spaces and comfortable modern rooms offering excellent views. There's a large (though not very private) pool terrace adjoining one of the lower levels, and a landmark restaurant and stylish bar on the top floor (see p.57). €125.

Hotel Lancelot

Avda Mancomunidad 9 ☎928 80 50 99, ⊜hlancelot@terra .es.Comfortable though slightly dated three-star seafront hotel with a great little rooftop swim-ming pool. The rooms, on four floors, are standard in style but good value and a decent size – ask for one with a balcony overlooking Playa del Reducto. The first-rate buffet breakfast is served in a dining room with lovely sea views. €75.

Hotel Miramar

Avda Coll 2 ☎928 81 26 00, ⊛www .hmiramar.com. Overlooking the historic Puente de las Bolas, this three-star seafront hotel has a cool, contemporary feel, and is brilliantly placed for Arrecife's busy shopping centre. Some rooms are rather plain, but the views from the sea-facing balconies are good, and there's a pleasant rooftop terrace. €73.

Apartments

Apartamentos Islamar

Avda Dr Rafael González Negrín 15 ☎928 81 15 00. A modest, very central block of seafront apart-ments with TV and phone. Each sleeps two and has a sea view. €40.

Guesthouses

Pensión Cardona

C/Dieciocho de Julio 11 ☎928 81 10 08. Above-average *pensión* with tidy self-contained rooms and a *cafetería*. The location is central and very handy for the clutch of nightspots on Calle José Antonio. €31.

Pensión San Ginés

C/Molino 9 ☎928 81 18 63. Away from the action of the commercial centre but not far from El Charco de San Ginés, this simple guesthouse has good-value en-suite rooms that are a little musty and airless but otherwise well kept. €23.

Shops

Adolfo Dominguez

C/José Antonio 8. Understated outlet for the latest collections from the classic Spanish fashion designer.

El Gourmet Tienda Delicatessen

C/Canalejas 6. Attractive deli selling edible treats such as ham, sausages, pickles, chocolate, coffee and wine.

Fiammetta

C/Inspector Luis Martín 3. Delightful costume jewellery and one-off bags made from brightly coloured fabrics.

La Galería

Arrecife Gran Hotel, Parque Islas Canarias. Perfectly positioned to tempt hotel guests but open to all, this is a small, swish collection of boutiques, plus a hairdressing salon.

La Santa Surf

Avda Dr Rafael González Negrín 5. One of the best of Arrecife's many surf shops, selling boards and funky clothing, both their own-label and international brands.

Silvestre Deportes

Avda Dr Rafael González Negrín 3. Cool sports and surf gear, including boards, bags and other accessories.

Urbanitas

C/José Antonio 10. Small boutique

with a select range of fresh, youthful urban clothing and trainers from labels such as Gas and By Pass.

Restaurants, bodegas and tapas bars

Altamar

Arrecife Gran Hotel, Parque Islas Canarias ☏928 80 00 00, ⊛www.arrecifehoteles.com. Glorious top-floor sea and city views – unique on this island of low-rise buildings – provide the stunning backdrop to a fine dining experience at this smart hotel restaurant specializing in Mediterranean cooking. Main courses average €15–18.

Arroz y Cañas

C/General Balmes 3 (corner of C/José Antonio) ☏928 80 35 66. Closed Sun eve. As the name suggests, one of the best places in town to try traditional Spanish rice dishes, washed down with beer. Above-average prices.

Bodegón Los Conejeros

Avda Rafael González Negrín 9 ☏928 81 71 95. Mon–Sat 7pm–midnight. An unassuming seafront entrance

▼ CASTILLO DE SAN JOSÉ

leads to this airy wine-cellar, very popular with discerning locals and highly recommended for its huge plates of very fresh, moderately priced food, including excellent salads, and superb Spanish and Canarian wine.

Castillo de San José

Ctra de Puerto Naos ☎ 928 81 23 21. Restaurant 1–3.45pm & 7.30–11pm, bar 11am–midnight. Book in advance. Midas-touch Manrique managed to turn the lower level of this fortress into a sleek temple to gastronomy. Like a showpiece of timeless 1970s design, the room is sleekly furnished with black chairs, leather-topped tables, and original wooden light fittings, and a sweeping arc of panoramic windows offers dynamic views of the port and the Mármoles pier. Even the washrooms are a work of genius – and they have their own harbour views. Serving imaginative and expertly presented Spanish and Canarian food, it's relaxed by day (when the *menu del día* is very good value) and smart in the evening (when main courses such as salmon with spinach, chicken breast with goat's cheese and sage, and grilled squid with green *mojo* cost around €12–15).

Chef Nizar

C/Luis Morote 19 ☎ 928 80 12 60. A comfortable, intimate and friendly place serving first-rate Lebanese specialities such as *kafta* and *baba ghanoush*, plus well-prepared grilled meat dishes at around €12 for a main course.

Domus Pompei

C/José Betancourt 19 ☎ 928 81 42 16. Daily 12.30–4.30pm & 8pm–midnight. Popular, cosy neighbourhood *trattoria* and *pizzeria* serving a good range of typical Italian dishes at decent prices, including main courses for under €10.

El Caracol

C/Río de Oro 17 ☎ 928 81 69 58. Closed Mon–Wed evenings & Sun. A chic, discreet little restaurant tucked away down a backstreet – an excellent recent addition to Arrecife's gourmet scene. Perfect for delicately spiced light meals such as lamb, ginger and mint meatballs or Indian-style vegetables at reasonable prices for a place of this quality.

La Montevideana

C/Carlos Sáenz Infante 30 ☎ 928 80 81 18. Mon-Sat 12.30–4pm & 8pm–midnight. Closed Sun. A small restaurant with bags of atmosphere, serving food (predominantly grills) from all corners of the Spanish-speaking world. Main courses average around €13.

La Puntilla

Ribera del Charco de San Ginés 52 ☎ 928 81 60 42. Closed Sun. The smartest of the lagoonside places, this quiet and pleasant bar-restaurant serves contemporary tapas and good fish dishes.

L'Arepera

C/Coronel Bens 9 (corner of C/Porra) ☎ 928 81 46 64. Atmospheric, volcanic stone-walled tapas bar. The house specialities are Venezuelan-style *arepas*, steamed and fried lumps of maize dough stuffed with meat or fish. Other excellent offerings include dates wrapped in crispy bacon, seafood salad, garlic mushrooms, *croquetas*, and good veggie options all for around €5 a portion – plus a small but delicious selection of puddings.

La Tinaja

C/Guenia 4 ☎928 81 44 96. Mon–Sat noon–4pm & 8pm–midnight, Sun noon–4pm. With tiled walls and wooden furniture, there's a very traditional Spanish feel to this place, which serves good tapas such as cod-stuffed peppers and local goat's cheese, plus classic Spanish and Canarian dishes: it's renowned for its Sunday lunchtime paella. Prices are above average.

Los Canarios

C/Leon y Castillo 39 ☎928 81 16 21. Rough-and-ready workers' eatery, very close to the main shopping area. From first impressions, it may seem a little intimidating to non-locals, but it's a good, cheap place to try simple Canarian food.

Pablo Ruiz Picasso

Centro Insular de Cultura El Almacén, C/José Betancort 33 ☎928 81 52 98. Part of César Manrique's El Almacén cultural centre, this pleasant, roomy bar-restaurant has a rustic feel, in keeping with its former status as a storehouse. It has a modest menu of light meals with a Canarian theme.

Pizzeria Italiana Gigi

C/Ruperto González Negrin 4. Open till midnight, closed Wed. First-rate pizza – probably the best in town. It's essentially a takeaway, but there are a few pavement tables if you'd rather eat on the spot. Everything is freshly made from scratch, and it's very popular, so be prepared to wait.

San Francisco

C/León y Castillo 12. Bang in the middle of the shopping centre, this is a cavernous, garishly lit basement tapas bar with a brisk, authentic atmosphere: a good place to try portions of anchovies, chorizo, roasted peppers or *papas arrugadas*.

Cafés and bars

Bar Andalucía

C/Luis Martín. This little pocket of southern Spain a few steps from Arrecife's principal shopping street makes a great, no-frills place to stop for a glass of wine.

Buzo's

C/Luis Morote 28. Evenings only, open till late. Small bar with a young, funky vibe, modern abstract art on the walls and volcano videos on screen.

Café Bar La Recova

C/Ginés de Castro y Alvarez 5. Large, atmospheric, rustic place serving drinks, tapas and sandwiches. Cheap and cheerful, it's highly popular with local shoppers.

Cafetería Rafael

C/Otilia Diaz. Closed evenings. Spacious tiled *cafetería* with a cheerful, Spanish feel, serving tapas, *churros* and *bocadillos*.

Crepería Canalejas

C/Canalejas 17. Closed Sat eve & Sun. Street-corner bar that's had a jazzy makeover, selling a small selection of tasty crepes, milkshakes, juices and sandwiches, plus good coffee.

El Linde

C/Canalejas 30. On a quiet corner, this chic café-bar furnished in dark wood has a contemporary vibe, and hosts occasional music and multimedia events.

Esencia de Luna

Pl Palmas 5. Closed Mon evening, Sat & Sun. Charming café with a New

▲ ALFRESCO CAFÉ ON ARRECIFE'S SEAFRONT

Age vibe, set on a tranquil and pretty church square close to the main shopping area, and serving good sandwiches.

Il Sole di Gelato
C/Canalejas 29 and Avda Mancomunicad 1. Congenial *gelaterias* serving fabulous Italian ice cream that tastes home-made, in a vast array of flavours.

La Minoca
Ribera del Charco de San Ginés 22. The best and friendliest of the café-bars with outdoor tables overlooking the city's peaceful central lagoon. An upbeat spot to enjoy a lunchtime beer with a crepe or a chunk of tortilla.

Moulin de Paris
C/Ginés de Castro y Alvarez 4. Closed evenings. French café on a quiet side street close to the heart of the shopping area, with a fine coffee menu and a good selection of *gateaux* and *patisserie*.

Rincón del Majo
Ribera del Charco de San Ginés 41. Lagoonside drinking place with a beach-bar feel. Live sessions from Spanish musicians from 11pm on Thurs & Sat.

Stars Bar
Arrecife Gran Hotel, Parque Islas Canarias. Panoramic views of the city and the volcanoes beyond plus a stylish, mellow atmosphere make this a sophisticated place to meet, and possibly the island's most impressive venue for sunset drinks.

Tasca Tambo
C/Luis Morote 24 (corner of C/José Betancort). Mon–Sat 8pm–3am. Very central tiny *tasca* serving up tapas and loud music for a young preclub crowd with a chilled, arty attitude.

Clubs

Calle José Antonio

C/José Antonio 59, 62, 71 & 76.
Wed–Sat 11pm–late. Free except
for special events. This clutch of
neighbouring nightspots – all
of which start warming up
after midnight from midweek
to Saturday – is the best area
on the island to get a feel for
the local (as opposed to tourist)
club scene. *Divino* (namesake
of the famous venue on Ibiza)
has regular live music sessions
and is the smartest of the bunch;
Seven specializes in laser shows
and massive video screens; *La*
Polinesia draws a lively student
crowd; while *Tsunami*'s surreal
trompe l'oeils make it – according
to the Spanish daily newspaper
El País – one of Spain's top 250
bars. Other venues include *Bar*
El 59, *El Convento*, *Black*, *Music*
Bar and *La Calle*.

Terraza La Biosfera

Avda Fred Olsen. Thurs, Fri & Sat
from midnight. Free except for special
events. A favourite spot for local
clubbers, this giant dome, just off
the seafront near the government
building west of town, hosts the
island's biggest music and dance
venue, with international DJs and
occasional live acts.

Puerto del Carmen

Lanzarote's first, and largest, resort, Puerto del Carmen is a cheerful jumble of beach umbrellas, bars, and chips-with-everything restaurants, backed by row upon row of neat little holiday villas, conveniently close to the airport. La Tiñosa, the old fishing village where it all started back in the 1960s, is still here – just – and the town that has grown up around it has the kind of genuine, down-to-earth atmosphere that purpose-built resorts can only dream of.

A major regeneration plan should soon bring the resort in line with the more modern developments else-where on the island – after four decades at the front line of package tourism, Puerto del Carmen's tacky, over-commercialized beachfront strip, Avenida de las Playas, is showing its age – but in the meantime tourists continue to flock here by the plane-load to enjoy the resort's easygoing, family-friendly character or to relax on its south-facing beaches, which seem to get more sun than anywhere else on the island.

Playa Grande

Puerto del Carmen's broad, pleasant main beach is the resort's pride and joy. With its signature blue and orange umbrellas, overlooked by a garden promenade planted with palms and hibiscus, Playa

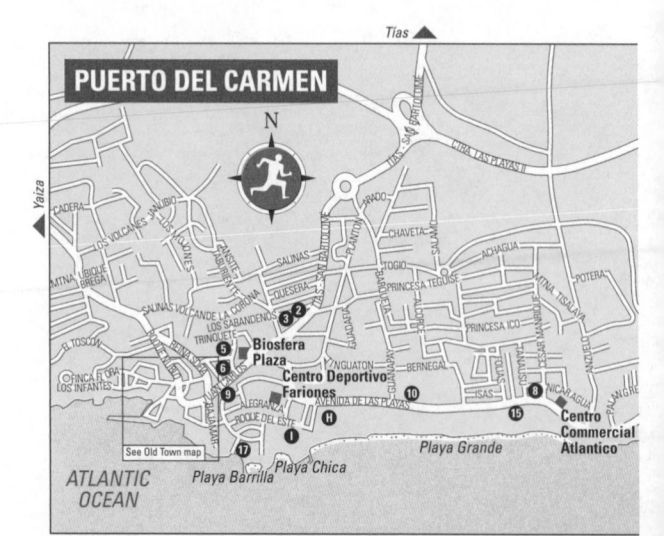

Arrival and information

Parking bays line most roads in Puerto del Carmen, and there are **car parks** at Punta Tiñosa in the Old Town and at the Biosfera Plaza shopping centre on Avenida Juan Carlos I. The town's **bus** (*guagua*) stops lie on a major route, *línea* #2, which has daily services from Arrecife via Playa Honda from 6.20am to 11.20pm (Mon–Fri every 20min, Sat & Sun every 30min) and six buses a day from Puerto Calero. The **tourist office** is on Avenida de las Playas (☎928 51 33 51; Mon–Fri 10am–10pm, Sat 10am–4pm).

Grande is an attractive sweep of sand. Around a kilometre long, it's easy to get to from all the centrally placed hotels and

▼ PLAYA GRANDE

holiday apartments, and well served by the restaurants and bars of the Avenida de las Playas. The water's great for swimming during the summer months.

Playa Chica and Playa de la Barilla

Small, sheltered and safe for snorkelling, these tucked-away coves are an appealing alternative to the main beach. Playa Chica is effectively the house beach of the *Hotel Los Fariones*; Playa de la Barilla is home to Safari Diving, a long-established scuba-diving station (see p.173), so sunbathers share the shallows with suited-and-booted divers.

El Rancho Texas ▲

Matagorda ▶

ACCOMMODATION

Apartamentos Cabrera	G
Apartamentos Fariones Playa	H
Apartamentos Floresta	A
Hotel La Geria	B
Hotel Los Fariones	I
Hotel Los Jameos Playa	C
Hotel San Antonio	F
Lanzarote Village	E
Riu Paraiso Lanzarote Resort	D

Playa de los Pocillos

EATING & DRINKING

Bäck Paradies	12
Bar Playa	17
Café La Ola	16
Catlanza Café	9
Cesars	10
Deutsche Bäckerei	1
Don Camillo	7
El Especiero	11
El Mirador La Playa	15
El Tomate	6
La Cañada	8
Mesón de Mariñeiro	13
Montmartre	6
O Botafumeiro	4
Quintins	2
Terraza Playa	14
Tomatissimo	5
Zafran	3

0   500 m

▲ OLD TOWN

– at least the Avenida doesn't pretend to be anything other than a neon-lit tourist strip. Pleasure boats have taken over the tiny harbour and, while old-style seafood restaurants still remain in abundance, the owners unload their fish from refrigerated vans instead of sorting through the daily catch.

The Old Town

The oldest and busiest part of Puerto del Carmen is its wharfside area, once an atmospheric fishing village called La Tiñosa but now so reconstructed – its storehouses and cottages converted into upbeat, tourist-friendly bars and eateries – that it's almost as tacky and manufactured as the Avenida de las Playas. Popular though the quarter may be with visitors, some may find the fakery a little nauseating

If beer, chips and holiday cheer are your thing, you'll be happy here, wherever you end up – for bar-crawl benders, it's the destination of choice. But with noisy theme pubs and tourist traps outnumbering the traditional restaurants and genuinely attractive tapas bars, it pays to be selective if you're looking for an authentic evening out.

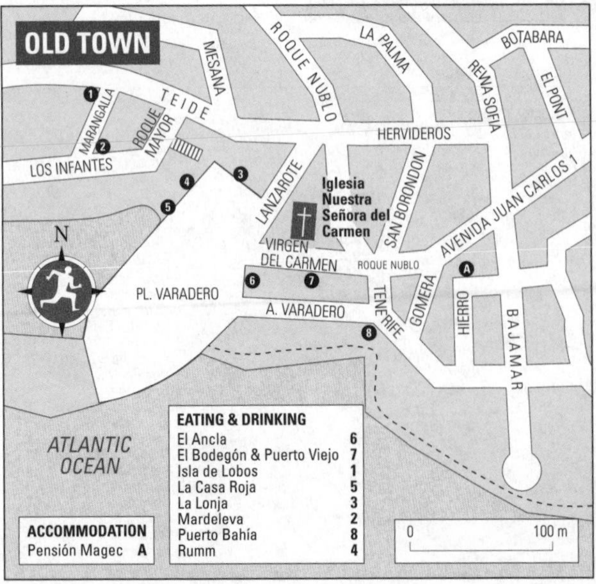

OLD TOWN

MESANA · ROQUE NUBLO · LA PALMA · BOTABARA · REWA SOFIA · EL PONT
TEIDE · MARANGALLA · ROQUE MAYOR · LOS INFANTES · HERVIDEROS
LANZAROTE · SAN BORONDON · AVENIDA JUAN CARLOS 1

Iglesia Nuestra Señora del Carmen

VIRGEN DEL CARMEN · ROQUE NUBLO
PL. VARADERO · A. VARADERO
TENERIFE · GOMERA · HIERRO · BAJAMAR

N

ATLANTIC OCEAN

EATING & DRINKING
El Ancla	6
El Bodegón & Puerto Viejo	7
Isla de Lobos	1
La Casa Roja	5
La Lonja	3
Mardeleva	2
Puerto Bahía	8
Rumm	4

ACCOMMODATION
Pensión Magec A

0   100 m

Events in Puerto del Carmen

The atmosphere in Puerto del Carmen steps up a notch during the town's **patronal fiestas**, which last for several weeks in July and August. The harbour is decked out with stalls, bars, fairground rides and a stage for musical events. This is a good time to see traditional dances featuring islanders of all ages dressed in peasant costume, accompanied by accomplished local *timple* players. On the **Fiesta de Nuestra Señora del Carmen** itself (July 16) a flotilla of decorated fishing boats sails out into the harbour.

Puerto del Carmen is also the focal point for annual professional athletics events including sections of the **Lanzarote Ironman** (see box on p.171).

Avenida de las Playas

Known locally as The Strip, Puerto del Carmen's six-kilometre-long seafront avenue is a classic ribbon development of shops, bars, restaurants and clubs catering for the tourist hordes. On the whole, it's an upfront, what-you-see-is-what-you-get kind of place: there's no real sleaze to be found here. In fact, brash though it is, there's a refreshing innocence to the avenida that helps give Puerto del Carmen more character than its younger, more purpose-built rival, Costa Teguise.

Most of the restaurants here – and there are literally hundreds to choose from – do their best to please tourist palates by offering an easy-going menu of international standards, even if that means favouring frozen ingredients over fresh. It's not all Irish pubs and English breakfasts, though – look carefully and you'll find the beginnings of a new breed of eating and drinking place created with the design-conscious young Euro-traveller in mind.

To escape the generally crowded beach, it's worth looking out for the steep flights of steps that lead down from the more built-up sections of the Avenida to the rocky shore – you may discover a tempting scrap of sand that you'll have all to yourself.

Los Pocillos and Matagorda

The broad, quiet Playa de los Pocillos to the east of town is backed by accommodation that's correspondingly peaceful and spacious, making Los Pocillos a popular area for family holidays. Further east still is Matagorda, a suburban quarter of timeshare bungalows and holiday

▼ ROCKY SHORE NEAR AVENIDA DE LAS PLAYAS

Activities in Puerto del Carmen

There's a moderate range of **sporting activities** on offer in Puerto del Carmen, and plenty of **excursions** to choose from, including coach tours and boat trips.

All the resort hotels have pools, and many have tennis courts, but the best **sports facilities** in town are at the Centro Deportivo Fariones (C/Alegranza 2, ☎928 51 47 90), a multi-sports centre near the *Hotel Los Fariones*. This is where the island's tennis tournaments are held; there are also squash courts, a large gym and a heated outdoor pool.

Several companies offer **watersports** such as parascending, powerboat and banana-boat rides. There are also a few scuba-diving outfits here, although the sites in the immediate vicinity aren't that great. If you'd rather churn up the dust on terra firma then try one of the out-of-town **go-karting** tracks or book a **quad-biking** trip. For operators' details, see "Essentials" (p.170).

apartments. Unfortunately, the beach here is rather narrow, and its close proximity to the airport means that aircraft noise shatters the peace at regular intervals.

El Rancho Texas

Near Puerto del Carmen ☎928 84 12 86, ☜www.ranchotexaslanzarote .com. Daily 9.30am–5.30pm. €14, children 2–12 years €9. This small Wild West theme park offers pony rides, a Native American village exhibit, and a creek to canoe in. Modest though the place may seem, there's enough to keep pre-teens happy for a whole day, with events such as meet-the-animals sessions, featuring eagles, crocodiles and racoons amongst others.

The park also hosts Country & Western nights with line dancing and live music for cowboys of all ages (Mon, Tues, Fri & Sat 7–11pm; €40, children €20 including a BBQ, soft drinks and sangria).

Hotels

Hotel La Geria

C/Júpiter 5, Playa de los Pocillos ☎928 51 04 41, ☜www.hipotels.com. Smaller than the other resort hotels, with a tranquil atmosphere and a palm-shaded pool garden

offering clear views of Los Pocillos beach. The rooms are rather characterless, though. €135.

Hotel Los Fariones

C/Roque del Este 1 ☎928 51 01 95, ☜www.grupofariones.com. The *Hotel Los Fariones* was one of the island's first tourist hotels, and while the rooms are now showing their age, there's still a civilised grandeur to the place. Conveniently close to both the Old Town and the Avenida, it has direct beach access: the view of the sea through the palms leaning decoratively over the pool is spectacular. Guests receive a small discount at the nearby sports centre (see above). €142.

Hotel Los Jameos Playa

Playa de los Pocillos ☎928 51 17 17, ☜www.los-jameos-playa.de. The top hotel in the Los Pocillos area, and arguably the best in Puerto del Carmen, this place impresses from the start with an atrium that's styled like a gigantic Canarian mansion, complete with timber galleries and lanterns. The theme continues with tiled floors, blue-painted balconies and whitewashed walls. The rooms are bright, and the pool area is beautifully designed – even the mini-golf, arranged beside a gurgling stream, is a work of art. Excellent, friendly service, and all the facilities you'd expect from a large four-star hotel. €136 (inland view) or €202 (sea view).

Hotel San Antonio

Avda Playas 84 ☏ 928 51 42 00, ⓦ www.hotelsanantonio.com. Built in the 1970s, the *San Antonio's* slightly dated style is matched by the attitude of its staff, with service that can be either frosty or slow. Its best points are its large and pleasant pools, direct access to a rocky stretch of beach, and reasonable prices. €112.

Riu Paraiso Lanzarote Resort

C/Suiza 4, Playa de los Pocillos ☏ 928 51 24 00, ⓦ www.riu.com. This all-inclusive four-star mega-resort was created by merging two seafront properties into one. Now so large that some guests have a hefty walk from their room to reception, it has taken on an impersonal character – not helped by its mediocre catering – but is comfortable for families and particularly popular with German tourists. From €154 (inland view) or €192 (sea view).

Apartments

Apartamentos Cabrera

Avda Playas 70 ☏ 928 51 36 94, ⓦ www.apartamentoscabrera.com. Three-storey block of small, simple apartments with an old-fashioned feel and limited facilities (there's no pool), but a fantastic location, perched right on the rocky shore and close to all the action on the Avenida. €52.

Apartamentos Fariones Playa

C/Acatife 1 ☏ 928 51 34 00, ⓦ www.grupofariones.com. This large, modern suite-hotel, adjacent to the *Los Fariones*, has a great beachside pool and, if you can stomach the concrete slab-like architecture, is one of the smartest self-catering places in town. The complex includes a PADI 5-Star scuba-diving centre, and all guests receive a small discount at the nearby Fariones sports centre (see p.66). €140.

Floresta

C/Mercurio 2, Pocillos ☏ 928 51 43 45. In a good, quiet location close to the Pocillos beach, this attractively landscaped complex has clean and competitively priced mini apartments equipped with basic kitchen facilities. €78.

Lanzarote Village

Avda Suiza 2 ☏ 928 51 13 44. Simple but pleasant three-star apartho-tel, a short walk from Playa de los Pocillos. The apartments are studio-style, each with a kitchenette and a terrace or balcony; they're moderately sized and sparsely furnished but are great value. €55.

Guesthouses

Pensión Magec

C/Hierro 11 ☏ 928 51 51 20, ⓦ www.pensionmagec.com. The only *pensión* in Puerto del Carmen, this is by far the cheapest place to stay in the area. Though small and simple, and with no parking, it is well kept, and the location – on a quiet backstreet of the Old Town – is very convenient. €24 (shared bathroom) or €30 (en suite).

Shops

Biosfera Plaza

Avda Juan Carlos I, 15. Mon–Sat 10am–10pm, Sun 11am–9pm. The island's busiest modern shopping centre, featuring high-street fashion brands such as Zara, The Body Shop, Levi's and Rip Curl, plus cafés and a children's play zone.

Bookswop

C/Timanfaya 4 and CC Costa Luz. Mon–Fri 9.30am–6pm, Sat 9.30am–1.30pm. The best places to find new and secondhand books in English.

Tienda Fundación César Manrique

Avda Playas 30. Mon–Sat 10am–6pm. Small outlet selling a selection of gifts incorporating Manrique's art and designs.

Restaurants, bodegas and tapas bars

Café La Ola

Avda Playas 35 ☎928 51 50 81, ⊕www.cafelaola.com. Daily 10.30am–3am, food served till 11pm. Like an upmarket slice of Ibiza airlifted in from the Med, this is a hip new departure for Puerto del Carmen. It's an all-day and late-night chillout venue serving drinks and Asian-fusion food, at above-average prices, in a space decorated like a fantasy Thai temple, with richly coloured silk cushions, lanterns and Buddhas. There's even a romantic four-poster bed on the sea-facing pool deck. The restaurant upstairs is more conventional, but has an interesting international mishmash of a menu.

Don Camillo

Avda Playas 67 ☎928 51 12 71. Busy, genial place serving up steaks and pizzas, desserts decorated with sparklers, and complimentary after-dinner liqueurs.

▲ STRELITZIA (BIRD OF PARADISE FLOWER)

El Ancla

Pl Varadero 12 ☎928 51 19 33. Shamelessly touristy, this big, bustling Old Town restaurant packs in the punters for huge plates of Canarian-style food or familiar international-style fare. Good value, with plenty of choices under €10.

El Bodegón & Puerto Viejo

Pl Varadero ☎928 51 52 65. Give the harbourside section of this busy restaurant a miss – it's a tourist trap serving uninspired standards – and head instead to the tapas bar at the back. Much more atmospheric, with hunks of *jamón iberico* hanging over the counter, this is a great place to enjoy a *tabla* (mixed grill) or a simple plate of manchego cheese and olives.

El Especiero

Avda Playas 42 ☎928 51 21 82. Closed Sun. With great views from its large sea-facing windows, this restaurant has the usual long menu of standard dishes but at lower-than-average prices. The paella is fantastic value at €7.50 per person (min of 2 people).

El Tomate & Tomatissimo

C/Jameos ☎928 51 19 85 & 928 51 42 53. Daily 7–11pm. A few paces apart near the Biosfera Plaza shopping centre, these twin restaurants are great little places to fill up on cheap, tasty Italian-European food. *Tomatissimo* is a pizzeria; *El Tomate* has a more international menu.

Isla de Lobos

C/Teide 9 ☎617 26 29 45. Tucked away on the far side of the Old Town, this simple, old-fashioned fish restaurant is a favourite of in-the-know locals. With most dishes less than €10, and a kids' menu for under €4, it's very affordable.

La Cañada

C/Cesar Manrique 3 ☎928 51 04 15. It's rare to find good-quality, authentic Canarian food in Puerto del Carmen, so it's worth eating here to find out what you've been missing – it's the best place around to try island standards such as roasted goat or kid and *papas arrugadas*. Main courses average around €12–15.

La Casa Roja

Pl Varadero ☎928 51 58 66. Daily 10am–11.30pm. Perched right on the harbour wall, this nautically themed restaurant occupies one of the few genuinely old buildings left in the Old Town. As well as the usual fish and grills there are tasty choices such as chicken with almonds, and local-style puddings such as *bienmesabe*.

La Lonja

Pl Varadero ☎928 51 13 77. This brightly lit, high-ceilinged harbourside building still smacks – more than most – of the days when La Tiñosa was a busy little fishing port. You can pull up a stool at the bar and take your pick from a fine array of tapas

(€3–11), or settle down at one of the outdoor tables for grilled fish or steak (€7–15).

Mardeleva

C/Los Infantes 10 ☎928 51 06 86. Closed Sun. A little out of the way (reached by climbing the steps to the right of *Rumm*), this unassuming neighbour-hood restaurant has a great little terrace with harbour views. It's a quiet and pleasant spot to share a jug of sangría or tuck into some keenly priced tapas (around €3) or a grill (most under €7).

Mesón do Mariñeiro

Avda Playas 56. Closed Mon. More authentic than most of the seafront restaurants, this place offers a great selection of tortillas and *revueltos*, plus plenty of other very reasonably priced choices, most of them under €10.

Montmartre

C/Jameos ☎928 51 30 48. One of Puerto del Carmen's very few French restaurants, this place has a cosy, old-fashioned atmosphere, serving classics such as beef bourguignon for €10.50–14.50.

Puerto Bahía

Avda Varadero 5 ☎928 51 37 93. Offering the usual fare at slightly above-average prices (mains €7.50–16.50), *Puerto Bahía* has the edge over its rivals due to its location in one of the Old Town's best spots, commanding great coastal views.

O Botafumeiro

C/Alemania 9, CC Costa Luz ☎928 51 15 03. Daily 1–4pm & 7pm–midnight. Galician restaurant serving specialities such as eel and hake. There's a good-value lunchtime menu (€11), but if you're ready to push the boat out you could go for a seafood *parillada* (mixed platter; €70 for 2).

Quintins

Avda Juan Carlos I, 25g ☎928 51 57 55. Mon–Sat 7–11pm. A welcome addition to the local restaurant scene, this sleek, spacious eatery has contemporary art on the walls, mellow jazz in the background and modern classics, such as veal parcels with celeriac mash and duck with cherries, on the menu, plus a good list of Spanish wine. British-run, the cooking, though ambitious, isn't quite as good the prices would suggest, but the presentation is top notch.

Terraza Playa

Avda Playas 28 ☎928 51 54 17. Puerto del Carmen has surprisingly few restaurants right on the shore, so to walk down the steps to the palm-shaded beach terrace at this endearing little place feels like a bit of a treat. The menu is nothing unusual but some dishes, such as prawns with avocado, are done very well. It's a good place for parents to enjoy lunch or a beer while keeping an eye on the kids as they paddle. Not to be confused with the chain restaurant *Terraza* up on the Avenida.

Zafran

CC Olivin, Avda Juan Carlos I, 25 ☎928 51 27 47. Mon & Wed–Sun 6pm–midnight. Take-away and delivery available. Quality Indian restaurant serving traditional Hindu cuisine, plus Spanish wine and Kingfisher and Cobra lager. Using careful combinations of spices, the chef will adjust the sauces according to whether you prefer your curry mild or fiery.

Cafés and bars

Bäck Paradies

Avda Playas, near C/Italia. Daily 10am–7pm. Open-air café serving big chunks of German-style cake and pretzels from a little pavilion overlooking the sea. There are loaves of German-recipe bread for sale, too.

Bar Playa

Playa de la Barilla. Unpretentious beach bar that's a favourite with clients from the nearby dive shop who come here to down a few post-dip beers. There's decent fish and chips on offer, too.

Catlanza Café

Avda Juan Carlos I. Small, cheerful English-speaking roadside bar where a large beer poured into a glass straight out of the freezer will set you back €2.

Deutsche Bäckerei

Avda Playas 89, Matagorda. Daily 9am–10pm. A fantastic seafront bakery-café that's excellent for breakfast, pitta-bread sandwiches, pastries, ice cream or cocktails. Its first floor terrace has great views of Playa de los Pocillos.

El Mirador La Playa

Avda Playas. At the east end of Playa Grande, and overlooking the beach, this is a pleasant spot for ice cream, beer or a light meal. There's live music from 9pm most evenings.

Clubs

Buddy's Jazz Club

C/Tenerife 18. Daily 10pm–3.30am. Old Town venue with live music every night; a welcome change from karaoke and cover versions.

▲ EL MIRADOR LA PLAYA

Centro Commercial Atlántico
Avda Playas.
The beating heart of Lanzarote's
tourist-oriented pub and
club scene is the Centro
Commercial Atlántico, a small,
unprepossessing concrete
complex that stirs into life at
night, when eager touts tempt
passers by with vouchers
offering free vodka shots and
flaming sambucas. Pick of
the bars are *Atomic Revolution*
(daily 8pm–late), for loud,
unsophisticated fun in the form
of cocktails, drinking games and
pool; *Big Apple* (daily 8pm–late),
a tired and tatty – but still
popular – bar with a dance
floor; and *Black and White* (daily
9.30pm–4am), one of Puerto
del Carmen's handful of gay
venues.

César's
Avda Playas 14. Daily 10pm–4am.
Popular club with a more
glamorous edge than many of
the resort's other offerings. It
makes a big show of its Ancient
Roman theme.

Rumm
Pl Varadero. Bar 7pm–3am, club
11pm–3am. This super-cool new
harbourside cocktail lounge and
club has a terrace inspired by a
Moroccan *riad* – all deep sofas,
lanterns and carpets – and an
icy-blue bar with a chillout vibe.
The club throbs to house music
every night.

San Bartolomé and Tías

San Bartolomé district is the perfect place to start exploring the sleek, chic, visionary world of Lanzarote's most celebrated artist, architect and cultural ambassador, César Manrique.

Manrique died in 1992 but his creative influence is still very much in evidence all over the island, and a visit to his former house, the architecturally fascinating Taro de Tahíche, is an absolute must. Home to the Fundación César Manrique, it stages excellent contemporary art and photography shows alongside a permanent collection of twentieth-century European works.

Two more examples of Manrique's work, the Monumento al Campesino and the Casa-Museo del Campesino, are found just outside San Bartolomé town, the district capital. A sleepy but pleasant place, San Bartolomé boasts one of the island's best folk museums, the Museo Etnográfico Tanit.

The rugged, arid interior of neighbouring Tías district is dominated by the brooding presence of Montaña Blanca, and dotted with hillside villages, some with commanding views of the sea. North of the mountain is wine-growing country, with *bodegas* to visit, local produce to sample and interesting rustic places to stay. The island's oldest winery, El Grifo, has a museum open to the public.

On the coast, a smart new promenade runs all the way from Arrecife to Puerto del Carmen, via the seaside suburbs of Playa Honda and Playa del Cable.

Visiting San Bartolomé and Tías districts

For maximum flexibility, the best way to explore the area is by **renting a car** (see p.167). Public transport to all but the main towns is infrequent (a complete bus timetable is available online at ⊛www.arrecifebus.com), but from Arrecife **buses** (*guaguas*) run to San Bartolomé (*líneas* #16 and #20; 11 buses a day Mon–Fri, 5 on Sat, 3 on Sun), Tías and Macher (*líneas* #5; #6 and #19; 16 buses a day Mon–Fri, 6 on Sat, 8 on Sun), Conil and La Asomada (*línea* #5; 1 bus a day Mon–Fri) and El Islote and Masdache (*línea* #14; 3 buses a day Mon–Fri). Buses from Arrecife run to Playa Honda and the airport every thirty minutes from 7.10am to 10.50pm (*línea* #4).

Three bus routes from Arrecife pass within walking distance of the **Fundación César Manrique**: *línea* #7 to Maguez (6 buses a day Mon–Fri, 4 on Sat, 3 on Sun), *línea* #9 to Orzola (3 buses a day Mon–Fri, 2 on Sat, 2 on Sun) and *línea* #10 to Los Valles (3 buses a day Mon–Fri).

Local **tour companies** include the area in their island itineraries; most large hotels can supply details.

Fundación César Manrique

Taro de Tahíche, near Tahíche ☏928 84 31 38, ⊛www.fcmanrique.org. July–Oct Mon–Sat 10am–7pm; Nov–June Mon–Sat 10am–6pm, Sun 10am–3pm. €7, children free. The visually stunning Taro de Tahíche was the private residence of César Manrique, who lived here from the late 1960s until the mid-80s, when he moved to his relatively low-key second home in Haría to avoid the uninvited guests who were forever dropping in at Tahíche. Since his death in 1992, the Taro has been privately managed as an art museum by the Fundación César Manrique.

César Manrique Cabrera (1919–1992)

The Lanzarote aesthetic – that distinctive combination of simple whitewashed houses and stark volcanic landscapes, unspoilt by billboards, ugly high-rise developments and, for the most part, litter – owes everything to one man, the individual who created much of the island's public art and all of its most imaginative architecture: **César Manrique**.

Born in Arrecife, Manrique studied architecture and art in La Laguna, on Tenerife, and in Madrid, going on to spend a chunk of his creative career in New York, fraternizing with the likes of Andy Warhol and John Bernard Myers. However, his heart remained firmly lodged in Lanzarote, and Canarian projects consumed most of his time, energy and passion during the latter half of his life.

A true polymath, Manrique is most celebrated for his architectural projects, but he was also an accomplished painter, sculptor, horticulturalist, ecologist and environmentalist. In matters relating to urban development and sustainable and responsible tourism, he was way ahead of his time – in the 1960s, Manrique, aware of Lanzarote's enormous potential as a tourist destination but mindful of the planning mistakes that blighted other Canary Islands and mainland Spain, began campaigning for controlled, sympathetic development that stuck to **traditional architectural styles** and colours. Thus, every building had to be low-rise and whitewashed, with green windows, shutters and doors (originally, the green paint left over from fishermen painting their boats was used; Manrique suggested the only other colours permitted for architectural timbers should be brown, if the house faced a volcano, or blue, if it faced the sea). He also knew that in order to attract discerning visitors, Lanzarote would have to offer more than just sun, sea and sand. With this in mind he set about creating seven unique **visitor attractions**: the Jameos del Agua; the Casa-Museo del Campesino; *El Diablo*, in the Parque Nacional de Timanfaya; the Mirador del Río; MIAC, at the Castillo de San José; the Cueva de los Verdes; and the Jardín del Cactus. He also designed distinctively quirky sculptures to brighten up key public locations: his wonderfully fanciful **juguetes del viento** (wind toys) add a dynamic splash of colour to the island's roundabouts.

Manrique's influence over the islanders, from decision-makers down to village property-owners, was impressive, to say the least, and at the time of his death in 1992, aged 73, his seven visionary projects were complete. A year later, UNESCO designated Lanzarote a World Biosphere Reserve in recognition of the islanders' respect for their unique environment, and the preservation of the landscapes that ignited Manrique's creative passions seemed secure. Today, Manrique's work is immaculately maintained by the island government and, thanks to the guidelines he hammered home, his vision lives on.

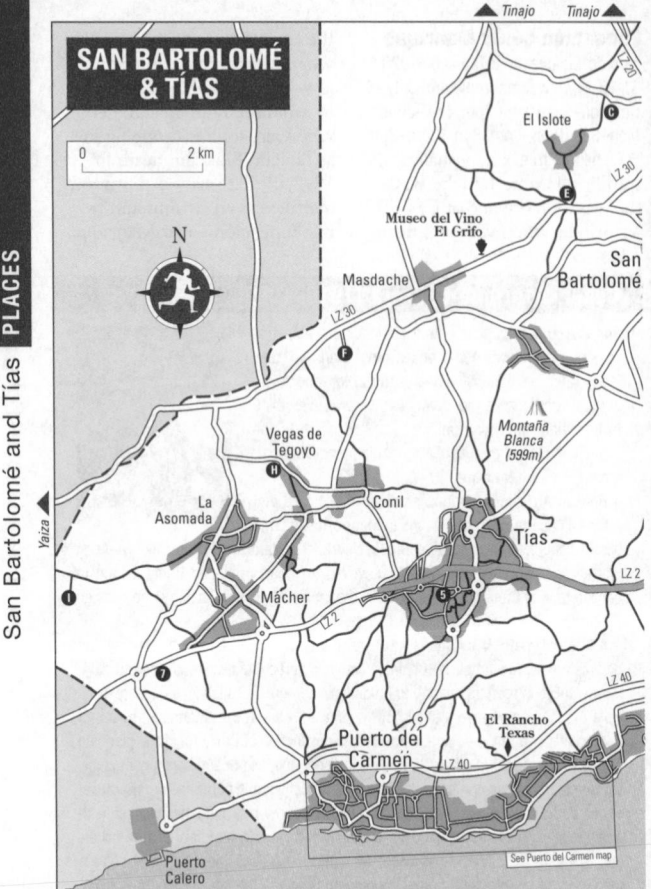

One of the cornerstones of Lanzarote's fascinating artistic and creative heritage, the *fundación* is an essential stop if you've already admired some of Manrique's creations elsewhere on the island and would like to find out what made this man of genius tick.

Manrique had an intuitive affinity with the volcanic wilderness of his island home, and the Taro de Tahíche, poised within a spectacular sweep of solidified lava, is perhaps the most revealing of his acts of

creative self-expression. In this one dwelling, completed in 1968, he managed to create a witty synthesis of traditional and futuristic architecture, inspired by, and working in close harmony with, the house's extraordinary natural surroundings.

He designed the house on two levels. The ground floor is styled as a traditional Canarian rural dwelling (a *taro* is a building with dry stone walls, sometimes used for maturing cheese),

Teguise

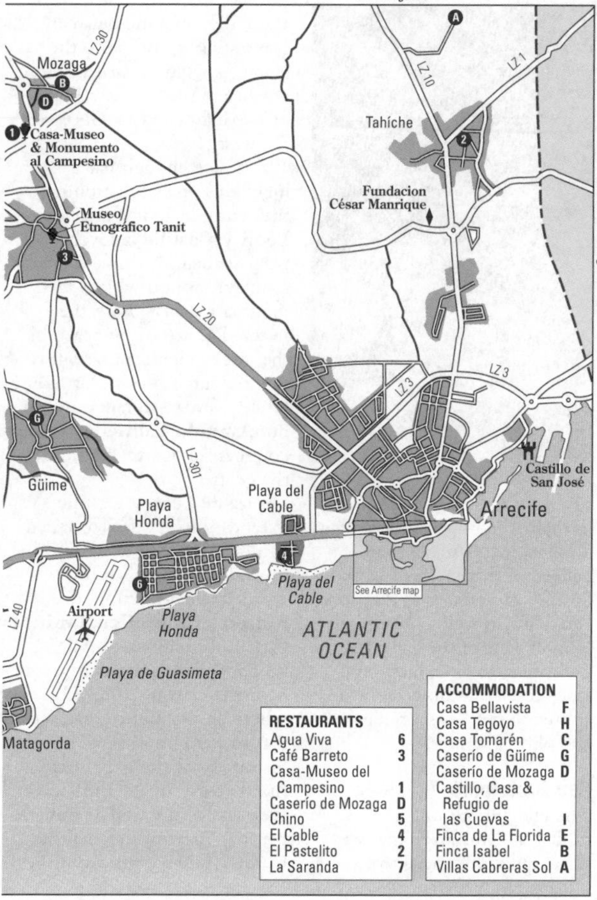

A

LZ 30

Mozaga
B
D

1 Casa-Museo
& Monumento
al Campesino

Tahíche

2

LZ 10

LZ 1

Museo
Etnográfico Tanit
3

Fundacion
César Manrique

LZ 20

Costa Teguise

LZ 301

LZ 3

LZ 3

G

Castillo de
San José

Güime

Playa
Honda

Playa del
Cable

Arrecife

LZ 40

6

Airport

Playa
Honda

Playa del
Cable

4

See Arrecife map

Playa de Guasimeta

ATLANTIC
OCEAN

Matagorda

RESTAURANTS	
Agua Viva	6
Café Barreto	3
Casa-Museo del Campesino	1
Caserío de Mozaga	D
Chino	5
El Cable	4
El Pastelito	2
La Saranda	7

ACCOMMODATION	
Casa Bellavista	F
Casa Tegoyo	H
Casa Tomarén	C
Caserío de Güíme	G
Caserío de Mozaga	D
Castillo, Casa & Refugio de las Cuevas	I
Finca de La Florida	E
Finca Isabel	B
Villas Cabreras Sol	A

complete with whitewashed facades and a colourful patio. Manrique's love of the *malpaís* glows through the architecture: large windows frame stunning views of volcanoes, and let the lava "flow into" the interior here and there. Underneath this are five adjoining lava caves dating from the island's eighteenth-century volcanic eruptions. The caves were formed naturally by trapped gases expanding just beneath the surface of the lava as it solidified, and Manrique

turned these into bubble-rooms decorated in über-modern late-60s style.

The colours he chose are the colours of vulcanology – black, white and red – and while the dominant style is minimalism at its sleekest, the burrow-like underground areas are softened by curvy passageways of glossy whitewash, and by a decorative pool with a soothing fountain.

While the lower floor bubble-rooms have been preserved more or less as Manrique lived

▲ FUNDACÍON CÉSAR MANRIQUE

at the dividing line between contrasting landscapes – the sandy, agricultural *jable* to the north, and the arid lava fields of Timanfaya and La Geria to the west.

It's a nice enough place: highlights of a stroll around the centre include **Plaza de León y Castillo**, a lovely palm-shaded square with a fountain, around which stand the smart *ayuntamiento*, the restored Teatro Municipal and the stocky eighteenth-century parish church of San Bartolomé, while a few restaurants and cafés dot **Avenida Palmeras**, in the commercial quarter southeast of the centre.

Plaza de León y Castillo extends into spotless terraced gardens that lead down towards the town's most worthwhile attraction, the **Museo Etnográfico Tanit**, at C/Constitución 1 (☎928 52 06 55, ⓦwww.museotanit.com; Mon–Sat 10am–2pm; €3), where all manner of artefacts record Lanzarote's social history, from the *majos* (its first known inhabitants) to the islanders of the mid-twentieth century. As your eyes adjust to the relative dimness of the

in them, the upper floor is now a gallery, with an excellent collection that includes work by Spanish greats such as Picasso and Miró, as well as Manrique himself. Part of the gallery is given over to an exhibition space for shows from renowned contemporary artists, sculptors and photographers.

San Bartolomé

The eponymous district capital of San Bartolomé is a small, quiet provincial town

▼ PLAZA DE LEÓN Y CASTILLO, SAN BARTOLOMÉ

main exhibition room – a former wine cellar that's still suffused with the heady aroma of old vintages – it's the sheer quantity of objects on display that impresses most: the walls are crammed with threshing boards, ancient pottery, fiesta costumes and musical instruments, including a *rascadera* made of bones, which bear witness to a folk culture that's now all but disappeared.

San Bartolomé's other historic features include a few windmills, once used to grind corn into *gofio* and now in various states of disrepair, and the **Casa del Mayor Guerra** (☎928 522 351), perched on the southwestern edge of town. Closed for restoration at the time of writing, this eighteenth-century country villa has been converted into a museum, craft shop and Canarian restaurant.

Monumento al Campesino and Casa-Museo del Campesino

Near Mozaga ☎928 52 01 36, ⊛www .cabildodelanzarote.com/cact. Museum daily 10am–5.45pm, craft workshops daily 10.30–5.15pm. Free. Bang in the middle of the island, Manrique's Monumento al Campesino (Farmworker Monument), subtitled *Fecundidad* (Fertility), is a tribute to Lanzarote's pastoral heritage, and the fortitude of the islanders who have, for generations, managed to make a living from this challenging terrain. A cubist conglomeration of white solids made from the water tanks of old fishing boats, it's a fifteen-metre-high metaphor for the harshness of island life, where the sea is a vital source of sustenance and water is cripplingly scarce.

Adjoining the monument is the Casa-Museo del Campesino, a museum and cultural centre that recreates a typical *Conejero* farmer's home. One of Manrique's earliest projects – it was completed in 1969 – it includes all the elements of traditional rural island architecture: whitewashed facades, turret-like chimneys, green-painted timbers and a central patio. Arranged around the patio is a series of craft workshops where, if you're visiting as part of an organized tour (or you happen to coincide with one), you can watch demonstrations of pottery- and basket-making, leatherwork, weaving and embroidery. Next to these is a wine shop showcasing local vintages, while the farmhouse kitchen, which operates as an excellent tapas bar (see p.81), is full of old-fashioned implements.

On the first floor there's a celebration of the artful simplicity of island architecture, with a collection of scale models of Lanzarotean churches, and a couple of rooms of hand-moulded ceramic objects and naïve rustic figures inspired by peasant culture and myth, the work of local archeologist and artist Juan Brito Martín.

PLACES San Bartolomé and Tías

▼ MONUMENTO AL CAMPESINO

Head back downstairs and into the restaurant (see p.81) and you enter another sphere: the hand of Manrique is very evident in this swaggeringly *modernismo* banqueting hall, excavated out of a pair of volcanic bubbles and connected to the central patio by a curving tunnel lined with blocks of lava and decorated with spot-lit replicas of ancient ceramic vessels.

Mozaga, El Islote, Masdache and around

The tidy village of Mozaga and its neighbour, the hamlet of El Islote, both well-to-do rural communities, make excellent bases from which to explore central Lanzarote, a wine-growing region with a rugged attractiveness unique to the island. In this harsh landscape, ancient-looking lichens and succulents cling to dynamic folds and fissures of solidified lava, and agave trees

▼ EL ISLOTE

tilt at improbable angles over the scene. In stark contrast to this natural chaos is the zen-like orderliness of the volcanic vineyards, with their neat ranks of crescent-shaped *zocos*, the low dry-stone walls that act as windbreaks for the vines. If you're planning an island wine tour (see box on p.98), it's definitely worth including this region.

The area around Masdache is particularly attractive, with smart country villas presiding over the farmland. Masdache itself has a striking church, Iglesia La Magdalena, built in the 1970s in traditional style, with an architecturally impressive first-floor balcony.

Museo del Vino El Grifo

Near Masdache ☎928 52 49 51, ⊛www.elgrifo.com. Daily 10.30am–6pm. Free. Founded in 1775 – it's thought that the palm tree outside the entrance is even older – the Museo del Vino El Grifo is situated in the oldest Canarian wine cellar still in use. The museum's displays focus on assorted bits of wine-making machinery, though the main reason most visitors are here is to try one of the *bodega*'s excellent wines – El Grifo is now Lanzarote's biggest producer, and one of the island's two best-known brands (the other major player being La Geria; see p.98). Visitors receive one free sample, and further tastings are very reasonably priced. It's worth trying the Barrica, their most traditional wine, aged in fresh barrels, or the Ana Moscatel, which has rich, but subtle, toffee and caramel notes, and an interesting aftertaste.

El Grifo is difficult to miss: it's on the LZ-30, its entrance signposted by Manrique's

▲ WINE SHOP, MUSEO DEL VINO EL GRIFO

Pájaro Grifo roadside sculpture depicting a flying griffin.

Tías and Mácher

The towns of Tías and Mácher are favourite hangouts of the island's expatriate British community: you'll find a lively mixture of British and Spanish businesses rubbing shoulders here. One reason to stop on Avenida Central, the main street in Tías, is the **Sala de Arte Ermita de San Antonio**, a former chapel that's now an art gallery, hosting exhibitions of painting, photography and sculpture (generally Mon–Fri 9am–1pm & 5–8pm, Sat 10am–2pm). The surrounding area is becoming something of a development hotspot – there's a new cod-Gaudí apartment complex, impossible to miss beside the LZ-2, while an 18-hole golf course, plus a complex of hotels and apartments, will be opening between Tías and Puerto del Carmen in 2007.

To get to one of Manrique's lesser-known **wind mobiles**, take the road from Tías to San Bartolomé: the *juguete del viento* is roughly halfway, on the roundabout right at the foot of Montaña Blanca.

Playa del Cable and Playa Honda

The coastal suburbs of Arrecife that stretch out into Tías district are a mixed bag of low-rent housing, beach bungalows and swisher executive villas, served by a couple of excellent restaurants. Playa del Cable is broad and low-key; a good way to appreciate it is to take a stroll along the promenade that runs from Arrecife to Matagorda, on the edge of Playa del Carmen. The walk from the *Arrecife Gran Hotel* (see p.52) to the old harbour in Puerto del Carmen (see p.64) is around 15km, so you could cover the whole distance in under three hours. On the way is Playa Honda's **Terraza Concorde**, where there's a market selling crafts, gifts and oddments on Saturdays (9.30am–4pm). You'll also skirt around the airport perimeter: exciting stuff when there are aircraft taking off overhead.

Hotels

Casa Tegoyo

C/Conil-Asomada 3 ☎928 83 43 85, ⊛www.tegoyolanzarote.com. Oozing character, this *hotel rural* occupies a creaky country mansion built around a leafy patio. All five rooms and six suites are dramatically elegant, and the bar is one of the cosiest places on the island to spend an evening. If that's not reason enough to stay here, there's also a stylish pool area with lovely vineyard views (marred, sadly, by the pylons that march through the plot), and a sauna. Doubles from €125, suites from €155.

Caserío de Mozaga

C/Mozaga 8, Mozaga ☎928 52 00 60, ⊛www.caseriodemozaga.com. A small, stylish country-house hotel in a sleepy village, the *Caserío de Mozaga* is a tranquil place, full of old-fashioned charm, with discreetly furnished bedrooms, pleasant gardens and useful extras such as Internet

▲ CASERÍO DE MOZAGA

access and satellite TV (there are plans to build a swimming pool, too). The restaurant is one of the island's best, so prepare yourself for a superb breakfast. €115.

Finca de La Florida

C/El Islote 90, El Islote ☎928 52 11 24, ⓦwww.hotelfincadelaflorida.com. On the edge of Lanzarote's winelands, this sixteen-room hotel has a decent restaurant (see p.82) and is popular with well-to-do locals as a venue for family celebrations. It has far more facilities than most rural hotels, including a garden with a small pool, a tennis court and a children's playground. Guests are also free to wander through the vineyards and orchard on the estate. The bedrooms are a little dated in style but have air-con and plenty of space; some have balconies with sweeping views of the winelands and the volcanoes beyond. €98.

Apartments and villas

Casa Bellavista

Masdache ☎928 84 57 23, ⓦwww.islaviva.com. A simple but charming two-bed rural house on a hillside with fabulous views of volcanoes and vineyards. Whitewashed stone walls and a pretty patio give the place a cosy atmosphere. €82.

Casa Tomarén

C/Tomarén 33, El Islote ☎928 52 08 18 or 676 45 30 08, ⓦwww.casaelmorro.com. Six lovely, well-equipped rural villas (sleeping 2–6 each) on a converted *finca* on the edge of the lava fields. The young Lanzarotean owner and his Indonesian wife have furnished the houses in east-meets-west style, and created one of the island's most peaceful and attractive swimming pools in a garden built in a *jameo* (volcanic bubble). Studio €60, villas from €90.

Caserío de Güime

C/La Entrada 35, Güíme ☎928 52 12 23 or 609 68 55 79, ⓦwww.caserioguime.net. Three attractively rustic one-bed single-storey villas, each with private pools and charming gardens, in a beautifully converted eighteenth-century *finca*. The quiet village location is popular with expats and within easy driving distance of Arrecife and the coast. €125.

Castillo, Casa & Refugio de las Cuevas

Valle de las Cuevas, La Asomada ☎928 51 11 59 or 606 63 34 09, ⓦwww.lascasascanarias.com. Three uniquely lovely apartments embedded into a cliff-face overlooking a secluded barranco, or small valley. There's a swimming pool on-site, and the ingenious design incorporates naturally occurring rocky hollows and caves. Beautifully decorated, charming and quite extraordinary. One-bed apartment €95, two-bed apartment €135.

Finca Isabel

C/Malvas 11, Mozaga ☎928 84 57 23, ☒www.islaviva.com. For those who dream of staying somewhere Manrique-esque, this converted farm comes pretty close. Its three apartments (two with two bedrooms plus one studio) are built around volcanic hollows containing perfect little swimming pools. Studio €85, two-bed apartment €120.

Villas Cabreras Sol

Las Cabreras ☎928 84 59 00, UK ☎0151 342 5359 or 07974 352998, ☒www.lanzarotesol.com. Three pleasant British-owned villas with private pools. Las Cabreras is a hamlet in open countryside, with far-reaching views right down to the sea, situated within easy reach of the Fundación César Manrique, Teguise and Arrecife. Good value for groups of four to six. From €103.

Restaurants and tapas bars

Agua Viva

C/Mástil 31, Playa Honda ☎920 82 15 05. Tues–Sat 1–4pm & 8–11pm. Well off the tourist trail on the airport side of Playa Honda, this top-end restaurant is a hidden gem. The interior has a welcoming country-house feel, the service is discreet and attentive, and the cooking is first class. French-inspired dishes (mains around €18) are prepared with an amazing lightness of touch, using interesting ingredients such as sea urchin caviar and, added to the fine sauces and amazing home-made puddings, make this a memorable place to eat.

Casa-Museo del Campesino

Near Mozaga ☎928 52 09 33, 52 01 36, ☒www.cabildodelanzarote.cact. Tapas bar 10am–5.45pm, restaurant 1–4.30pm. With a choice of jaunty green-painted tables in the sun or rustic tables inside, and folk songs on the stereo, the tapas bar is an atmospheric place to sample delicacies such as goat's cheese and marinated octopus for €4–5 per plate. Downstairs, the vast and architecturally impressive restaurant specializes in Canarian fare, with a menu featuring *sancocho*, *bienmesabe* and *frangollo*, and *malvasía* wine. The sampler menu is good value at €18; main courses are €7–15. Canarian musicians play here from time to time.

Caserío de Mozaga

C/Mozaga 8, Mozaga ☎928 52 00 60, ☒www.caseriodemozaga.com. Daily 1–3.30pm & 8–11pm. The restaurant of this charming rural hotel, open to non-residents, is a firm favourite of in-the-know well-heeled locals. The main dining room is airy and elegant, with huge windows overlooking the surrounding countryside. By night, it's softly lit and fabulously intimate. Friendly service and impeccably prepared Canarian and French-inspired cooking help make this the perfect setting for a romantic treat. Above-average prices, but worth it.

▼ CASA-MUSEO DEL CAMPESINO

PLACES San Bartolomé and Tías

Chino

Avda Central 61, Tías, ☎928 83 36 74. Daily noon–4pm & 7pm–midnight. This large, brightly lit mid-price place is the island's best Chinese restaurant. The owner prefers to steer clear of over-commercial international-style "Chinese food" in favour of authentic cuisine, travelling back to China twice a year to check out new recipes. Excellent *dim sum* with subtle flavours.

El Cable

C/Cactus, Ciudad Jardín, Playa del Cable ☎928 80 56 49. Restaurant daily noon–4pm & 8pm–midnight, bar noon–midnight. The informal style of this restaurant, and the quality of the food, don't really justify its highish prices, but there are some interesting choices on the menu (such as steak with truffle sauce or mushroom and saffron risotto) and the setting is wonderful. The terrace hangs right over the shore, with great coastal views.

Finca de La Florida

C/El Islote 90, El Islote ☎928 52 11 24, ⓦwww.hotelfincadelaflorida.com. Daily 7–9pm. Good service, fresh ingredients, simply prepared dishes and great views of the adjoining winelands make this hotel restaurant a decent, if unadventurous, choice.

La Saranda

Mácher (on the LZ-2 to Yaiza) ☎649 00 24 94. Closed Sun eve and Mon.

You'll have to polish up your Spanish before visiting this rustic restaurant – instead of showing you a written menu, the waiters rattle off the choices, typically generous plates of hot tapas to share for €5–8 a portion. It's a superb place to savour good country cooking, and the atmosphere is fantastic when a guitar and *timple* trio serenades the tables late on Friday nights. Excellent house wine, too.

Cafés

Café Barreto

Avda Palmeras 20, San Bartolomé. Mon–Fri & Sun 8am–2pm & 5–11pm. Bright, clean, dynamic urban café with Internet access and a big choice of excellent fresh juices, sandwiches and crepes, all reasonably priced. Come here on a Sunday morning for *chocolate con churros*.

El Pastelito

Avda N Torre 22, Tahíche (on the LZ-1 to Jameos del Agua). Daily 8am–8pm. One of the island's best bakery-cafés. Delicious pastries, cakes, sandwiches and bread (including healthy wholemeal and seeded varieties) are all freshly made on the premises. They also have good coffee and a superb line in tarts and gateaux for special occasions.

Playa Blanca

Playa Blanca, Lanzarote's southernmost resort, is a fresh-faced, family-friendly collection of hotels, villas, apartments and restaurants, strung out along a remote stretch of coast with fabulous views of Fuerteventura. Once a simple fishing community, Playa Blanca has been developing at full tilt since the early 1980s, growing far beyond the original village into a sizeable tourist town that's particularly popular with British visitors. A good deal of thought has gone into making it the most pleasant of the island's holiday hotspots, and its newest addition, the swish Marina Rubicón, is decidedly upmarket. If you're planning to explore the island in depth, or you're a serious clubber, you might prefer a base that's more central – perched on the edge of the empty, mountainous Rubicón desert (Los Rostros) and the _malpaís_ of a dormant volcano, Montaña Roja, Playa Blanca is the most isolated of the resorts, stranded in the corner of Yaiza district. But for families looking for a reasonably priced, relaxing beach break, it's perfect: there's a wealth of accommodation options; clean, safe beaches; and enough in the way of activities, excursions and ice-cream shops to keep young ones more than happy. It's easy for sun-worshippers to escape the crowds, too, by heading for the glorious golden sands of Punta del Papagayo, an attractive headland east of town, or the even emptier beaches of Fuerteventura, a short ferry-ride away.

Playa Blanca village

There's still something of a village feel to the heart of Playa Blanca, particularly the area around **El Varadero**, the original fishing harbour, where modest apartment buildings with sun-trap balconies line the traffic-free seafront and children play in the church square. The old fishermen's cottages are now nearly all gone, replaced by new complexes that spread well into the surrounding desert, but,

---

Arrival and information

The most convenient way to reach Playa Blanca is by **renting a car** (see p.167). Otherwise, from Arrecife **buses** (_guaguas_) run to Playa Blanca via Tías and Yaiza (_línea_ #6; 12 buses a day Mon–Fri, 6 on Sat, 8 on Sun), stopping near the El Varadero–Avenida Playa Blanca roundabout and near the port.
The **tourist office** is on El Varadero (℡928 51 90 18; July–Sept Mon–Fri 9am–1.30pm, Oct–June Mon–Fri 9am–2pm).

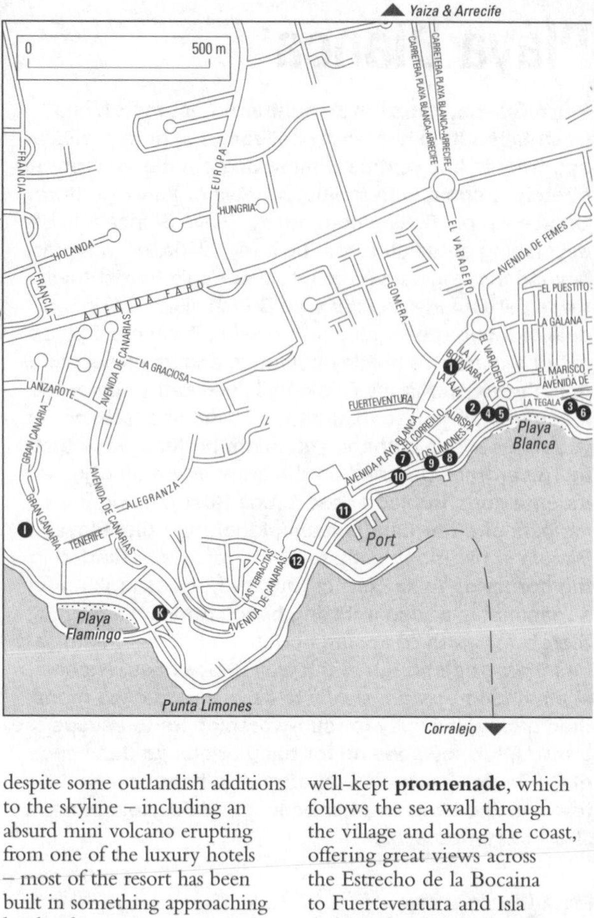

Yaiza & Arrecife

B & Montaña Roja

Playa Blanca

Port

Corralejo

despite some outlandish additions to the skyline – including an absurd mini volcano erupting from one of the luxury hotels – most of the resort has been built in something approaching local style.

Probably the most appealing part of Playa Blanca is its well-kept **promenade**, which follows the sea wall through the village and along the coast, offering great views across the Estrecho de la Bocaina to Fuerteventura and Isla de los Lobos. It's perfect for strolling, and safe for cycling. In the village, the promenade

Ferries to Fuerteventura

Two companies ply the route between Playa Blanca and Corralejo in northern Fuerteventura (see p.148), carrying vehicles and foot passengers. **Naviera Armas** (Playa Blanca ☎902 45 65 00, Corralejo ☎928 86 70 80, ⊛www.navieraarmas .com; €21 return, children €11, 2 adults plus car €64) make the trip in twenty minutes, with six sailings daily each way. **Líneas Fred Olsen** (Playa Blanca ☎902 10 01 07, ⊛www.fredolsen.es; €27 return, children €13, 2 adults plus car €78) run a high-speed catamaran service, crossing in twelve minutes, with seven sailings daily each way during the week and five at weekends. They also provide a free shuttle bus for passengers from Playa Blanca to Puerto del Carmen and Arrecife.

▲ Punta del Papagayo

PLAYA BLANCA

EATING & DRINKING
Aromas	1
Café del Mar	15
Casa Pedro	8
Casa Roja	16
Don Camillo	9
El Almacén de la Sal	5
El Bodegón del Maño	14
El Horno de la Agüela	3
El Pastelito	4
Galería del Sol	6
Irish Anvil	12
L'Artista	6
La Cofradía	11
La Cuadra	10
La Giralda	17
La Terracita	7
Romántica	2
Rooftops	12
Típico Canario	6
Varadero del Rubicón	13

ACCOMMODATION
Apartamentos Bahía Blanca Rock	C
Apartamentos Gutiérrez	G
Apartamentos Rubimar	J
Apartamentos Sun Beach	A
Bungalows Playa Flamingo	K
Casa del Embajador	H
Hesperia Kamezí	B
Hesperia Playa Dorada	F
Hotel Gran Meliá Volcán Lanzarote	L
Hotel Lanzarote Princess	D
Hotel Princesa Yaiza	E
Hotel Timanfaya Palace	I

PLACES Playa Blanca

is lined with relaxed, tourist-friendly eateries, many of them reasonably authentic, with menus offering a familiar combination of tapas, grills and international favourites. More of the same are dotted along the next street back, **Calle Los Limones**; the best of these have small, sunny terraces overlooking the sea. With the resort ribboning along the coast, it's a good plan to book accommodation within easy walking distance of the centre if you're thinking of eating out frequently.

Playa Dorada, Playa Flamingo and Playa Blanca

Playa Blanca's beaches are pleasantly small, with fine, pale sand and turquoise water that's shallow enough to warm up in the sun. Safe and sheltered from the wind, they're excellent for young children. The most popular beach in the resort, Playa Dorada, lies just east of the village, within easy walking distance of the most central hotels and apartments. West of the port area is the smaller and quieter Playa Flamingo, backed by a row of palms. In the centre of the village, Playa Blanca itself is a tiny stretch of sand that gets some exciting waves when the Fuerteventura ferries roll in.

Marina Rubicón

Playa Blanca's smart new marina, east of the main resort area, is Lanzarote's most upmarket

▼ PLAYA DORODA

boom zone. Built in a style that lovingly recreates vernacular architecture in idealized form (there's even a large "chapel" housing a contemporary art gallery; see p.90), its high property prices have attracted shops, bars and restaurants that are smarter – and pricier – than elsewhere, making it the place to come for designer fashions, quality cuisine, cocktails, or, for that matter, ships chandlery. For relaxation, there's a lovely open-air public pool (daily 10am–7pm; €5).

Castillo de las Coloradas

Also known as the Torre del Aguila, this simple, thick-walled fortified tower dates from 1743, and is the only original structure in this newly built neighbourhood. Set in a commanding position on the cliffs at the eastern end of Playa Blanca – just a short stroll from the *Gran Meliá Volcán* – it was built by Spanish settlers as a defence against Berber pirates.

At the time of writing, a plan was in place to restore the tower and turn it into a museum (the Museo del Rubicón), documenting the history of the surrounding Yaiza district.

Punta del Papagayo

For the very best beaches, you need to head out of town and take the bumpy, dusty track into the Reserva Natural Protegido de los Ajaches (entry €3 per car; if walking from central Playa Blanca, allow 45min), at the southern limit of which is the Punta del Papagayo, with a series of lovely sandy coves that are good for swimming and almost completely undeveloped. The broad beach you reach first, **Playa Mujeres**, is popular with families; there's a kiosk here but no restaurant, so you'll need to bring your own shade and supplies. The smaller, more distant coves are secluded sun traps: **Playa del Papagayo**, the most famous, is a perfect horseshoe of pale sand and turquoise water, sheltered by dark cliffs and overlooked by a couple of laid-back beach cafés selling drinks, snacks and ice cream; a short walk further south is the clothing-optional haven of **Puerto Muelas**; and beyond this, on the other side of the headland, is **Caleta del Congrio**.

▼ PUNTA DEL PAPAGAYO

Activities and day-trips

The majority of visitors to Playa Blanca come here to make the most of the beaches, but there are plenty of activities on offer, too. Energetic children and sporty adults will love **Kikoland**, on the seafront next to the *Hotel Princesa Yaiza* (€6, family €12, plus an hourly fee for some sports), which offers tennis, football, basketball, volleyball and table tennis, plus, for kids, a playground, mini-disco, bouncy castle and other supervised activities.

Playa Blanca is also a good starting point for **scuba diving** trips to Isla de los Lobos, to explore its underwater lava caves, and divers are served by several diving centres, including the particularly good Marina Rubicón Diving Center (see p.173).

The resort's main port is the departure point for **pleasure-boat trips** to Punta del Papagayo, Corralejo and Los Lobos, and for submarine and glass-bottom boat tours (see p.170).

At the time of writing, developers were planning a major new **sports complex** at the east end of Playa Blanca including football pitches, athletics facilities, swimming pools, tennis courts and a sports hall. The first phase is due to open in 2007. Also opening in 2007 is a new 18-hole, par-71 **golf course**, set on the lower slopes of Montaña Roja. It's been designed to be as environmentally friendly as possible: by using the area's natural contours to collect rainwater and dew, the site's water consumption should be kept to a minimum.

Montaña Roja

For an enjoyable hike, it's easy to climb Montaña Roja, the extinct 197-metre volcano that dominates the west end of the resort. You can either walk all the way from the village, starting with a thirty-minute stroll from El Varadero to Montaña Baja on the west side of the cone, or you can drive to the same spot and pick up the trail from there. Montaña Baja is within ten minutes' walk of the crater rim, from where you can reach the peak in a round trip of an hour or so. It's particularly pleasant in spring, when a fuzz of vegetation colours the slopes.

Hotels

Casa del Embajador

C/Tegala 30 ☏928 51 91 91, ⊛www .casadelembajador.com. Though officially a hotel rural, the twelve-room Casa del Embajador occupies a prime seafront spot on a quiet backstreet in central

▼ PARASCENDING, PLAYA BLANCA

Playa Blanca. Effectively, the resort grew around it – the building is around 100 years old – and it's an oasis of elegance and restraint in the midst of all the modern development. The facilities are relatively simple – there's not even a pool – but the atmosphere is comfortable and relaxed. The rooms, though a little cramped, have glorious elevated views over a garden terrace to the straits beyond, where, at night, the lights of Fuerteventura twinkle on the horizon. €150.

Hesperia Playa Dorada

Avda Papagayo ☎928 51 71 20, ⊛www.hesperia-playadorada.com. This stark, modernist four-star resort hotel makes no concessions to local architecture or style, and its rooms are on the small side, but its public areas have a spacious, airy atmosphere. It's also very well positioned, right on Playa Dorada and within easy walking distance of the village. €130.

Hotel Gran Meliá Volcán Lanzarote

C/Castillo, Urb Castillo del Aguila ☎928 51 91 85, ⊛www.solmelia .com. A resort-style hotel that attracts business travellers, the *Gran Meliá Volcán* is often quiet by day, with none of the sunlounger wars you might find in the package-holiday places. With an imaginative design – inspired by Lanzarotean village architecture – it should be beautiful, but there are some bizarre touches, not least the replica volcano that sits over the atrium. The layout is awkward to navigate, too, and the rooms are rather fussily decorated. However, such quibbles are outweighed by the catering, which is every bit as good as you'd expect from a

five-star luxury hotel – breakfast is superb. What's more, the marina's great restaurants are practically on the doorstep. €216.

Hotel Lanzarote Princess

C/Maciot ☎928 51 71 08, ⊛www .h10.es. A step down in style and locale from its sister resort, the *Timanfaya Palace*, this hotel is nevertheless worth considering for its good-sized rooms and large, palm-shaded pool area. The food is well prepared, and there are plenty of free activities for all ages. €110.

Hotel Princesa Yaiza

Avda Papagayo ☎928 51 92 22, ⊛www.princesayaiza.com. This massive five-star luxury resort has large, stylish, comfortable rooms, making it an appealing option for families who need space to spread out. The location is a big hit with kids, too, as it's right on a great beach, Playa Dorada, and next door to

▼ HOTEL PRINCESA YAIZA

the Kikoland sports complex (free for guests; see p.87). It's by no means a families-only place, however: architecturally imaginative, with beautiful pool terraces, five restaurants and a spa, it has the relaxed, confident atmosphere of a hotel that knows it's an excellent choice by any standards. €250.

Hotel Timanfaya Palace

C/Gran Canaria, Urb Montaña Roja ☎928 51 76 76, ⊛www.h10.es. Unquestionably palatial, the much-praised four-star *Timanfaya* Palace is lavishly designed in Moorish-Spanish style and generously laid out in a good seafront location, close to Playa Flamingo. On clear days, the pool area and the sea-facing rooms have lovely views of Fuerteventura and Isla de los Lobos. €156 (inland view) or €180 (sea view).

Apartments and villas

Apartamentos Bahía Blanca Rock

C/Janubio ☎928 51 70 37, ⊛www .h10.es. Family-friendly complex of 200 apartments in vaguely Canarian style, with an attractive pool area. Although not on the beach, it's very close to Playa Dorada and the Kikoland sports complex (see p.87). €54.

Apartamentos Gutiérrez

Pl Nuestra Señora del Carmen 8 ☎928 51 70 89. In the heart of Playa Blanca village, these simple townhouse apartments are a good bet if you're on a budget and resort-style complexes aren't your thing. Facilities are limited, though, and there's no pool. €36.

Apartamentos Rubimar

C/Cocinilla 2, Urb Castillo del Aguila ☎928 51 92 66. New low-rise four-star aparthotel with spacious one-, two- and three-bed suites, arranged around a large pool terrace. A little stark but still a good, reasonably priced option if you'd like to be close to the marina's various facilities. €63.

Apartamentos Sun Beach

C/Janubio ☎928 51 83 59. Not on the seafront, as the name would suggest, but still less than ten minutes' walk from Playa Dorada, this basic aparthotel goes down well with British package holidaymakers as it's clean, peaceful and well laid out, with decent pools. €55.

Bungalows Playa Flamingo

C/Limones ☎928 51 73 00. Very family-oriented, the Playa Flamingo complex is right on the beach of the same name, and has good pools. The bungalows are simple but equipped with the essentials, and the village is a pleasant ten- to fifteen-minute walk away along the coastal promenade. €55.

Heredad Kamezí

C/Mónaco ☎928 51 86 24, ⊛www .heredadkamezi.com. One of the best self-catering options on the island, this superb collection of luxury serviced villas is set in an attractive coastal plot at the Montaña Roja end of Playa Blanca, a three-kilometre drive from the centre. With roomy, chic, Manrique-inspired architecture, they're very well equipped and have several eco-friendly features, including solar-heated water and private seawater pools. Inland view €230, direct sea view €255.

PLACES Playa Blanca

Shops

Café del Mar Shop

Marina Rubicón. Sells branded clothing and, of course, the latest Café del Mar chillout compilations.

Canariensis

Marina Rubicón. Designer clothes shop stocking international brands such as Boss, Calvin Klein and O'Neill, and a big selection of unmistakably loud tops from Custo, the outré T-shirt designers from Barcelona.

Mercadillo de Marina Rubicón

Marina Rubicón. Wed 9am–2pm. Busy little wharfside market that's good for picking up souvenirs such as locally made jewellery and ornaments.

▼ MARINA RUBICÓN

Mercadillo de Playa Blanca

Off the road to Femés, at the corner of C/Concha. Wed & Sat 9am–2pm. Small, twice-weekly open-air tourist market with stalls selling T-shirts, hats, crafts and oddments.

Sammer Gallery

La Ermita, Marina Rubicón ☎610 58 32 51. Daily 10am–10pm. Bright, spacious contemporary art gallery showcasing the work of Spanish artists in a beautifully recreated "village chapel".

Restaurants, bodegas and tapas bars

Aromas

C/La Laja 1 ☎928 34 96 91. Mon–Sat 1–4pm & 6.30–11pm. The most upmarket restaurant in central Playa Blanca, with an award-winning chef whose excellent menu is inspired by traditional island cooking. Dishes include *ajoblanco* soup with almonds and grapes, rabbit stew with *papas arrugadas*, and *tollos* (Canarian dried fish) with onion sauce.

Casa Pedro

Avda Marítima 17 ☎928 51 79 65. Closed Thurs. A cut above most of the seafront places in the village, and relatively untouristy, this is a medium-sized restaurant with refreshingly old-fashioned values. It specializes in generous platefuls of fresh local fish (typically €11–12 for a main course) but also serves decent steaks.

Casa Roja

Marina Rubicón ☎928 13 60 70. Daily 1–4pm & 7–11pm. With a creative menu including dishes such as

▲ PUNTA DEL PAPAGAYO

sea bass with green *mojo*, and couscous and veal with ratatouille and truffles, this is one of the marina's better restaurants, though rather over-priced.

Don Camillo

Avda Marítima ☎ 928 51 77 78. Like its counterpart in Puerto del Carmen, this is a family-friendly mid-price grill with a good selection of huge, juicy steaks.

El Almacén de la Sal

Avda Marítima 20 ☎ 928 51 78 85, ⊛ www.almacendelasal.com. Closed Tues. One of the better seafront options, *Almacén* is an attractive – though fairly pricey – place with a dignified, traditional atmosphere, serving excellent fresh fish and seafood such as mussels, clams and squid, plus grilled meat and local specialities.

El Bodegón del Maño

Marina Rubicón 52b ☎ 928 51 87 12. Closed Thurs. Smart eatery with an imaginative menu including sirloin with chestnut sauce, champagne-steamed king prawns, home-made Spanish-style puddings, and gourmet versions of Canarian tapas. An attractive position – overlooking the moorings – but prices are high, even for the marina.

El Horno de la Agüela

C/Tegala 10 ☎ 928 51 78 25. Daily 1–4pm & 7–11pm. A first-rate traditional-style Spanish restaurant specializing in meat dishes. The excellent-value king-size steaks and roasted cuts of local kid, pork and lamb are succulent and superb.

L'Artista

C/Tegala 20 ☎ 928 51 75 78. A friendly and cosy Italian restaurant set back from the promenade, with effervescent staff and plenty of appealing dishes, including a good range of vegetarian options. Decent pizza, but variable pasta.

La Cofradía

Puerto de Playa Blanca. The local harbour-workers all head here for the catch of the day. The decor and service may seem rough-and-ready but if you like the idea of being served a whole octopus, freshly caught and at an everyday price, this is the place.

La Cuadra

C/Limones 65 ☎ 928 51 87 81. Pleasant, unpretentious restaurant with sea views, serving simple, well-prepared fish and grills at moderate prices.

La Giralda

Marina Rubicón 8 ☎ 928 51 91 90. In a quiet spot at the eastern end of the marina, *La Giralda* manages to be both upmarket and relaxed, and is one of the best places to eat in the area, thanks to its excellent Andalusian cooking – including succulent tapas such as grilled baby cuttlefish and mini broad beans with bacon – and delicious home-made desserts. The tapas are particularly good value at €2–4, while main courses average around €18.

La Terracita

C/Limones 51. A great lunchtime stop, with more of a Spanish feel than most, this little place has a good long list of tasty tapas and salads, and a tiny terrace overlooking the sea.

Romántica

C/Limones 6 ☎928 51 71 66. A place that plays up to its syrupy name, with a romantic atmosphere, good food from the grill and fine wine list including some notable Rioja Gran Reservas.

Típico Canario

Avda Marítima. A good place to try Canarian food in Playa Blanca, this restaurant serves freshly grilled rabbit, kid and fish, plus good *papas arrugadas con mojo*.

Cafés and bars

Café del Mar

Marina Rubicón. Daily 10am–2am. From the people who turned José Luis Delgado's Ibiza chillout hotspot into an international brand, this self-consciously cool waterside café serves cocktails and sandwiches, and hosts the odd party and event. The music selection – and mood – is mellow, in trademark *Café del Mar* style. Live DJ sets on Fridays and Saturdays from 9pm.

El Pastelito

C/Limones 9. Closed Tues. One of central Playa Blanca's few decent European-style cafés, *El Pastelito*

serves good coffee and German-recipe cake, and has plenty of breakfast options.

Galería del Sol

C/Tegala 22. 1pm–late. Closed Thurs. Just off the seafront on the east side of the village, and with great views across the resort, this cosy little British-run bar is one of Playa Blanca's best, and is always busy with expats and holidaymakers.

Irish Anvil

CC Punta Limones 31. Friendly bar, usually packed out with tourists and English-speaking expats, that stays open after midnight – a rarity in Playa Blanca. It also has a short menu of pub grub, and hosts regular live music.

Rooftops

CC Punta Limones 33. 8pm–late. Cheerful and unintimidating disco-bar popular with twenty-something tourists. Live music from local bands on Fridays.

Varadero del Rubicón

Marina Rubicón. Daily 9am–5pm. Pleasant, down-to-earth wharf-side café-bar near the marina office, serving coffee, ice cream and a great-value traditional-style *menú del día* (€7) – the kind of typically Spanish lunch that's hard to find on the islands.

Yaiza and Timanfaya

Southwestern Lanzarote contains some of the island's most dramatic landscapes – stark volcanic cones and calderas, valleys devoured by lava, and mountainsides dotted with what must be the weirdest vineyards in the world.

There's an appealing detachment and emptiness to the region that gives it an atmosphere unlike anywhere else on the island. The attractive villages of Yaiza, Uga and Femés have breathtaking views of unspoilt countryside, and the wine region of La Geria lies within a protected area with an untouched-by-time tranquillity – all are great places for rustic restaurants, congenial *bodegas* and quirky places to stay. On the coast, the shiny new marina town of Puerto Calero, its sleepy neighbour Playa Quemada and the fisherman's refuge of El Golfo lie in wild, remote areas a world away from the well-trodden tourist resorts.

The region's principal resort, Playa Blanca is surrounded by wilderness, too: it lies at the limit of Los Rostros, a barren plain near the island's southernmost tip, closer to Corralejo on neighbouring Fuerteventura than to Arrecife. But the biggest – and most fascinating – wilderness of all is the Montañas del Fuego de Timanfaya, an unearthly expanse of volcanic peaks that heads the list of Lanzarote's must-see attractions.

Yaiza

Universally praised as one of Lanzarote's prettiest villages, and home to some of the island's finest rural restaurants and hotels, Yaiza is a quiet,

Visiting Yaiza district and Timanfaya

For maximum flexibility, the best way to explore the area is by **renting a car** (see p.167). Otherwise, there's a regular **bus** (*guagua*) service from Arrecife, Tías and Mácher to Uga, Yaiza and Playa Blanca (*línea* #6; 12 buses a day Mon–Fri, 6 on Sat, 8 on Sun) and an infrequent service from Arrecife, Tías and Mácher to Femés (*línea* #5; 3 buses a day Mon–Fri), but no other state-run public transport in this part of the island. Local **tour companies** include the area in their island itineraries, and coach trips to the Parque Nacional de Timanfaya run daily from all the resorts; most large hotels can supply details. Whether visiting Timanfaya independently or on an organized trip, your entry fee includes the Ruta de los Volcanes coach tour around the peaks and craters. Hiking in the national and natural parks is strictly limited, and only possible on a pre-booked guided walking tour (see p.104).

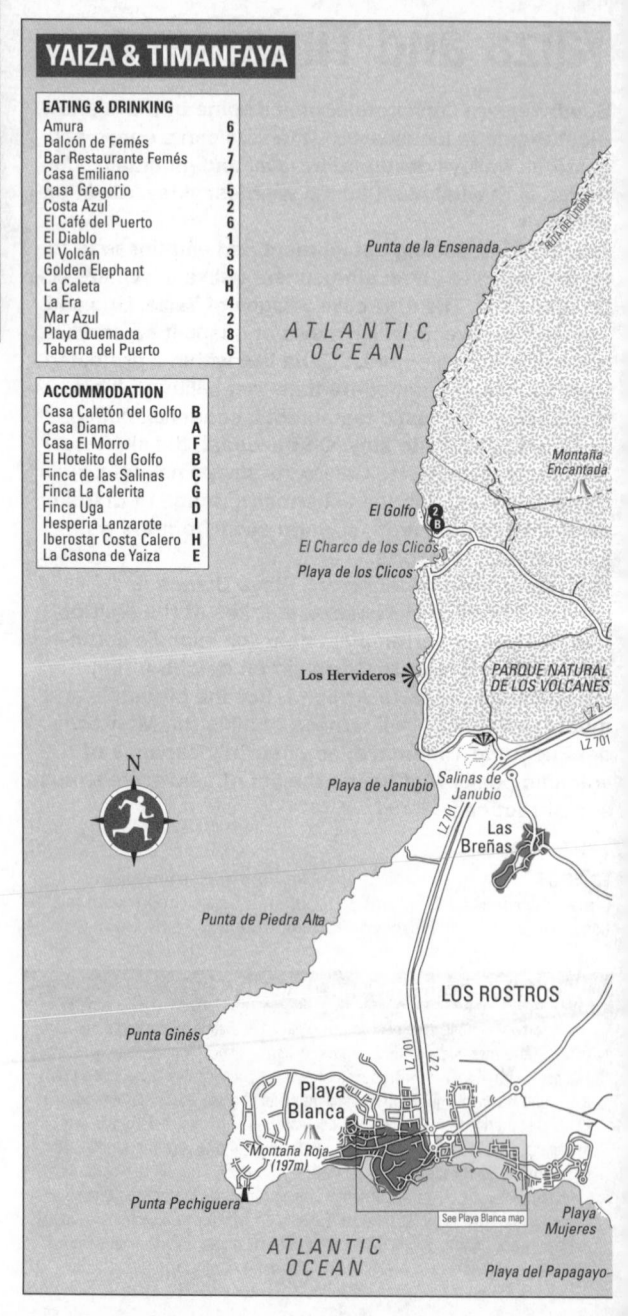

YAIZA & TIMANFAYA

EATING & DRINKING
Amura	6
Balcón de Femés	7
Bar Restaurante Femés	7
Casa Emiliano	7
Casa Gregorio	5
Costa Azul	2
El Café del Puerto	6
El Diablo	1
El Volcán	3
Golden Elephant	6
La Caleta	H
La Era	4
Mar Azul	2
Playa Quemada	8
Taberna del Puerto	6

ACCOMMODATION
Casa Caletón del Golfo	B
Casa Diama	A
Casa El Morro	F
El Hotelito del Golfo	B
Finca de las Salinas	C
Finca La Calerita	G
Finca Uga	D
Hesperia Lanzarote	I
Iberostar Costa Calero	H
La Casona de Yaiza	E

Punta de la Ensenada

ATLANTIC OCEAN

Montaña Encantada

El Golfo

El Charco de los Clicos

Playa de los Clicos

Los Hervideros

PARQUE NATURAL DE LOS VOLCANES

LZ 701

Playa de Janubio

Salinas de Janubio

Las Breñas

Punta de Piedra Alta

LOS ROSTROS

Punta Ginés

Playa Blanca

Montaña Roja (197m)

Punta Pechiguera

See Playa Blanca map

Playa Mujeres

ATLANTIC OCEAN

Playa del Papagayo

N

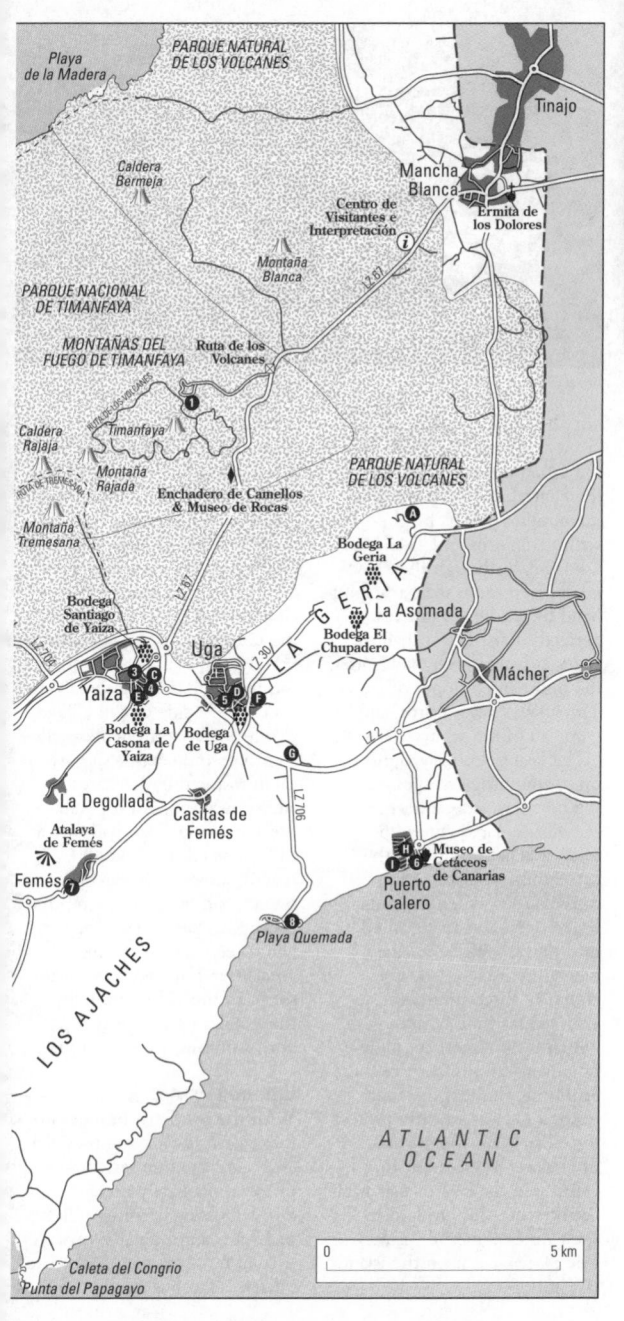

Playa
de la Madera

PARQUE NATURAL
DE LOS VOLCANES

Tinajo

Caldera
Bermeja

Mancha
Blanca

Ermita de
los Dolores

Centro de
Visitantes e
Interpretación

Montaña
Blanca

PARQUE NACIONAL
DE TIMANFAYA

MONTAÑAS DEL
FUEGO DE TIMANFAYA

Ruta de los
Volcanes

Caldera
Rajaja

Timanfaya

PARQUE NATURAL
DE LOS VOLCANES

Montaña
Rajada

Enchadero de Camellos
& Museo de Rocas

Montaña
Tremesana

Bodega La
Geria

La Asomada

Bodega
Santiago
de Yaiza

Uga

Bodega El
Chupadero

Mácher

Yaiza

Bodega La
Casona de
Yaiza

Bodega
de Uga

La Degollada

Museo de
Cetáceos
de Canarias

Casitas de
Femés

Atalaya
de Femés

Puerto
Calero

Femés

Playa Quemada

LOS AJACHES

ATLANTIC
OCEAN

0   5 km

Caleta del Congrio
Punta del Papagayo

▲ YAIZA

unassuming little place. Its beauty is partly the result of the villagers' efforts to keep the central, shady square and surrounding streets bright with geraniums and absolutely immaculate, though they have been given more than a helping hand by nature – Yaiza sits, perfectly poised, in a shallow valley surrounded by volcanoes, the multi-hued slopes of Timanfaya to the north, and glimpses of the sea to the west.

The lava fields flow right up to the village fringes on the northern side; indeed, the village narrowly escaped total destruction during the cataclysmic volcanic eruptions of the 1730s, when Timanfaya broke open and lava gushed into the valley. The village's best-known landmark is a clutch of three-hundred-year-old farming buildings, which were almost the only houses in Yaiza to survive these eruptions. Supervising their restoration was an early project for César Manrique, whose idea of creating a restaurant that celebrated the best of Canarian country life was brought to life with *La Era*, one of the very best places to eat on the island (see p.109).

Yaiza's natural focal point is the pleasant **Plaza de los Remedios**, with its traditional church. Small, but still rather grand, its pillars and pulpit are made of dark volcanic rock, and it has five decorated altars. Nearby are a few **art galleries**, all of which merit a quick visit: the Casa de Cultura opposite the church, which opens for special exhibitions; Galería Yaiza on the west side of the village (Mon–Sat 5–7pm), which sells paintings and ceramics, most of them inspired by Lanzarotean landscapes; and, a short walk to the south, the cellar galleries at the *Casona de Yaiza* hotel (see p.106), showing works by its co-owner, and mounting temporary displays by other painters.

For keen walkers, there's a great four-hour **walk** from the south of the village uphill to the Atalaya de Femés (see p.97), with stunning views en route.

Uga and Femés

With the southern beaches no more than twenty minutes' drive away, and the fine restaurants of Yaiza practically on the doorstep, the charming village of Uga is a good place to stay if rural tranquillity appeals. The village is famous for the smoked

Fiesta de Nuestra Señora de los Remedios

A highlight of Yaiza's village calendar is the **Fiesta de Nuestra Señora de los Remedios** on 8 September, when villagers attired in traditional costume join together in a *romería*, or religious pilgrimage, with much cheerful celebration to follow.

salmon from its *ahumadería* (on the road to Yaiza); *salmón de Uga* features on upmarket restaurant menus all over the island.

The picturesque hamlet of Femés, perched on a saddle in the Agache mountains, has fabulous views reaching down to Playa Blanca and across the Estrecho de la Bocaina to Fuerteventura and Isla de los Lobos. The village church, the **Ermita de San Marcial del Rubicón**, is one of the island's oldest, dating from 1630, and the focus of a major fiesta in late June or early July.

Above the village, bristling with telecommunications masts, is the **Atalaya de Femés** lookout, one of Lanzarote's highest points.

La Geria

The dramatic volcanic countryside just to the north of Uga, known as La Geria, is the heart of Lanzarote's **winelands**.

▼ LA GERIA

You'd be forgiven for thinking that viticulture would be totally impossible on an island with no freshwater springs, rivers or streams – but the *Conejeros* have devised a method of farming that takes advantage of the fact that *picón* (volcanic gravel, mined on the island) traps just enough droplets of dew to nourish a vine.

La Geria is a *paisaje protegido*, protected because of the particular way in which the landscape has been sculpted by this process: you'll see hillsides carefully scattered with fine *picón*, punctuated by rhythmic patterns of *zocos* – low, crescent-shaped dry stone walls made of volcanic rocks, each one built to protect a single vine against the prevailing wind. By the summer, each *zoco* shelters a healthy plant, its leaves and fruit a vivid green against the soil – "like emeralds lying in a black velvet case", as one writer described them. The grape that's most characteristic of the area is the *malvasía*, a crisp white.

As you'd expect, this is a good region to sample wine, with a number of excellent *bodegas* (wineries) open to the public (see box on p.98). It's also a highly attractive area to tour by car or bicycle.

El Golfo and El Charco de Los Clicos

Isolated by great expanses of lava, El Golfo is one of Lanzarote's remotest coastal villages, perched right on the edge of the island's volcanic

The wine routes

Lanzarotean viticulture is labour intensive – the grapes have to be harvested by hand – so even the biggest producer, El Grifo, produces little over a million litres of wine each year. The boutique wineries may produce as few as 30,00 liters. As a result, the wines produced within the few square kilometres of Lanzarote's wine-lands are surprisingly varied, and it's well worth taking a **winery tour** to investigate the subtleties, and perhaps do a little buying: while good local wine generally costs €6–8 in the shops, it's cheaper direct from the wineries.

Some local tour companies organize winery tours (the resort hotels can supply details), but the best way to see the area is to travel by car with a designated driver or, if you're prepared to approach the tastings with restraint, devise a cycling itinerary that includes La Geria and the areas around Masdache and Mozaga (see p.78), and Mancha Blanca.

The best *malvasía* is reckoned to come from El Grifo, Reymar and Vega de Yuco, but the following wineries are all worth a stop.

Bodega de Uga On the LZ-2, Uga ☏928 83 01 47. Small, congenial *bodega*. See p.107.

Bodega El Chupadero Just off the LZ-30 from Uga to Masdache ☏928 17 31 15, ⊛www.el-chupadero.com. German-owned boutique winery. See p.107.

Bodega El Grifo C/El Islote 121, Masdache ☏928 52 40 36, ⊛www.elgrifo.com. Venerable *bodega* and museum. See p.78.

Bodega La Geria On the LZ-30 from Uga to Masdache ☏928 17 31 78, ⊛www .lageria.com. Daily 9am–6pm. Guided tours (€3) Tues & Thurs at noon. The second biggest producer on the island, *Bodega La Geria* has been in business since the late 1800s – it makes a very popular, crisp and citrussy *malvasía* (though some of the small wineries produce better ones) and some decent oaky reds. Guided tours of the winery last for an hour and include a wine and cheese tasting. If you'd like to skip to the tasting then a barman will serve you straight from the barrels for next to nothing; you can also buy wine by the bottle or case. The *bodega* has its own chapel, a tiny, pretty roadside building, where special masses are held at harvest time.

Bodegas Los Bermejos C/Bermejos 7, La Florida, near El Islote ☏928 52 24 63. Mon–Fri 10am–6pm. This small winery produces very successful wines in distinctive slim flask-shaped bottles. Their 2003 *malvasía* was a classic.

Bodegas Reymar Plaza de los Dolores 19, Mancha Blanca ☏928 84 07 37. Mon–Fri 9am–6pm. This boutique winery, a little over a decade old, produces just 30,000 bottles per annum, including a highly regarded *malvasía*.

Bodegas Vega de Yuco C/Vegueta 127, La Vegueta ☏609 21 70 14. Mon–Fri 10am–2pm. A relatively new boutique-style operation that aims high, cultivating top-quality grapes and producing 250,000 bottles of wine per year.

wilderness. It's also one of the best places on the island to eat fresh fish – though tiny, the village has a dozen fish restaurants, many of which have tables right on the edge of the rocky bay that neighbours Playa de los Clicos. Rustic as these places may seem, eating here is not particularly cheap, but the quality of the fish on offer – invariably the catch of the day – makes them good value nonetheless. El Golfo's cul-de-sac atmosphere makes it a peaceful place to spend time, and, since its modest seafront faces west, it's a particularly mellow spot to listen to the waves breaking on the dark shore as the sun sinks into the sea.

▲ EL CHARCO DE LOS CLICOS

Just to the south of El Golfo is an unusual natural landmark, El Charco de los Clicos (sometimes, confusingly, also called El Golfo), a curiously green-coloured lagoon that's separated from the Atlantic by an expanse of black beach known as Playa de los Clicos. You're not allowed near the edge of the lagoon, and the beach itself isn't recommended for swimming, but it's a dramatic spot, made all the more so by the bizarrely molten-looking dark strata of the cliffs which enclose the beach like the walls of an amphitheatre. This is actually the remains of the crater of an extinct volcano, which must have been the scene of some extraordinary explosions at the time of the eruptions; as molten magma hit the sea the water would have vaporised with spectacular force. The unusual colours and textures of the rock faces have inspired a number of photographers and filmmakers, most recently the celebrated Spanish film director Pedro Almodóvar.

Salinas de Janubio

The Salinas de Janubio salt pans are a reminder of the time when salt was a crucial food preservative and sea-salt production was one of Lanzarote's major industries. It's a good area for bird-watching, with an interesting variety of sea birds and some secluded black-sand beaches.

Puerto Calero

Founded in the late 1980s and growing steadily ever since, Puerto Calero is a swish, upmarket marina development – impressive-looking yachts crowd the quayside, and real estate prices here are some of the highest on the island for newly built property.

In the heart of the sleek waterfront area is a shiny new attraction all about dolphins and whales, the **Museo de Cetáceos de Canarias** (CCM; ☎928 51 57 73, ⓦwww .museodecetaceos.org; daily

▼ PUERTO CALERO

Fiesta de la Vendimia

Harvest time in La Geria is August (for white grapes) and September (for red). *Bodega La Geria* hosts the **Fiesta de la Vendimia**, a traditional grape-trampling festival, in mid-August – winery workers dressed in traditional costume load up camels with freshly harvested *malvasía* grapes, which are then transported to a large stone vat. That's when the barefoot stamping free-for-all begins. It's all for show, of course – these days the grapes destined to be made into wine are collected by small tractor then steam-washed, and pressed by machine.

10am–6pm, closed the first Thurs of the month, 1 Jan, 6 Jan & 25 Dec; €11, children under 7 free). You can't miss the entrance – it's marked by the skeleton of a Bryde's whale. Aiming to educate visitors in matters relating to cetacean biology and behaviour, the exhibits draw on two decades of investigation and research. On display are images and models of marine mammals – including the rarely studied Cuvier's beaked whale – plus skeletons and other biological material; you can hear recordings of the animals, too. Explanations of how whales and dolphins breathe, sleep, communicate and detect objects are given in Spanish, English and German. There's a strong conservation message and the museum is keen to remind us that it's everyone's responsibility to protect the marine environment.

Puerto Calero also has a good choice of waterfront restaurants, a few shops and a small but chic contemporary art gallery, La Galería de Arte (Tues–Sat 11am–2pm & 5–9pm, Sun 5–9pm).

Playa Quemada

There's an otherworldly tranquillity to this scruffy fishing hamlet, which makes it an appealing antidote to the resort areas further along the coast for lunch or a lazy afternoon. It's possible to pick your way along the rocky shore to a secluded dark-sand beach, or you could just settle yourself in one of the clutch of untouristy bar-restaurants and watch the fishing boats bobbing in the natural bay.

Mancha Blanca

Mancha Blanca is a rural village surrounded by tidy fields in which neat rows of crops stand out against the dark volcanic *picón*. It pre-dates Timanfaya's last eruptions in the eighteenth century, and was lucky to survive: in 1735, the lava spewing out of the calderas in a northeasterly direction came to an abrupt stop just as it threatened to engulf the village.

Legend has it that it was Mancha Blanca's patron saint, Maria, Virgen de los Volcanes, who saved the village from destruction, and she is honoured at a large chapel, the **Ermita de los Dolores**. The chapel is rather plain, making the richly robed statue of the Virgin behind the altar all the more impressive.

The **Fiesta de la Virgen de los Volcanes** (Sept 15) celebrates the miracle with a grand *romería*, in which locals dressed in traditional costume make a ritual pilgrimage to the chapel, and a major rural craft fair is held, marking the end of

▲ ERMITA DE LOS DOLORES, MANCHA BLANCA

the summer. One of the biggest fiestas of the year, it's attended by people from all over the island.

Centro de Visitantes e Interpretación

Crta Yaiza-Tinajo, near Mancha Blanca ☎928 84 08 39. Daily 9am–5pm. Free. The Centro de Visitantes e Interpretación is the main visitor centre for the Parque Natural de los Volcanes and Parque Nacional de Timanfaya, the two parks that together make up Lanzarote's largest inland protected area. It's just under a kilometre outside Mancha Blanca, on the road to the clutch of volcanoes at the parks' heart, which are known collectively as the Montañas del Fuego de Timanfaya. Although some visitors come here after they've toured Timanfaya's Ruta de los Volcanes, it's a much better idea to drop in for an hour or so beforehand, as the informative displays and explanations are likely to enhance your understanding and appreciation of the surreal volcanic landscape. There's a particularly good audiovisual presentation on the sequence of eruptions and the more recent colonization of the lava fields by insects and plants. You'll need to bring your own headphones to hear the commentary in English.

The visitor centre is also the starting point for hikes along the Ruta de Tremesana, a highly recommended way of

PLACES Yaiza and Timanfaya

▼ PARQUE NATURAL DE LOS VOLCANES

getting to know the volcanoes far more intimately than the coach tours can allow (see p.104).

Montañas del Fuego de Timanfaya

☎928 84 00 57, ⊛www.cabildodelan-zarote.com/cact. Daily 9am–6.45pm. Coach tours (35min; included in entry fee) every half hour til 5pm. €8. The Montañas del Fuego de Timanfaya (Timanfaya Fire Mountains) are without doubt Lanzarote's blockbuster natural attraction. Southern Lanzarote's present-day landscape owes much of its appearance to the eighteenth- and nineteenth-century volcanic eruptions that, catastrophically, devoured numerous hamlets and much of the island's richest agricultural terrain. Nowhere is the potency and violence of these eruptions more graphically apparent than in the *malpaís* surrounding Montaña Timanfaya and its near neighbours, which have been part of the Parque Nacional de Timanfaya since 1974. There's visible evidence all around of the melting and fusing of rocks. In places, the

▼ NATIONAL PARK EMBLEM, TIMANFAYA

petrified lava is so wrinkled and contorted that, with eyes half shut, you can imagine it flowing still.

Montaña Timanfaya, also known as Pico del Fuego, is one of the island's highest peaks; surrounding it are 35 more volcanic cones, of which Montaña Rajada (with its deep-red caldera) is one of the most impressive. Active but slumbering, they appear utterly arid and devoid of life, but in fact are home to over eighty species of bird, and to one species of lizard (the Haría lizard) found nowhere else on the planet. Over 300 desert-adapted plant species also cling to life here: windborne particles of organic matter that settle on the otherwise barren rock give them a foothold. Human encroachment in this extraordinary environment has been so minimal since the last eruptions that the Parque Nacional de Timanfaya, and the Parque Natural de Los Volcanes that surrounds it, are areas of significant scientific interest and the subject of ongoing research.

To visit the Montañas del Fuego, you join a **Ruta de los Volcanes coach tour** – sit on the right-hand side for the best views along the way. You're driven along a sinuous route that gives you the chance to admire some of the hundred or so craters that simply didn't exist until Timanfaya blew its top twenty-six terrifying times between 1730 and 1736. The route was designed by artist Jesús Soto (who also worked on the Cueva de los Verdes in northern Lanzarote; see p.139) to include some staggering perspectives – at one point the coach drives right through an open-roofed cave.

▲ ECHADERO DE LOS CAMELLOS, TIMANFAYA

There's a multilingual, recorded commentary throughout. You'll discover that much of our knowledge of the eighteenth-century eruptions comes from the detailed diary of Don Andrés Lorenzo Curbelo, a plucky parish priest who lived close to the limit of the lava flow in Yaiza, and survived. His descriptions are terrifyingly graphic: at one point he recorded that "the earth suddenly opened up and an enormous mountain rose from the heart of the earth and from its apex shot flames which continued to burn for 19 days". The eruptions filled the sky with ash so thick that the islanders barely saw the sun at all for six years. Fortunately, nobody died as a result of the disaster – the emission of toxic gases was very low and the lava flow was slow enough for villages to be evacuated in plenty of time – but the effect on the island economy was catastrophic. Lanzarote's fertile fields of cereal and livestock had provided food for the entire

archipelago – but much of this fine agricultural land was totally destroyed by lava. It took many years of painful economic adjustment, and a burgeoning tourist scene, before the islanders could look back and say that Timanfaya had actually brought more benefits than it had taken away.

The coaches start and finish on the **Islote del Hilario**, the elevated central area under which the subterranean temperature is highest – it's thought that pockets of boiling magma have been trapped here since 1736. The geothermal tricks you'll be treated to here, such as water being poured down a hole and rocketing back out again as steam, are graphic proof of the fact that the temperature climbs to over 600°C just 13m below the surface. The biggest sideshow of all is the outdoor geothermal barbecue at *El Diablo*, Cesár Manrique's rather wonderful glass-walled restaurant that sits like a frisbee in the centre of the national park, and to which

Could it happen again?

While there's every possibility that Montaña Timanfaya could erupt again, there's absolutely no chance of it happening unexpectedly. Lanzarote's advance warning systems – including 140 seismographic sensors, more than most other volcanic regions in the world – are so sophisticated that the island has become a centre of research and discussion for leading vulcanology and volcanic geophysics experts from around the globe. There are data collection stations in the Jameos del Agua, Cueva de los Verdes and the Montañas del Fuego – the main surveillance system (sited at La Casa de los Volcanes at the Jameos del Agua; see p.139) transmits data every four hours to Madrid – while manual readings of subterranean temperatures are taken at various survey points once a week. Any change on the slopes or distances between survey points is detected with theodolites and tiltmeters designed to detect changes in slope smaller than one part per million. Barometric readings and water levels measurements are also monitored.

Even if an eruption were to take place, it would, say experts, occur slowly, with ample time to evacuate those affected.

all tour parties gravitate (see p.108).

Back down on the southern approach-road to the Montañas del Fuego you can choose to take a short ride on a camel train from the **Echadero de Camellos** (daily 8am–4pm; €10 for a camel with 2 seats), a reminder that dromedaries were once the island's most important working animals. There's also an excellent exhibition centre, the **Museo de Rocas** (Mon–Fri 8am–3pm; free), displaying information on the park and on the use of camels in traditional farming.

Ruta de Tremesana and Ruta del Litoral

Mon, Wed & Fri mornings. Booking ☎928 84 08 39, or in person at the Centro de Visitantes e Interpretación, near Mancha Blanca. Free. Hiking through the Parque Nacional de Timanfaya and the Parque Natural de los Volcanes is by far the best way to appreciate both the subtlety and brutality of this extraordinary place. Visitors are not permitted to walk in the park on their own, however – it's potentially damaging both to

the environment (the volcanic crust, and the fragile plant species that inhabit it, are vulnerable to erosion) and to you (4–5km beneath the surface, the molten magma is close enough for the ground to be hot underfoot in some places). To experience more of the Montañas del Fuego than you can see through the window of a coach, sign up for a guided walk along the Ruta de Tremesana in the south of the park.

Numbers on this two-hour, 3.5-kilometre walk are strictly limited and restricted to able-bodied adults only (although there's no climbing involved). You need to reserve a place at least a week or two in advance, and then reconfirm two days beforehand.

The well-worn cliché that Timanfaya is like a lunar landscape rings so true, and the silence is so unearthly, that you may have the words "one small step, one giant leap" buzzing in your brain all the way. But while the lava flows are positively majestic in their hugeness and harshness, close inspection will reveal delicate feathery lichens and fine seams of elements and oxides that paint the rocks in shades of violet, ochre and grey.

The Spanish and English-speaking national park guides who conduct the walk are very well informed in geology and vulcanology, and they stop the group at regular intervals en route to explain significant details relating to the park's history, topography and flora.

If the Ruta de Tremesana has given you a taste for hiking in the park, it's worth considering the longer – and tougher – Ruta del Litoral, which follows the rugged coastline at the park's western limit for 10km from Playa de la Madera to El Golfo, and can be walked either with or without a guide (around 5hr).

Hotels

El Hotelito del Golfo
Avda Golfo 10, El Golfo ☎928 17 32 72. Charming little place close to El Golfo's profusion of fish restaurants, with a pristine swimming pool and small but tidy rooms, some with sea views. €55.

Finca de las Salinas
C/Cuesta 17, Yaiza ☎928 83 03 25, ⊛www.fincasalinas.com. Attractively situated, with distant Timanfaya as a jaw-dropping backdrop, this elegant eighteenth-century mansion has comfortable suites and, in an annexe surrounding a small but delightfully curvy pool, roomy doubles. Despite being overdue for a revamp (the decor, though stylish, is a little tired), it's still atmospheric, and the restaurant is good. €150.

Hesperia Lanzarote
Urb Cortijo Viejo, Puerto Calero ☎828 08 08 00, ⊛www.hesperia-lanzarote .com. Arguably the most stylish of Lanzarote's large five-star hotels, with elegant public areas and rooms that leave many others looking decidedly twentieth century, this is a good choice if you're happy to be on the coast but away from the action. The spa is one of the island's best. From €111 (inland view) or €130 (sea view).

Hotel Iberostar Costa Calero
Puerto Calero ☎928 84 95 95, ⊛www .iberostar.com. Though huge, this sleek, spotless four-star hotel spreads itself wide, rather than high, and is sensitively designed using local materials such as whitewash and dark stone in uncompromisingly modern style. The bar, and the best rooms, have great coastal views towards Fuerteventura and Isla de los Lobos. Facilities include fabulous pools, a spa and a scuba diving centre, and the atmosphere is much warmer than first impressions might suggest; it's also good value. €92 (inland view) or €108 (sea view).

▼ HOTEL IBEROSTAR COSTA CALERO

La Casona de Yaiza

C/El Rincón 11, Yaiza (on the south side of the village, signposted from La Era) ☎928 83 62 62, ☒www.casonadeyaiza .com. Surrounded by glorious volcanic hills and fields with distant views of Timanfaya, this small, beautiful rural hotel and restaurant was once a manor house and winery. It's now one of Lanzarote's loveliest places to stay: the spacious rooms and suites are individually decorated with Baroque-style murals and ceiling paintings by Barcelona-based artist Germán Carregálo, and the overall effect is exquisitely romantic. Downstairs, the former cellars have become art galleries where guests can relax. There's an excellent restaurant on the premises, and La Era, one of the best places to eat on the entire island, is within walking distance. €135.

Apartments and villas

Casa Caletón del Golfo

Avda Marítima 3, El Golfo ☎928 52 40 04. This converted fisherman's cottage has bags of character, with cosy, old-fashioned decor, three en-suite bedrooms, and a private gate to the rocky beach. €90.

Casa Diama

La Geria ☎928 84 57 23, ☒www .islaviva.com. Simply furnished two-bed villa and one-bed apartment (sharing a small pool) in a winelands *casa rural* with sweeping views of Parque Nacional de Timanfaya. €120.

Casa El Morro

C/Morro, Uga ☎928 83 03 92 or 629 33 28 37, ☒www.casaelmorro.com. Five hillside villas that share an attractive pool terrace. In a thoughtfully converted old property, the villas (sleeping 3–5 each) are comfortable, with well-chosen, characterful decor. €100.

Finca La Calerita

Crta Arrecife-Yaiza km 17, near Uga ☎928 81 65 86, ☒lacalerita@lanzarote.com. Four simple apartments in open countryside, with views towards the sea, and a decent-sized swimming pool. Studios from €62, two-bed apartment €144.

Finca Uga

C/Agachadilla 5, Uga ☎629 37 22 20, ☒www.fincauga.com. Simple village house converted into three compact, characterful studio apartments, each sleeping two on mezzanine areas over the living space. From €61; generous reductions for longer stays.

Restaurants, bodegas and cafés

Amura

Puerto Calero ☎928 51 31 81. Closed Mon. The elegant terrace at this upmarket restaurant has the best views of all the harbourside places in the marina, looking southwest towards the open sea. On offer are imaginative dishes such as squid with coconut, Iberian pork with goat's cheese and quince jelly, and apple ravioli with lychee sorbet. The building, a fine reproduction of a Canarian mansion, is a popular choice for wedding parties. There's live guitar and *timple* music from 9pm on Fridays. Main courses €12–18.

Balcón de Femés

Pl San Marcial 9, Femés. This busy spot has a fairly traditional Canarian menu, and the views across Los Rostros to Playa Blanca certainly have "wow factor", but the food is indifferent and the service can be rather hurried, so if you're after more than a drink, you're better off at *Casa Emiliano*.

Bar Restaurante Femés

Pl San Marcial, Femés. Closed Thurs. On the square near the church, this down-to-earth place lacks the glamorous views of *Balcón de Femés* and *Casa Emiliano* so is always much quieter, though its menu of reliable Canarian favourites such as grilled fish and fried kid is very similar.

Bodega de Uga

Uga (on the LZ-2) ☎928 83 01 47. 1–3pm & 7pm–midnight. Closed Thurs. Booking advisable. This is one of the best places in the region to sample excellent Lanzarotean *malvasías*, fine Riojas and vintage Ribera del Dueros, Castile's most famous wine. There's a boutique vineyard attached to the *bodega*, a tiny and intimate place, with a lovely garden terrace, where you'll be served a plateful of specialities with your wine, including ham, olives, local cheese, smoked salmon from Uga's *ahumadería* and (when available) camel meat. It's not cheap (typically €40 per person for tapas), but the atmosphere is superb, especially on evenings when there's live music. There's a celebratory fiesta when the new wine is ready (Oct or Nov).

Bodega El Chupadero

Just off the LZ-30 from Uga to Masdache ☎928 17 31 15, ☏www.el-chupadero.com. Tues–Sun noon–10pm. Fabulous, funky little

bodega attached to a German-owned boutique winery that produces a particularly fine, fruity *moscatel*. Outside, you can enjoy surreal views of the tranquil winelands, Montaña Chupaderos, and the distant sea; inside, the place has an arty feel and a mellow, jazzy vibe, especially when the owner kicks off a DJ set. The superb tapas menu (from €5) includes lentil soup, dates with bacon, tomatoes with basil, and crepes with cactus jam, and the wine is delicious.

Bodega La Casona de Yaiza

C/El Rincón 11, Yaiza (on the south side of the village, signposted from La Era) ☎928 83 62 62, ☏www.casonadeyaiza.com. Daily 7–11pm; closed Thurs. Open to non-residents, this excellent hotel restaurant is a quiet, intimate place for a simple but delicious meal expertly prepared by the Argentinian chef. Specialities include gently spiced dishes such as tiger prawn and scallop *simbal*.

Bodega Santiago de Yaiza

Los Rostros (on the Tinajo road, outside Yaiza) ☎928 83 62 04. Tues–Thurs 11.30am–10pm (Fri & Sat til 11pm) & Sun 11.30am–6pm. A brilliant addition to Yaiza's first-class dining scene, this rustic but sophisticated *bodega* has cosy interior dining areas and a sunny terrace shaded by a magnificent magnolia tree. The menu includes plenty of good tapas plus interesting dishes such as beef with peaches, and chicken breast with apple. The prices are moderate for food of this quality, and the wine is superb.

Casa Emiliano

C/La Plaza 10, Femés ☎928 83 02 23. Closed Mon. At first glance, you might imagine this rustic little place with its flower-filled terrace garden would have an inferior view to that of its rival the *Balcón de Femés*, but it's actually better – and the atmosphere is friendlier, too. Locals come here for modestly priced rabbit and goat dishes, and overall it's much less of a tourist trap.

Casa Gregorio

C/Uga 15, Uga ☎928 83 01 08. Closed Tues. Set in the middle of the village, this simple place specializes in Canarian dishes such as baked *cabrito*, *sancocho* and *bienmesabe*; there's also a long selection of standard Spanish fish and meat dishes, and local wine from the barrel. A good choice for lunch at weekends.

Costa Azul

Avda Marítima 7, El Golfo ☎928 17 31 99. At the southern end of El Golfo, with beachside tables and good views. Like all the restaurants in the village, it serves excellent grilled fish, but is also a great spot for sunset drinks.

El Café del Puerto

Antiguo Varadero 6, Puerto Calero. Busy with locals, this European-style café spills out onto the esplanade at the east end of the marina and has a good line in fresh sandwiches, cakes and ice cream.

El Diablo

Islote del Hilario, Parque Nacional de Timanfaya ☎928 17 31 05; restaurant noon–3.30pm, bar 9am–4.45pm. Carefully constructed of heat-resistant stone, glass and tiles, this miracle of engineering is a hot-spot in more ways than one. César Manrique's late-60s design is chic, as you'd expect, and the views of volcanoes from the panoramic windows are truly superb. The unique selling point is the geothermal barbecue, and most people go for the grills, for the novelty value, but they're disappointing – other choices, such as the generous salads, are a better bet.

El Medianero

Bodega La Geria, on the LZ-30 from Uga to Masdache ☎928 17 31 78. This *bodega* café-bar is big enough to accommodate the coach parties that call in here every day. Sandwiches and

▼ GEOTHERMAL BARBECUE, EL DIABLO

tapas are good value at €2–3, and there is, of course, plenty of wine to wash them down.

El Volcán

Pl Remedios 4, Yaiza. Closed Sun eve. Impossible to miss as you drive through the village (it's on the main road near the church), this rustic restaurant serves hearty Spanish food, including a couple of local specialities: *potaje canario* and *puchero canario*. Above-average prices, but the portions are vast.

Golden Elephant

Antiguo Varadero 4, Puerto Calero ☎928 51 02 53. Take-away available. Not the most atmospheric of Thai restaurants but reasonably priced and a good choice if you're looking for a change from Canarian or European cuisine.

La Caleta

Hesperia Lanzarote, Cortijo Viejo, Puerto Calero ☎828 08 08 00, ☻www .hesperia-lanzarote.com. Closed Mon. First-class hotel restaurant with an inspired menu that takes Canarian themes and gives them a gourmet twist. Dishes include steak cooked in *malvasía* wine or salt cod with thyme; desserts include *gofio* ice cream. Main courses €10–17.

La Era

El Barranco 3, Yaiza (signposted from Pl Remedios) ☎928 83 00 16, ☻www .la-era.com. Closed Mon. Booking recommended. Much praised, and rightly so, *La Era* is an absolute must for anyone wishing to sample Canarian cuisine at its very best. The setting is charming – quaint little dining rooms leading off a central patio, and

a pretty courtyard behind – the menu superb, and the service friendly but discreet. Traditional recipes are the starting point for all the dishes, so you'll find plenty of classic ingredients, such as *papas arrugadas*, *mojo* and *gofio*, used with considerable imagination and flair. Pudding fans will adore the option that lets you sample a little bit of everything. There's a suitably excellent wine list, too – including a *malvasías* from *La Era's* own vineyard. Well worth the above-average prices.

Mar Azul

Avda Golfo 42, El Golfo ☎928 17 31 32. Serves possibly the freshest fish in El Golfo, with a small sheltered upstairs terrace offering great sea views, plus beachside tables.

Playa Quemada

Avda Marítima 16, Playa Quemada ☎928 17 07 37. Daily 11am–11pm. A genuine atmosphere, good fresh produce and an unrivalled location, right on the rocky shore, make this simple little place a good choice for local-style fish and grills. Main courses €8–15.

Taberna del Puerto

Paseo Marítimo 17, Puerto Calero ☎928 51 28 82. Offering one of the most authentic Spanish/Canarian menus of all the harbourside places, this unpretentious restaurant serves generous plates of top-quality tapas (€4–6) such as stuffed courgettes, or prawns with dates and *jamon serrano*, plus plenty of substantial fish and meat dishes (€7–11). It also has a great selection of Spanish wine.

Costa Teguise

The sun-and-fun resort of Costa Teguise is wholly geared to mass-market tourism and makes little pretence otherwise. Boasting a string of breezy but decent beaches, a purpose-built coastal promenade, a water park and golf club, and an abundance of amenable restaurants, it has plenty to offer. Its village-style square, Plaza del Pueblo Marinero, is convivial enough, and the most attractive beach, Playa de las Cucharas, is an excellent place to learn to windsurf.

Despite all this, Costa Teguise's fortunes have flagged in recent years. While it's not an unattractive place – the architecture is varied, there's plenty of greenery to soften the scene and the overall scale is modest compared to the mega-resorts found on some of the other Canary Islands – the resort is dominated by substantial modern hotel and apartment complexes, some of them monolith-like temples to tourism, and a stale and rather forced holiday atmosphere hangs over its commercial centres, where raucous karaoke, cheesey drag shows, and bars with widescreen TVs are the standard fare.

Things in Costa Teguise may gradually change, however: improvements and additions such as a new aquarium and theme park are already in the pipeline, and local politicians are even considering rebranding the place "Costa del Amor" – the Coast of Love.

Playa de las Cucharas

Costa Teguise's biggest and best beach, Playa de las Cucharas, is an impressive arc of golden sand where the activity of choice is flaking out under a brightly coloured sunshade.

The breezy but safe Cucharas bay is good for swimming and, particularly, windsurfing – this is where most of the island's windsurfing instructors set their students loose on the open water (see box on p.112). The best conditions for windsurfing tend, of course, to be the worst for sunbathing: you'll need a windbreak to avoid a sandblasting on blustery winter days.

Arrival and information

From Arrecife, daily **buses** (*guaguas*) run to Costa Teguise from 6.40am to 11.40pm (Mon–Fri every 20min, Sat & Sun every 30min), stopping at Pueblo Marinero and the *Hotel Gran Meliá Salinas* (*línea* #1).

The **tourist office** is currently in the Centro Commercial Los Charcos on Avda Islas Canarias (☏928 82 71 30; Mon–Fri 9.30am–1pm); at the time of writing, a new office was being built next to Plaza del Pueblo Marinero.

▲ HOTEL GRAN MELIÁ SALINAS

The first hotel to be built on Playa de las Cucharas was the *Gran Meliá Salinas*, as remarkable a landmark today as when it opened in the 1970s, when there was little to see in the area beyond lava fields and salt pans (hence the name "Salinas"). With César Manrique originals in the public areas, including richly textured paintings and beautiful fossil-like carved murals, plus a stunning indoor tropical garden and outdoor pool area – also designed by Manrique – the *Meliá Salinas* is an impressive complex that's well worth visiting even if you're not staying (see p.115). The indoor courtyard garden is particularly intriguing: open to the sky, its mood changes as the day passes – with fountains and pools among the tropical greenery, it's fresh by morning, and alive with the cheery croaking of frogs in the evenings.

Sadly, the resort that grew up around the *Meliá Salinas* has not lived up to its potential, and these days the hotel stands out like an overdressed adult at a teenagers' party – dignified but nonetheless rather out of place. Spreading south from the hotel, around Playa de las Cucharas

and beyond, is a sprawl of development that, despite regular nods towards traditional local style, is unremittingly commercial. The resort continues inland, too, so most of the holiday flats are some distance from the beach.

Playa de los Charcos, Playa del Jablillo and Playa Bastián

North of Playa de las Cucharas is Playa de los Charcos, a quiet bay ringed by a narrow strip of pale sand. Playa del Jablillo, to the south of Cucharas, is a safe, shallow beach that's child-friendly but otherwise less appealing than its neighbour, partly because it looks towards Arrecife's industrial fringes, and partly because it's close to some of the resort's tackiest hangouts. Further south is a long, open, rocky stretch called Playa Bastián, which, despite being close to the centre of the resort, feels isolated and a little desolate.

Coastal promenade

Stretching the length of the resort, Costa Teguise's six-kilometre seafront footpath is perfect for strolling or pottering on a bike or a pedal cart (available to rent throughout

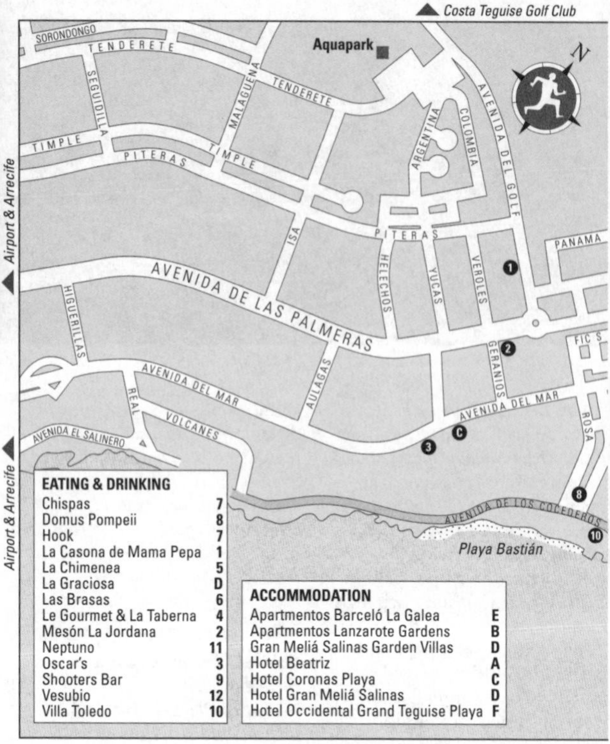
Costa Teguise Golf Club
Airport & Arrecife
Airport & Arrecife
Aquapark
SORONDONGO
TENDERETE
TENDERETE
SEGUIDILLA
MALAGUEÑA
TIMPLE
TIMPLE
PITERAS
PITERAS
ARGENTINA
COLOMBIA
AVENIDA DEL GOLF
ISA
PANAMA
AVENIDA DE LAS PALMERAS
HELECHOS
YUCAS
VEROLES
HIGUERILLAS
FIC S
GERANIOS
AVENIDA DEL MAR
AVENIDA DEL MAR
AULAGAS
REAL
VOLCANES
AVENIDA EL SALINERO
ROSA
AVENIDA DE LOS COCEDEROS
Playa Bastián
EATING & DRINKING
Chispas 7
Domus Pompeii 8
Hook 7
La Casona de Mama Pepa 1
La Chimenea 5
La Graciosa D
Las Brasas 6
Le Gourmet & La Taberna 4
Mesón La Jordana 2
Neptuno 11
Oscar's 3
Shooters Bar 9
Vesubio 12
Villa Toledo 10
ACCOMMODATION
Apartmentos Barceló La Galea E
Apartmentos Lanzarote Gardens B
Gran Meliá Salinas Garden Villas D
Hotel Beatriz A
Hotel Coronas Playa C
Hotel Gran Meliá Salinas D
Hotel Occidental Grand Teguise Playa F

the resort). A gentle walk from end to end is likely to take you an hour and a half, if you're not distracted by the beaches and bars along the way. Punctuating the scene are a few large sculptures: stylised windmills and a rather less successful metal abstract on the southern lip of Cucharas bay. The path is lit at night and is generally safe.

Catch the mighty wind

The coast of eastern Lanzarote is regularly claimed to be one of the best **windsurfing** spots in the world: beyond the relatively calm waters of Las Cucharas bay, where rookies learn the ropes, conditions get exciting enough to satisfy the experts, and Costa Teguise hosts high-octane **tournaments** from time to time. The most prestigious of these is the Professional Windsurfers Association Championships (@www.pwaworldtour.com), which takes place in July, when the trade winds are at their strongest. When the ocean is particularly "gnarly" you'll see an impressive display of back loops, donkey kicks and helicopter manouevres from serious boarders.

Several outfits in Costa Teguise offer **tuition and equipment rental**, among them the world-renowned Club Nathalie Simon (see p.174).

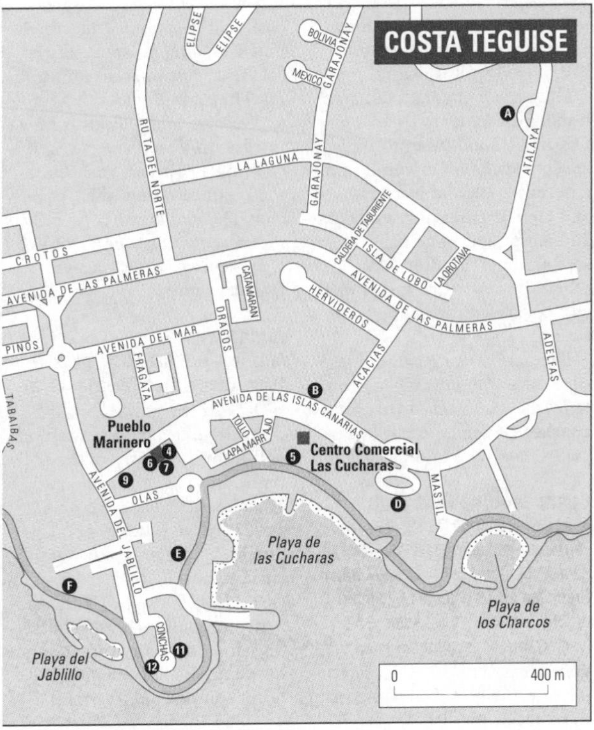
COSTA TEGUISE
ELIPSE
BOLIVIA
MEXICO
GARAJONAY
ATALAYA
RU TA DEL NORTE
LA LAGUNA
CROTOS
AVENIDA DE LAS PALMERAS
CATAMARAN
CALDERA DE TABURIENTE
ISLA DE LOBO
LA OROTAVA
HERVIDEROS
PINOS
AVENIDA DEL MAR
DRAGOS
FRAGATA
ACACIAS
ADELFAS
AVENIDA DE LAS ISLAS CANARIAS
TABAIBAS
Pueblo Marinero
TOLLO
LAPA
MARRAJO
Centro Comercial Las Cucharas
MASTIL
OLAS
AVENIDA DEL JABLILLO
Playa de las Cucharas
Playa de los Charcos
CONCHAS
Playa del Jablillo
0
400 m

Plaza del Pueblo Marinero

By far the most atmospheric corner of the resort, Plaza del Pueblo Marinero manages to retain something of a fishing-hamlet feel in its jumble of whitewashed buildings, green-painted timbers and shady trees.

▼ WINDSURFING CLASS, PLAYA DE LAS CUCHARAS

It'll come as no surprise, then, to hear that César Manrique had a hand in its design.

The main entrance is an arch leading off Avda de las Islas Canarias. Good times to visit are for lunch, when you'll find a decent choice of restaurants and tapas bars serving reasonably authentic food in genial surroundings, or after dark, when the rustic drinking holes and cocktail joints swing into action.

The bars do a roaring trade on Friday evenings when, from 6pm, there's a popular tourist **market** selling a hotchpotch of crafts, silverware and other gifts.

Costa Teguise Golf Club

Avda Golf ☏ 928 59 05 12, ⊛ www .lanzarote-golf.com. Daily May–Sept 8am–8pm, Oct–April 7.30am–7.30pm. Green fee for 18 holes €65 (winter) or €55 (summer), for 9 holes €52 (winter) or €44 (summer). For a good many visitors to Costa Teguise, the golf club is the main draw. It has an 18-hole, par-72, pro-standard course, plus a driving range and a practice green, and is extremely well kept – a labour of love on this arid island – with plenty of landscaped areas planted with grass, cacti, palms and shrubs. It's such an

▼ 18TH HOLE, COSTA TEGUISE GOLF CLUB

oasis that it's one of Lanzarote's bird-watching hotspots, albeit one that's not open to non-golfers. The club provides buggies and tuition, and sells kit from a small shop. Visitors are advised to bring a copy of their handicap certificate from their home club. The clubhouse, a friendly spot to enjoy post-golf drinks, is particularly attractive, with fantastic views of the 18th hole.

Aquapark

Avda Teguise ☏ 928 59 21 28. Daily 10am–6pm. €21, children (2–12yrs) €15. Near the golf club and a short drive or taxi ride (around €4) from the centre of the resort, this is a child-pleasing complex of slides, tubes and games. Though not as good as the newer, bigger Baku Water Park in Corralejo, Fuerteventura (see p.150), it can be a fun alternative to the beach, particularly on windy days. Be warned: none of the pools are heated, so the water can be cold in winter.

Hotels

Hotel Beatriz

C/Atalaya 3 ☏ 928 59 08 28, ⊛ www .beatrizhoteles.com. This massive, slab-like four-star complex, sited well away from the coast, is completely out of character for Lanzarote, where most developments are required to conform to local style. Inside, it's impressive, though rather impersonal, with gurgling waterfalls and tall atria hung with greenery. The rooms are larger than average, with views of an attractive pool and garden. An on-site wellness centre offers treatments including thalassotherapy (€18) and "chocotherapy" (a chocolate body wrap and anti-stress massage, for €99). €146.

Hotel Coronas Playa

Avda Mar 26 ☎928 82 66 40. A hit with British package holiday-makers, this hotel might be rather plain and concrete in style but it's well-run, with attentive staff, a large pool and spotless, good-sized rooms, each equipped with air-con and mini-fridge. €90.

Hotel Gran Meliá Salinas

Avda Islas Canarias ☎928 59 00 40, ⊛www.solmelia.com. Famous for being part-designed by César Manrique (see p.111), this huge beachfront place was the island's first five-star deluxe hotel, with all the elegance, comfort and service you'd expect. The rooms have attractive sea views, and the pool area is delightful. If you really want to push the boat out you could opt for a private villa – the most expensive accommodation option on the island (see below). €265.

Hotel Occidental Grand Teguise Playa

Avda Jablillo ☎928 59 06 54, ⊛www .occidental-hoteles.com. Large, uncompromisingly designed

concrete four-star right on the shore, close to the busiest – and tackiest – of Costa Teguise's commercial centres. Grand as the hotel's main entrance may be, some of the rooms are in need of a revamp, but in all other respects it's a comfortable and competitively priced choice for an undemanding package holiday. €114.

Apartments and villas

Apartamentos Barceló La Galea

Paseo Marítimo ☎928 59 05 51 ⊛www.barcelo.com. Self-catering aparthotel in a good position close to Playa Las Cucharas. The clean, good-sized apartments and studios equipped with basic kitchen facilities represent good value. It's also child-friendly, with three pools and energetic entertainment staff. €55.

Apartamentos Lanzarote Gardens

Avda Islas Canarias 13 ☎928 59 01 00, ⊛www.h10.es. One of the better aparthotels, this well-cared-for place has a great pool garden, jaunty geraniums on all the balconies, and a good family-friendly atmosphere.

Gran Meliá Salinas Garden Villas

Avda Islas Canarias ☎928 59 00 40, ⊛www.solmelia.com. The last word in luxury, these ten gorgeous villas are discreetly furnished with plump sofas, four-poster beds and elegant detailing. Each has a private pool and garden, and benefits from the hotel's top-notch "Royal" service. €1260.

▼ GRAN MELIÁ SALINAS

Shops

Bongo

Paseo Marítimo, near C/Olas. Original women's clothing, bags and contemporary jewellery, all with a funky, colourful twist.

Clean Ocean Project

C/Olas. Daily 10.30am–1.30pm & 5–9pm. Excellent little clothing shop run by a Fuerteventura-based organization that aims to encourage young people in the Canaries and Cape Verde Islands to care for their marine environment. Snazzy "Save the Ocean" T-shirts and surf gear for all ages.

Restaurants, bodegas and tapas bars

Domus Pompei

C/Tabaiba 2 ☎928 82 71 12. Cosy, characterful Italian restaurant in the quiet Playa Bastián area, serving classic pizza and pasta dishes at moderate prices.

La Casona de Mama Pepa

Avda Campo de Golf 25 ☎676 30 96 30. Closed Mon. Down-to-earth Spanish and Canarian cooking with dishes such as *ropa vieja de pescado* and snails with brandy, wine and bacon. Not the cheapest, but good value.

La Chimenea

CC Cucharas ☎928 59 08 37. Closed Sun. In the busy commercial centre close to the beach, this Italian restaurant has brisk, efficient, service, decent food and reasonable prices.

La Graciosa

Hotel Gran Meliá Salinas, Avda Islas Canarias ☎928 59 00 40. Daily 7.30pm–midnight. Booking recommended. The approach to this esteemed establishment – through the hotel's exotic indoor gardens – heightens the anticipation, and it doesn't disappoint. Elegant and dressy, it sets high standards with select dishes such as lobster with mushroom and leek sauce, sirloin with *foie gras*, and lamb with a sesame crust. Three courses start at around €45, plus wine. By far the best place in Costa Teguise to celebrate a special occasion.

▼ BEACHFRONT CAFÉ, COSTA TEGUISE

Las Brasas

Pl Pueblo Marinero ☎928 59 07 61. Tues–Sun from 8pm. An independent-minded little restaurant that prides itself on its short, carefully presented mid-priced menu as a break from the bland, crowd-pleasing places elsewhere in the resort. Choices include steak, lamb chops and prawns.

Le Gourmet & La Taberna

Pl Pueblo Marinero. Closed Thurs. *Le Gourmet* is stylish and attractive, with a good menu of Italian standards, and decent wine. Attached is *La Taberna*, a touristy but appealing tapas bar with courtyard tables under a spreading tree. Its brilliantly illustrated menu might be enough to tempt even the most nervous eater into trying something new: selections of hot and cold tapas and *pinchos* to share are good value at €10–12.

Mesón La Jordana

CC Lanzarote Bay 10–11, C/Geranios ☎928 59 03 28. Closed Sun. A short distance from the heart of the resort, this great little place's reliable Mediterranean-style dishes make the most of local produce such as fish, rabbit and kid. Above-average prices.

Neptuno

CC Neptuno 6, Avda Jablillo ☎928 59 03 78. Closed Sun. Tucked away in a quiet corner, and far less touristy than most, this place is worth seeking out for its carefully prepared Spanish and European dishes such as *parillada de pescado* or bourguignon fondue. Moderately priced, it's good value, and they take pride in their wine here, too.

Oscar's

Avda Mar 24, Las Coronas ☎928 59 04 89. Daily from 7pm. Closed Thurs. Some distance from the beach, this relaxed, characterful restaurant has a lovely leafy terrace, and a stylish interior decorated with messages from well-wishers. It's a good place for meat dishes, including surf and turf, or duck breast with orange sauce, plus other multinational classics, all moderately priced.

Vesubio

Playa del Jablillo ☎928 80 46 75. Great little pizzeria-grill with a terrace that has far-reaching coastal views and plenty of inexpensive choices on the menu.

Villa Toledo

Los Cocederos, CC Playa Bastián ☎928 59 06 26. Restaurant and café in a great location on the esplanade, with two fabulous terraces overlooking Playa Bastián. The enormous menu (mostly under €10) includes a good choice of salads and veggie dishes.

Bars

Chispas

Pl Pueblo Marinero. Daily 7pm–late. Cheap-and-cheerful drinking hole, popular with locals, in an atmospheric part of town.

Hook

Pl Pueblo Marinero. Busy late-night bar where generously proportioned cocktails ensure a lively ambience.

Shooters Bar

CC Tandarena. Welcoming place that's popular with a crowd of regulars who come here to play pool or catch up on the latest sporting action or UK soaps on the giant-screen TV.

Teguise and Tinajo

The historic town of Teguise, capital of Teguise district and once of the whole island, is a delightfully elegant little backwater. It's rather sleepy most days, but springs into life on Sunday mornings, when its colourful weekly market is in full flow and the streets and squares are jammed with stalls, buskers and milling crowds. The area surrounding Teguise and its neighbouring small country towns of Tiagua and Tinajo is known as El Jable. This is Lanzarote's rural heartland, where painstakingly watered fruit, vegetable and cactus farms make the most of the sandy but fertile *jable* terrain. There's a genuine, down-to-earth feel to the villages here that's unmatched elsewhere on the island, making it a good place to stay in a *casa rural*.

North of the resort town of Costa Teguise, the eastern coastline up to Charco del Palo and beyond is wild, rocky and sparsely developed, making it an appealing destination for those seeking solitude, while for die-hard sports fans, the coast north of Teguise is the destination of choice – La Santa is home to a world-class multi-sports centre, which hosts the Lanzarote Ironman each year, and nearby Famara and the northwest shores are the island's prime spots for surfing and kiteboarding.

Visiting Teguise and Tinajo districts

For maximum flexibility, the best way to explore the area is by **renting a car** (see p.167). Public transport to all but the main towns is infrequent (a complete bus timetable is available online at www.arrecifebus.com), but from Arrecife three **bus** routes serve Teguise (*línea* #7 to Haría and Maguez, #9 to Orzola and #10 to Los Valles), with a total of ten departures a day Monday to Friday (6 on Sat, 5 on Sun). Two of these routes (*líneas* #7 and #9) also stop at the Jardín del Cactus (8 buses a day Mon–Fri, 6 on Sat, 5 on Sun). *Línea* #10 serves Los Valles twice a day (weekdays only). Two bus routes from the capital serve Tiagua (*líneas* #16 and #20) with a total of 11 departures a day Monday to Friday (5 on Sat, 3 on Sun). *Línea* #16 continues to Mancha Blanca, Tinajo and La Santa (8 buses a day Mon–Fri, 5 on Sat, 3 on Sun). *Línea* #20 serves La Caleta de Famara three times a day (weekdays only).

Teguise's **Sunday market** is served by four buses from Costa Teguise (*línea* #6) and Puerto del Carmen (*línea* #11) and by one bus from Playa Blanca (*línea* #12); buses leave the resorts between 9am and 10.15am and return between noon and 1.15pm. If driving, you can park in one of the fields on the edge of town that become dusty makeshift **car parks** at the weekend.

Local **tour companies** run Teguise-market specials and include the Jardín del Cactus on larger tours of the island; most large hotels can supply details.

Teguise

Undoubtedly Lanzarote's most attractive town, Teguise was the island's administrative centre and cultural powerhouse until 1852, when the port of Arrecife was deemed a better-located choice of capital. These days, Teguise has a tranquil, dignified atmosphere, and it's a pleasant place to potter about, browsing for gifts in shops or stopping for lunch and a glass of wine on a quiet side street. You'll have to stay elsewhere, though, as the town has no hotels – the nearest accommodation is in nearby Nazaret (see p.128).

Teguise was founded in the early fifteenth century and, along with Betancuria on Fuerteventura, is the Canary Islands' oldest settlement. Teguise escaped the worst of the damage caused by the island's volcanic eruptions (see p.102), and many fine buildings from the eighteenth and nineteenth centuries still stand, a good few of which have been carefully restored over the last couple of decades, their whitewash dazzling on bright days. The heavily carved wooden doors and balconies of the grander mansions speak volumes about

▲ TEGUISE

Teguise's former affluence: timber has always been scarce on the island, and only the wealthy could afford to adorn their houses with it.

The focal point of the town is the Plaza de la Constitución, on which the **Iglesia de Nuestra Señora de Guadeloupe** stands – the church tower is Teguise's principal landmark, easily visible in the distance if you're approaching from the

▼ SUNDAY MARKET, TEGUISE

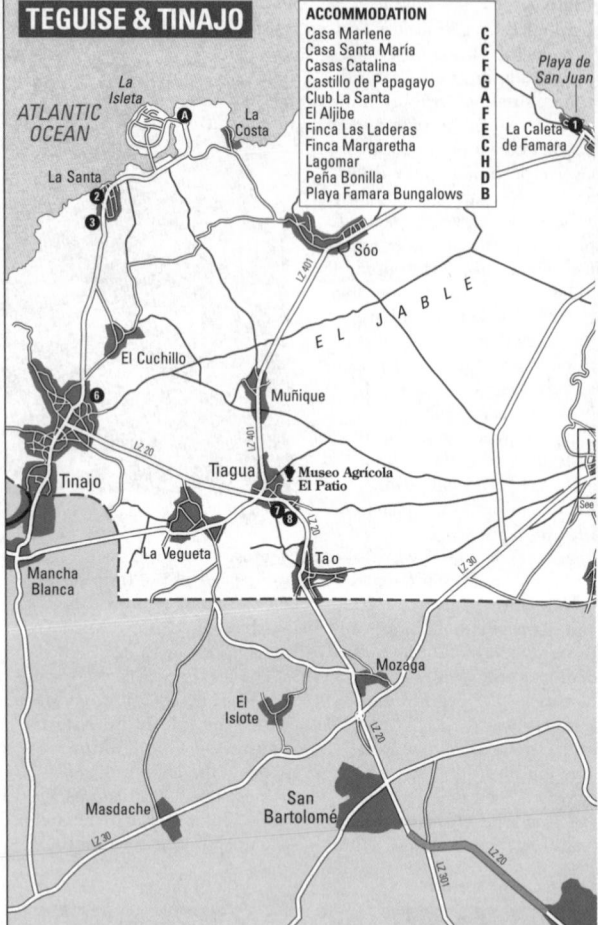

TEGUISE & TINAJO

ACCOMMODATION
Casa Marlene	C
Casa Santa María	C
Casas Catalina	F
Castillo de Papagayo	G
Club La Santa	A
El Aljibe	F
Finca Las Laderas	E
Finca Margaretha	C
Lagomar	H
Peña Bonilla	D
Playa Famara Bungalows	B

north or southwest. On the west side of the square is the elegant eighteenth-century **Casa-Museo Palacio Spínola** (☏928 84 51 81; Mon–Fri 9am–3pm, till 4pm in winter, Sat–Sun & public hols 9am–2pm, till 3pm in winter; €6), the restoration of which was overseen by César Manrique; it's open to the public as a fine example of a Canarian stately home. Standing on the south side of the square is what must be one of the most elegantly rustic banks in the world, the Caja de Canarias, in a converted fifteenth-century tithe barn, **La Cilla de Diezmos y Primicias**.

On nearby C/Marqués de Herrera is another notable building, the **Palacio del**

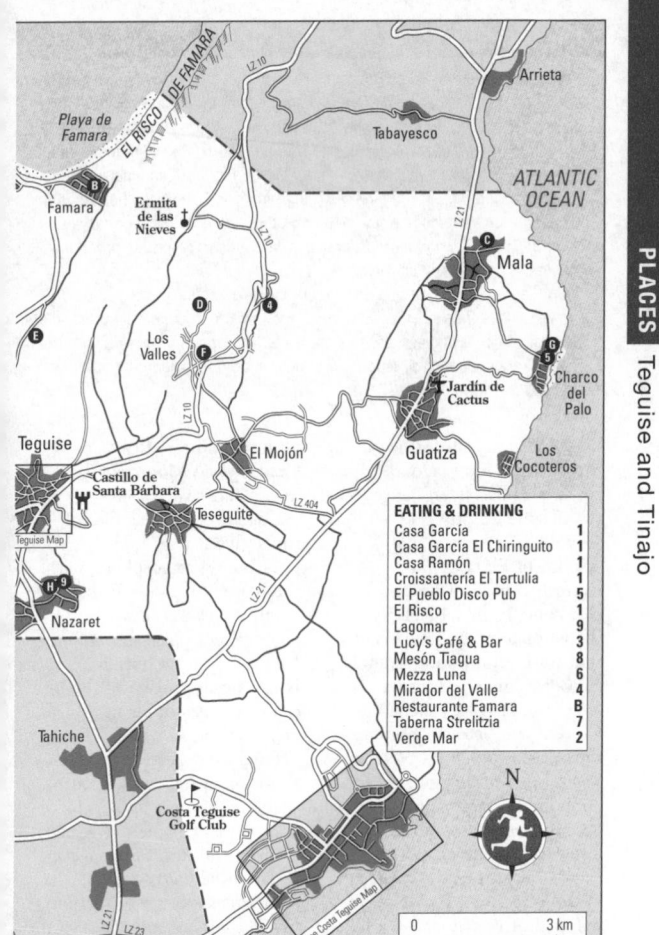

EATING & DRINKING

Casa García	1
Casa García El Chiringuito	1
Casa Ramón	1
Croissantería El Tertulía	1
El Pueblo Disco Pub	5
El Risco	1
Lagomar	9
Lucy's Café & Bar	3
Mesón Tiagua	8
Mezza Luna	6
Mirador del Valle	4
Restaurante Famara	B
Taberna Strelitzia	7
Verde Mar	2

Marqués, built between 1423 and 1455 and now privately owned – its charming patio is an upmarket wine bar (see p.132). East of the *palacio*, **Castillo de Santa Bárbara**, the chunky sixteenth-century fortress that overlooks Teguise, was originally built as a watchtower to guard against North African pirates and marauders. Your most likely reason to make the uphill trip is to admire the sweeping views, but there's also a museum here, the Museo del Emigrante Canario (☎928 84 59 13; daily 10am–4pm, till 5pm in winter; €3), with artefacts relating to the emigration of Canarians to America in the eighteenth and nineteenth centuries. This

Teguise market

On Sundays, Teguise undergoes a complete change of character when its famous weekly **market** (Mercadillo de Teguise; 10am–2pm) swings into action. Stalls sprawl all over town, but if it's quality crafts and artisan-made produce you're look-ing for then the best street to aim for is **C/José Antonio**, off Plaza Clavijo y Fajardo. Elsewhere, there's an abundance of cheap jewellery, clothing and tourist tat, but don't be too put off – with a little searching you'll find interesting offerings from the bizarre, such as found-object garden sculptures or volcano-shaped candles, to the exotic (there's always a good showing of West African traders offering to braid your hair or haggle over carvings).

All of Teguise's shops, restaurants and bars have their doors wide open on Sundays – in fact, you may discover some you never knew existed if you've only visited on a weekday before. During market hours, you'll also find a row of mobile snack bars in Parque la Mareta, selling all sorts of drinks and snacks, from *churros* to *bratwurst*.

risky and desperate path was chosen by many islanders whose livelihoods had been destroyed by volcanic eruptions and drought.

South of Plaza de la Constitución, on C/Santo Domingo 1, the large, lofty chapel of Teguise's seventeenth-century Dominican convent has been converted into a contemporary art gallery, the **Centro de Arte de Santo Domingo** (☎928 84 50 01; Mon–Fri 10am–3pm, Sun & public hols 10am–2pm; free), staging temporary shows and installations. The chapel's elaborate altarpiece – dedicated to the Virgen del Rosario but stripped of its statuary – still survives.

Tiagua and Tinajo

The small towns of Tiagua and Tinajo lie in the heart of the rural area in which most of the island's fruit and vegetables are grown. Sand carried inland on the prevailing northeasterly winds settles in this region, producing a rather bleak, flat, fertile terrain known locally as El Jable. On clear days, the road from Tao to Tiagua offers fantastic views across the sandy plains to Famara,

with the offshore islands of La Graciosa and Montaña Clara set in an azure sea beyond.

Tiagua's solid agricultural roots give it a grounded, unassuming atmosphere; with the Museo Agrícola El Patio on the outskirts of town, it's an excellent place to explore Lanzarote's rural heritage. Tiagua is also home to two of the best gourmet restaurants in the rural areas (see p.131 and p.132).

Tinajo is a quiet little town of flat-roofed houses with onion-shaped chimneys and, in its central plaza, some particularly ancient and impressive *drago* trees. These hardy agaves, sometimes known as "dragon's blood trees", were sacred to the aboriginal islanders.

Museo Agrícola El Patio

C/Echeyde 18, Crta Sóo-Tiagua ☎928 52 91 34 or 928 52 91 06. Mon–Fri 10am–5.30pm, Sat 10am–2.30pm. €5. Built in 1845, this peaceful and attractive traditional farm, complete with windmills, live-stock and gardens of flowers, vegetables and cacti, has been converted into an illuminating museum of country life. It's a little dry and lacking in interac-tive exhibits, so kids may end

Castillo Santa Bárbara

up fidgeting, but for interested adults it's an insight into many island traditions.

The heart of the museum is the grand **manor house**,

full of objects and images that celebrate the efforts of a community that, over the course of 150 years, struggled to make a living in an unforgiving

Fiestas in Teguise

Teguise's patronal festival, the **Fiesta de Nuestra Señora del Carmen** on July 16, is a great time to see locals dressed in traditional costume and hear musicians playing the *timple*, a Canarian instrument that originates from Teguise. You might catch some Canarian *lucha* (wrestling) bouts, too. There's more fun and games **between Christmas and Epiphany**, and during **carnaval** in February, when the local brand of merry-making includes the *Danza de los Diabletes* (Dance of the Little Devils) – a chance for locals to disguise themselves in red-and-black-patterned suits and devil masks and dash about scaring people. Around the time of **Corpus Christi** in June, you may see the Plaza de la Constitución decorated with elaborate carpets of coloured salt, depicting saints and holy icons.

▲ MUSEO AGRÍCOLA EL PATIO

environment – and succeeded. It quickly becomes apparent that the museum is not about the objects themselves – wooden barrows, earthenware pots, well-worn tools – but about what they represent: a slower, harder way of life, moulded around earthly rhythms. Enlarged sepia photos show a man loading a camel with water drawn from a well, peasants posing proudly with heavily laden donkeys, and children sorting corn cobs and grinning at the camera from under their bonnets, while commentaries mourn the loss of folkloric skills in this age of mass production. The farmworkers' quarters at the back of the manor house are presented as they might have been in the early twentieth century: a dark, soot-blackened kitchen, a patio with a stone water distiller and, in the simple bedroom, a bed strung with ropes in place of slats or springs.

Outside in the yard is a highlight of the museum, the **bodegón** – a recreation of an old wine shop – where you can sample the estate's present-day house vintages and excellent, salty goat's cheese.

La Santa

La Santa is a nondescript village on a grubby, rocky shore, but the area has become synonymous with sport on Lanzarote, thanks to the sports resort of *Club La Santa*, which lies on the edge of a coastal lagoon 1km outside the village (see p.128). In addition to its year-round programme of activities and events, the club hosts important sporting fixtures including the La Santa Surf Pro Surfing championship in October, an international contest that's the highlight of the island's surfing calendar and acts as a European qualifier for the WCT Surfing World Championships, and the Lanzarote Ironman challenge in May (see box on p.171)

Playa de Famara and La Caleta de Famara

By far the most impressive beach on this side of the island, the nine-kilometre-long Playa de Famara made a profound impression on César Manrique during his formative years. The artist spent happy summers here as a child, and in later life his affection for the place stoked his

Surf's up

Some local surfers, in their more gung-ho moments, claim that Lanzarote is Europe's answer to Hawaii. Far-fetched though that might be, parts of the island – Famara, La Santa and the northern coast – are blessed with some first-class swells.

Thanks to Lanzarote's long history of volcanic activity, the ocean along this stretch bears little resemblance to the benign waters lapping the tourist beaches of the south. The violent collision of boiling lava and cold sea produced a system of over twenty shallow reefs around the north of the island. Because Lanzarote has no continental shelf to act as a drag on wave movement, incoming waves whipped up by the trade winds travel in from deep water, hit the lava reefs, and swell to six feet – and often much higher – before breaking with force onto the northern shores.

Famara, with its long sandy beach and consistent conditions, is surf central, and would-be wave riders are well catered for by its surf schools (see p.174), all of which are buzzing from October to April. Some surfers graduate on to the more demanding swells at **Playa de San Juan** and, further west, the coastline near **La Santa**, where classic breaks include El Quemao (a powerful left-breaking wave that's strictly for experts), the infamous Morro Negro and the ominously named Slab.

passion for defending the natural environment.

The beach, which faces northeast, has treacherous undercurrents and is better for surfing and fishing than swimming, though plenty of people spend sunny days chilled out behind the *zoco*-like stone windbreaks dotted about the sand. On haze-free days, the view across the water to the islands of La Graciosa, Montaña Clara and Alegranza is stunning.

Most people staying on this part of the coast base themselves right behind the beach, in one of the distinctive and interesting Norwegian-designed modernist bungalows (see p.128), built here as holiday homes in the 1970s, but it's also possible to find lodgings in Famara's main settlement, La Caleta de Famara, a kilometre to the west. With sandy streets and the kind of bars where fishermen hang out with surfers and kiteboarders, this is one of the most relaxed villages on the island and a pleasantly low-key place to spend time.

The wild, scrubby heathland inland from the village is a protected area that's attractive in spring, when blossoming rare plants carpet it with a soft, green fuzz.

▼ PLAYA DE FAMARA

El Risco de Famara

El Risco de Famara, part of the Parque Natural del Archipiélago Chinijo, is the closest Lanzarote has to a mountain range; 23km long, it includes the island's highest peak, the Peñas del Chache (670m). Rare flora flourish on the cliffs, including a high concentration of endemic species such as the silver-leafed *algodonera* and the pretty dandelion-like *Reichardia famarae*. The rough terrain makes for some bracing hiking, and the cliffs are also Lanzarote's best-known launch site for hang-gliders (see p.172) – in the right conditions, you can fly all the way up to the far north of the island and back from here.

Los Valles

The hamlet of Los Valles has a couple of excellent places to stay (see p.128), making it a fine base from which to explore the surrounding Paisaje Protegido de Tenegüime, an

▼ SANTA MARGARITA, GUATIZA

attractive protected upland area. It's good for bird-watching, and is home to some rare endemic plant species including the inconspicuous, russet-coloured *tajose*, plus a small but far from inconspicuous forest of wind turbines.

Guatiza

The pretty, Moorish-looking village of Guatiza, 8km east of Teguise, lies in an area bristling with prickly-pear farms – in fact, there are plots of the plants right in the middle of the village, dusted with the tell-tale white bloom that indicates the presence of the cochineal beetle (see box on p.127). At its centre is an attractive late-nineteenth-century chapel, Santa Margarita, built in simple colonial style with an onion-dome tower.

Jardín del Cactus

Near Guatiza ☎ 928 52 93 97, ⊛ www .cabildodelanzarote.com/cact. Daily 10am–6.45pm. €5 including a drink.

On the outskirts of Guatiza, César Manrique's Jardín de Cactus is a surreal yet glorious garden devoted to the presentation of spiny plants as art objects. Completed in 1990, it was one of his last Lanzarotean projects, and his favourite: he devised it as a celebration of the island's cultural and botanical heritage. There are cacti everywhere – over 1000 varieties are represented, including specimens from America and Madagascar, as well as the Canaries – with beds of them ranked on terraces of fine black *picón*, tumbling down from a small, windmill-topped hill into an amphitheatre-like open space once used as a *picón* quarry. Dotted among the plants are bizarre, sculptural pillars of volcanic rock, left behind by the miners. After you've admired the

▲ JARDÍN DEL CACTUS

of the whole garden from the elegantly canopied café.

As a project, the garden offers a magnificent reminder of the sheer fertility of Lanzarote's austere-seeming terrain; the only blot on this aesthetic treat is the super-sized cactus sculpture in the car park.

Charco del Palo

Charco del Palo is one of Lanzarote's quietest resorts. Tucked away on a rocky stretch of coast, the seclusion suits its regular visitors down to the ground, in particular the German naturists who first adopted it in the 1970s and have been coming back ever since. The resort is small, with

cactus specimens at close range from the tiered pathways, you can take in the excellent views

Red gold

Apart from a sideline in jam and syrup making, the cactus farms in and around Guatiza are dedicated to the production of **cochineal**. Thought to have been discovered by the Aztecs, who used it as a war paint, this distinctive carmine red pigment – made from drying and crushing the larvae of the tiny cochineal beetle, whose distinctive colour comes from their diet of *tunera* cacti juice – has, over the centuries, been much prized as a colour for princely gowns, paints, cosmetics and, famously, Campari.

When the Spanish conquistadors came across cochineal in sixteenth-century Mexico, they quickly recognized it as a key commodity, on a par with gold. Shipped back to Europe, it created a sensation – the red it produced was brighter, deeper and longer lasting than anything anyone had ever seen – and cochineal soon came to account for one fifth of Spain's gross income. Striving to maintain a trade monopoly, the Spanish fiercely guarded the secrets of cochineal cultivation, and it wasn't until the eighteenth century that microscopes brought the mystery of the source of the red powder to light.

The Spanish had struggled to introduce the beetle in Europe but they discovered that conditions were perfect in the Canary Islands: on Lanzarote, the first cochineal farms, in Tiagua, Guatiza and Mala, opened in the 1830s. By the nineteenth century, carmine red was being used to dye everything from carpets to cardinals' robes and had been mixed into pigments used by great artists such as Rembrandt and Turner. But the tide turned for the cochineal trade with the development of cheap and effective chemical dyes, and general demand for red pigments flagged when the fashionably attired began to prefer blue and black fabrics over crimson and scarlet. Gradually, Lanzarote's cactus farms began to falter.

Today, though, their fortunes have recovered. Many confectionery, cosmetics and textile producers now prefer organic dyes to chemical alternatives, and Lanzarote, as one of the few places in the world where cochineal beetles are still bred, is well-placed to corner the market.

neat rows of holiday bungalows, and an atmosphere that's relaxed enough for people to leave their clothing behind when walking from house to house, rambling along the beach or visiting some of the restaurants. The beach has pale sand and a natural lagoon that makes a perfect swimming pool. There are also some interesting diving and snorkelling sites just offshore (see p.173 for operator details).

Apartments and villas

Apartamentos Castillo de Papagayo

Charco del Palo ☎928 17 31 76, ⓦwww.charco-del-palo.com. Attractive clothing-optional apartments and villas in various sizes and styles, scattered all over the village of Charco del Palo, and managed by a German naturist tour operator. Most are comfortably equipped and some have private pools. From €80.

Apartamentos LagOmar

C/Loros 6, Nazaret (signposted "Museo") ☎928 84 53 69, ⓦwww.lag-o-mar.com. Two small stylish guest villas (each sleeping two), tucked away to the side of one of the island's most impressively located restaurants (see p.131). Decorated with whitewash, volcanic stone and contemporary art, each has a kitchenette, a terrace and use of a pool. €90.

Bungalows Playa Famara

Urb Famara ☎928 59 25 58, ⓦwww.bungalowsplayafamara.com. With the Famara cliffs as a striking backdrop, this intriguing collection of semicircular single-storey villas is a real mixed bag.

The houses are all individually owned, and while some are dated and rather forlorn, the best ones are sleek and chic, with private pools and zen-style gardens. Many are also naturist-friendly. From €75.

Casas Catalina

C/San Isidro Labrador 12, Los Valles ☎928 52 80 19 or 902 36 33 18, ⓦwww.rural-villas.com. Sharing a good-sized heated swimming pool, these two neighbouring villas in a former farmhouse are comfortably furnished in a pleasant rustic style, sleeping up to four each, with free use of mountain bikes. From €120.

Club La Santa

Urb La Santa ☎928 59 99 99 or UK enquiries 0161 790 9890, ⓦwww.clublasanta.com. Huge, highly rated family sports-resort with impressive facilities and an exhaustive (and potentially exhausting) programme of daily events, from martial arts to minigolf, included in the price; extras include scuba diving and surfing. There's an overwhelmingly institutional feel to the place, and the mini-apartments, which sleep two to six and have a kitchenette, are dated and plain, but you'll probably be far too busy to care. From €104.

El Aljibe

C/San Isidro Labrador 12, Los Valles ☎928 52 80 19 or 902 36 33 18, ⓦwww.rural-villas.com. Utterly lovely, this stone-walled former water store has been converted into a unique rural retreat for two, with a vaulted gallery-style bedroom above a cosy open-plan living space with a state-of-the-art stereo system – so you can appreciate the acoustics to the full. There's also an attractive sea-water pool in a good-sized garden, shared with the *Casas Catalina*. €160.

Estudio Chimida

C/Jaime Balmes 14, Teguise ☎928 84 57 23, ☺www.islaviva.com. A rare find in Teguise, this apartment is small, bright, comfortable and reasonably priced, with a tiny terrace (but no pool). It's situated near the edge of the village, but only a short walk from the centre. €55.

Finca Las Laderas

C/Las Laderas 2, Famara ☎607 59 14 47 or 699 30 87 31, ☺www .fincalanzarote.de. Two single-storey, one-bedroom apartments in a simply furnished nine-teenth-century farmhouse with a small, shared pool. Remote, rustic setting, a short drive from Famara beach. From €50.

Finca Margaretha, Casa Santa María & Casa Marlene

C/Cangrejo 31, Mala ☎928 52 95 89, ☺www.lotus-del-mar.com. On the outskirts of the village of Mala, these attractively designed holi-day villas have good views of open countryside and a relaxed, New Age atmosphere. Good value for an away-from-it-all stay. From €42.

Peña Bonilla

Los Valles ☎928 84 57 23, ☺www .islaviva.com. These two diminutive, but charming, one-bedroom villas have a pleasantly rough-edged rustic atmosphere and bags of character. They share a small attractive pool. €85.

Shops

Arena Negra

C/Higuera, Teguise. Cutting-edge fashion from Diesel, Custo and Camper.

Arte Cerámica

Avda Acorán 43–45, Teseguite ☎928 84 50 57. Mon–Fri 11am–5pm. A German expat couple exhibit their original ceramics and paintings, much inspired by aboriginal Canarian themes, at this studio-gallery.

Casa de la Palmera

Pl Constitución, Teguise. Sells local products including aloe vera, jewellery, wine, jars of *mojo*, and tasty cactus jam.

La Lonja Fundación César Manrique

Pl Dieciocho de Julio, Teguise. Shop selling Manrique-branded post-ers, clothing, tiles and books.

La Route des Caravanes

Pl Clavijo y Fajardo, Teguise. Bazaar-style luxury emporium piled high with Moroccan throws, mirrors, lamps and slippers.

Malvasía

Pl Constitución, Teguise. Fine deli and wine cellar stocking local delicacies such as honey, rum and artisan-made cheese.

Tierra

C/Higuera, Teguise. Delectable ceramics inspired by Canarian ethnic art and symbology.

Restaurants, bodegas and tapas bars

Acatife

C/San Miguel 4, Teguise ☎928 84 50 37. This redoubtable restaurant claims to be Lanzarote's oldest restaurant. In an atmospheric mansion right in the middle of Teguise, it serves substantial fare such as fish with sea salt and

PLACES

Teguise and Tinajo

▲ LA GALERÍA, TEGUISE

rabbit in red wine. While the style of cooking might seem dated and uninspired, prices are very moderate (€8–10 for most main courses), and you can't fault the service.

Bodega Santa Bárbara

C/Cruz 5, Teguise ☎ 928 84 57 38. Mon–Fri & Sun 11am–5pm. A charming bodega with a tiny, cool, leafy patio, serving scrumptious plates of tapas (€6–9). An excellent place to dive into on a Sunday to escape the market-day crowds.

Casa García

Avda Marinero 1, La Caleta de Famara ☎ 928 52 87 10. Mon, Tues & Thurs–Sun noon–midnight. Big and bright, so good for large gatherings, this popular, reasonably priced restaurant specializes in fish dishes and home-made pizza.

Casa Ramón

C/Marinero 31, La Caleta de Famara. Closed Tues. An unpretentious, friendly and spacious bar-restaurant with brisk, efficient service, this place serves phenomenal paella, plus plenty of other choices, all at reasonable prices.

Cejas

Pl San Francisco 5, Teguise ☎ 928 84 51 01. Tues–Sat noon–4pm & 7–11pm, Sun (café-bar only) 8am–2pm. Elegant restaurant and café-bar with an elaborate and rather pricey menu including wild boar with wild mushrooms and chestnut sauce, and duck *confit* with citrus fruit and honey. Main courses €15–19.50.

El Risco

C/Montaña Blanca 30, La Caleta de Famara ☎ 928 36 63 97. Mon–Wed & Fri–Sun 12.30–10pm. Unassuming, but still the best spot to eat in Famara, this harbourside restaurant is a bright, friendly family-run place serving great local fish, fresh salads and home-made desserts at very reasonable prices. It used to belong to relatives of César Manrique, and works by the great man, including jaunty fish prints and a wall-mounted collage that's a total one-off, celebrate the connection.

El Ryad

C/León y Castillo 3, Teguise ☎ 928 84 59 31. Tues–Sat from 7.30pm, Sun 10.30am–10pm. An immaculate Moroccan restaurant with a tantalizing menu of *tagines* and couscous (typically €12–21), and lighter meals at lunchtime on Sundays. Belly dancers entertain at weekends.

Ikarus

Pl Dieciocho de Julio, Teguise ☎ 928 84 53 32. Tues–Thurs 11am–6pm, Fri 11am–10.30pm, Sat 7–10.30pm, Sun 10am–2pm. Fairly pricey but fashionable and arty bar-restaurant in an interesting building with a smart covered courtyard, serving good beer and bistro-style food such as vegetable curry with sesame and almonds, or crispy duck with red cabbage and *cassis* sauce.

La Galería

C/Nueva 8, Teguise. Daily 10am–4pm (Tues–Fri & Sun til 10pm). Mellow little *taberna* and trendy gallery space, with a short menu of tapas and salads for around €4–7. On a quiet sidestreet off the main square, it's a good place to stop for a bite during the Sunday market; it also sometimes hosts evening live music sessions.

LagOmar

C/Loros 6, Nazaret (signposted "Museo") ☎ 928 84 56 65, ⓦ www.lag-o-mar.com. Tues–Sat noon–midnight, Sun noon–6pm. Part *haute-cuisine* restaurant, part smart cosmopolitan nightspot, *LagO-mar's* setting is jaw-droppingly dramatic. The garden restaurant is dominated by a sculpted-looking cliff-face, in which a cave has been turned into a bar, while the focal point is a turquoise ornamental pool, from which winding walkways lead to private nooks and lookouts. Designed by César Manrique in the 1970s as part of a residence that was once earmarked for actor Omar Sharif (hence the name), it's showing its age, and the service can be indifferent, but you can't fault the cooking. Fresh and imaginative, it aims high, with prices to match.

Mesón Tiagua

Avda Guanarteme 19, Tiagua ☎ 928 52 98 16, ⓦ www.meson-tiagua.de. Mon & Wed–Sat 7–11pm, Sun 1–4pm & 7.30–11pm. Appearances can be deceptive: from the outside, it's easy to mistake this for a roadside café, but hidden within is a cosy restaurant with smart linen, soft lighting, and one of the most imaginative gourmet menus on the island, prepared by the German chef who also owns *El Caracol* in Arrecife. His idea was to bring city-style dining to the country – dishes such as beef stuffed with gherkins and bacon, chicken with spicy peanut garlic pesto, and vegetable tempura with curry sauce use creative combinations of herbs and spices, and are excellent value at €9–15.50 for a main course. The desserts are also superb. With only seven tables, it's worth reserving in advance.

Mezza Luna

Avda Cañada 22, Tinajo ☎ 928 84 01 41. Closed Tues. Attractive restaurant that's the best place on this side of the island for pizza and other Italian specialities.

Mirador del Valle

Los Valles ☎928 52 80 36. Daily 11am–7pm. This viewpoint restaurant, halfway round a hairpin bend, overlooks terraced farmland typical of the area. Rustic in style with a pleasant panoramic terrace, it has a standard menu of meat and fish dishes at moderate prices.

Palacio del Marqués

C/Herrera y Rojas 9, Teguise ☎928-84 57 73. Mon–Fri noon–6pm (till 8pm in summer), Sun 10am–3pm. A perfect place for lunch on a sunny day, particularly for wine buffs, this *bodega* is tucked away in the lovely courtyard of what is thought to be the oldest mansion on the Canary Islands (completed in 1455). The German owners, wine experts with a superb cellar of Spanish and Lanzarotean vintages, offer delicious plates of cheese, olives and tapas to accompany your choice (typically around €11.50 per person, with free portions for kids).

Restaurante Famara

Playa Famara Bungalows, Urb Famara ☎928 84 51 32. Situated in the heart of the bungalow complex but open to all, this place has a decent, though unremarkable, menu of fish and meat dishes at standard prices. Design-wise, it's so trapped in a 1970s time warp that it feels rather funky.

Taberna Strelitzia

Avda Guanarteme 55, Tiagua ☎928 52 98 41. Daily from 7.30pm. Cosy, intimate, cluttered with rustic odds and ends and suffused with delicious aromas, this

place is a real find. It's just like a French country inn that's been bundled up and transplanted from rural Provence, kitchen and all. The cooking is truly superb, with fabulous ingredients and inspired sauces, and you're free to nose around the well-stocked cellar to choose the perfect accompanying wine. The pièce de resistance is a chintz-filled private upstairs room that's perfect for a romantic evening for two. Above-average prices, with starters from €10.50 and main courses averaging €16, but definitely worth it.

Verde Mar

C/Sena Encarnación, Pl Iglesia, La Santa ☎928 84 08 58. Tues–Sun from 6.30pm. British-run place that's generally busy, largely because it's the best restaurant in a village where most eating options are thoroughly mediocre. Specialities include chicken-liver salad, and oriental tuna with noodles; vegan dishes are also available.

Cafés and bars

Café Jaleo

Casa Santiago, C/Flores, Teguise ☎928 84 56 63. Mon–Wed 10am–5pm, Thurs–Fri 10am–5pm & 7–11pm, Sun 10am–4pm. With masses of character, this gallery-café has one of the healthiest light menus around, including great veggie options such as lentil curry, vegetable *albondígas* and goat's-cheese quiche. The cool, eclectic style incorporates lampshades made from vintage teacups, and decorative installations from locally based artists. Hosts regular live jazz and tango sessions.

Casa García El Chiringuito

C/Marinero 16, La Caleta de Famara. Closed Mon. Visiting kiteboarders mingle with the locals at *Casa García El Chiringuito*, the busiest bar in La Caleta de Famara. As well as drinks and tapas, there are light meals on offer.

Croissantería El Tertulía

C/Marinero 20, La Caleta de Famara. A great stop for breakfast on the run, this tiny bakery serves top-notch pastries, tasty *empanadas* and good coffee, all at decent prices.

Croisantería La Despensita

C/San Miguel, Teguise. Selling coffee, pastries, sandwiches and ice cream, *La Despensita* is one of the few places in Teguise open at breakfast time.

El Pueblo Disco Pub

Centro Commercial, Charco del Palo. Late-opening bar oriented to German holidaymakers. It's right in the middle of Lanzarote's naturist resort, but most people arrive clothed.

La Bodeguita del Medio

Pl Clavijo y Fajardo, Teguise. A tiny rustic wine bar and deli that spills out onto the square on market days, serving drinks and tapas (around €4 a portion).

Lucy's Café & Bar

Avda Marinero, La Santa. Daily 10am–11pm. Clued-up café on the road to Tinajo at the edge of La Santa village, serving delicious fruit smoothies, salads and protein drinks to fitness fanatics on an outing from the nearby sports complex, as well as sandwiches, burgers and ice cream for the not-so-dedicated.

Haría and the north

Northern Lanzarote is by far the greenest part of the island, particularly in spring, with terraced fields marching down verdant hillsides and, in the Haría valley, a liberal sprinkling of palm trees shading well-tended gardens. After the winter rains, the slopes and banks are bright with wild flowers, and even in the driest of summers evergreens lend colour to the landscape. It's a great area for a drive – some roads have thrilling hair-pins and heart-stopping views – and, if rural seclusion is far more your scene than busy beach resorts, it's a good place to stay, too.

The regional capital, Haría, is an inland village so pleasant that César Manrique chose it for his semi-retirement, while the coastal villages of Punta Mujeres and Arrieta are also worth a visit for their secluded coves and rustic fish restaurants. Orzola, near the island's northern tip, is the jumping-off point for Isla de la Graciosa, a sleepy, near-empty island that offers the ultimate in away-from-it-all tranquillity. You can look down on La Graciosa from the Mirador del Río, which has some of the very best views in the Canaries.

The main attractions lie underground, though, at Lanzarote's most famous lava caves: the Cueva de los Verdes and the Jameos del Agua. No cold drips down the back of your neck here – prepare yourself instead for spectacular lighting, impressive cathedral-like spaces, über-cool bars and atmospheric background music.

Haría

Haría is an attractive, tranquil village where palm fronds, geraniums and bougainvillea provide splashes of vivid green, pink and vermillion against the dazzling whitewash. There's a sense that it's passed its heyday,

Visiting Haría district

For maximum flexibility, the best way to explore Haría is by **renting a car** (see p.167). Otherwise, two **bus** (*guagua*) routes cover the area: *línea* #9 to Arrieta, Punta Mujeres and Orzola, which makes stops within walking distance of the Jameos del Agua and Cueva de los Verdes (3 buses a day Mon–Fri, 2 on Sat, 2 on Sun), and *línea* #7 to Arrieta and Haría (5 buses a day Mon–Fri, 4 on Sat, 3 on Sun). You can catch these buses in Arrecife, Tahíche, Nazaret, Teguise, Guatiza and Mala. Local **tour companies** include the area's highlights in their island itineraries; most large hotels can supply details.

Fiestas in the north

Festival time in **Haría** district is midsummer, with bonfire parties held to mark the Fiesta de San Juan on June 24. In Caleta del Sebo, on **Isla de la Graciosa**, fishermen decorate their boats and parade around the harbour to celebrate Nuestra Señora del Carmen on July 16, when the whole village gets together for a seafood feast. **Carnaval** in February is lively, too, with costumes, processions and musical events.

with faded-looking mansions and derelict plots here and there, but it's still a good place to enjoy a glimpse of provincial Canarian life: you'll see the locals exchanging banter in the shady squares and smoky bars. Haría's traditional atmosphere attracted César Manrique to spend his last years here: his former house near the southern edge of the village is closed to the public, but his simple grave can be found in the cemetery, marked by his favourite variety of cactus.

The village's very neat pedestrian avenue, the Plaza de Haría, is the scene of a **craft market** on Saturday lunchtimes (10am–2pm); though significantly smaller than Teguise's Sunday *mercadillo* (see p.122), it's much more relaxed, and the quality of items on offer is reasonably high, with artisans selling cheese, cactus jam and homemade bread, plus crafts including lace, locally inspired paintings, and jewellery made from silver and lava.

Arrieta and Punta Mujeres

Arrieta and Punta Mujeres are unassuming fishing villages, a couple of kilometres apart, with small, appealingly subdued resort areas. There's a sandy beach with a playground at Arrieta's Playa de Garita, and the villages each have a clutch of seafood restaurants, many of which have terraces overlooking the rocky shore, a pleasant prospect on days when it's not too windy.

The area's most notable landmark is the Manrique **juguete del viento** sculpture on the Arrieta roundabout: painted red, its gyrating cone-shaped appendages have earned it the nickname "Madonna sculpture". The road that leads north from here to Punta Mujeres and beyond is one of the most scenic coastal routes on the island (see box on p.138). Punta Mujeres is even quieter

▼ MONTE CORONA, HARÍA DISTRICT

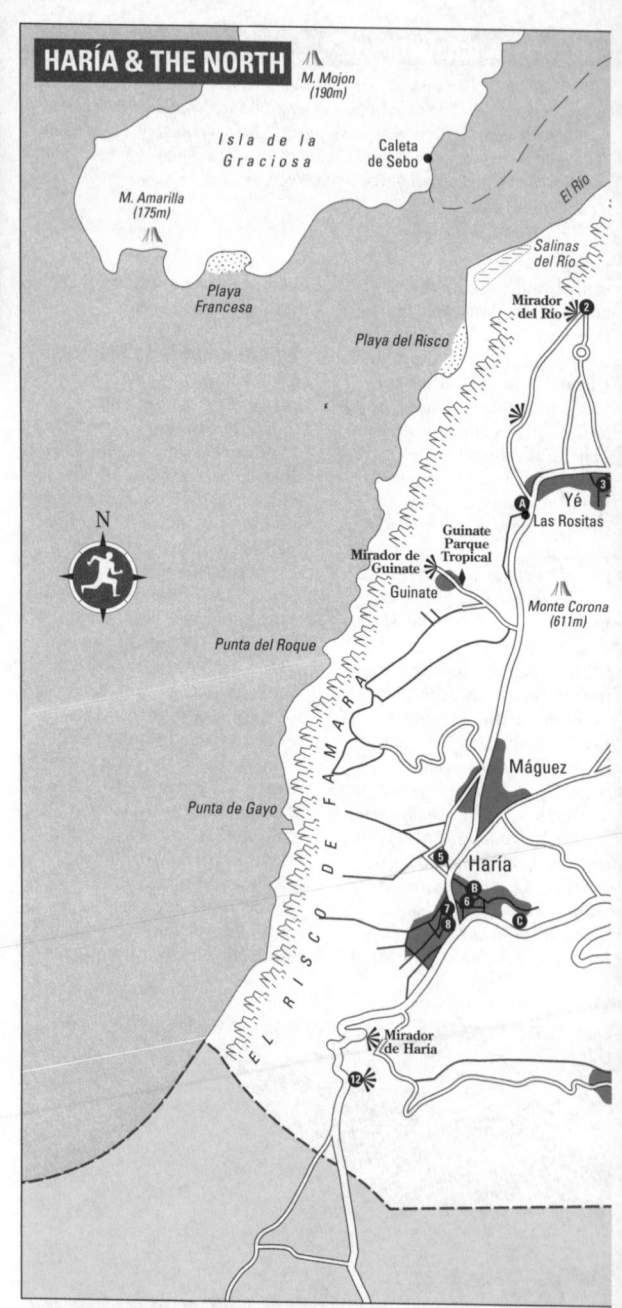

HARÍA & THE NORTH

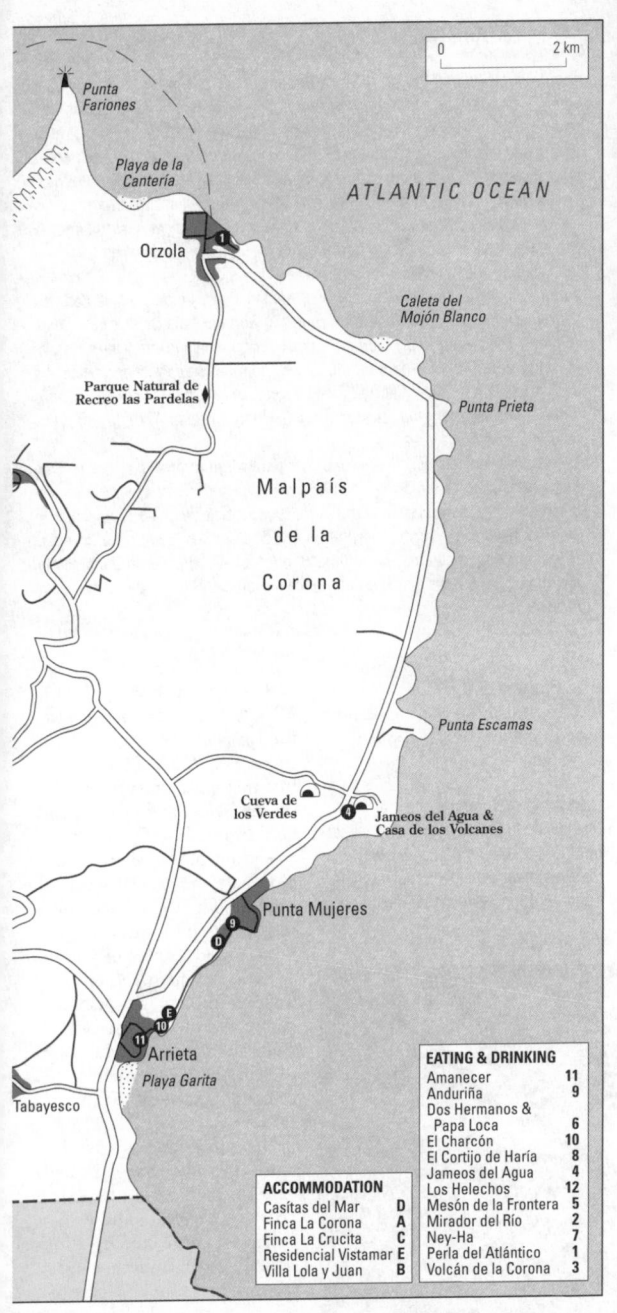

ACCOMMODATION

Casitas del Mar	D
Finca La Corona	A
Finca La Crucita	C
Residencial Vistamar	E
Villa Lola y Juan	B

EATING & DRINKING

Amanecer	11
Anduriña	9
Dos Hermanos & Papa Loca	6
El Charcón	10
El Cortijo de Haría	8
Jameos del Agua	4
Los Helechos	12
Mesón de la Frontera	5
Mirador del Río	7
Ney-Ha	2
Perla del Atlántico	1
Volcán de la Corona	3

Scenic drives

Approaching Haría on the **LZ-10 from Teguise**, you'll see plenty of Canary date palms – remarkable on this island where so few trees grow – as the landscape unfolds. It's an inspiring drive, with hairpins to get the pulse racing and several lofty *miradores* from which to admire the sweeping vistas; the northeast coast is rarely out of sight. A short, bumpy westward detour will take you to the Ermita de las Nieves (Chapel of the Snows), said to mark the island's coldest spot. On clear days, you can enjoy spectacular views from the cliffs near here to Playa de Famara and the ocean beyond. Northwest of Haría, minor roads wend their way through the dark, dramatic lava fields of the Malpaís de la Corona. You'll have the tarmac almost to yourself here as it loops around Monte Corona, one of northern Lanzarote's highest peaks (not to be confused with Montaña Corona near Costa Teguise). Long extinct, this volcano's most recent eruption predates those of Montaña Timanfaya by well over 4000 years, and the *malpaís* landscape seems eerily ancient. A fuzz of primitive-looking vegetation clings to the craggy volcanic debris – an indicator of the ecosystem that might take hold on Timanfaya in a few thousand years' time.

The region's other classic drive is the **LZ-1 from Arrieta to Orzola**, a coastal route that passes close to the Jameos del Agua and Cueva de los Verdes. The remote landscape here is singularly dramatic, with succulent plants and lichens softening the dark folds of the rugged *malpaís* on one side and, on bright days, an azure ocean sparkling on the other. On the northernmost stretch, beyond Punta Prieta, are impromptu lay-bys, giving access to the most picturesque of the northeastern beaches (see p.141).

than Arrieta – this, for those looking for a low-key, neon-free seaside experience, is the key to its appeal.

Jameos del Agua

Malpaís de la Corona, 4.5km northeast of Arrieta ☏ 928 84 80 20, ⊛ www .cabildodelanzarote.com/cact. Daily 10am–6.45pm, evening opening

▼ JAMEOS DEL AGUA

Tues, Fri & Sat 7pm–2am. €8 (day), €9 (eve). Created in the 1960s, the Jameos del Agua, or water caves, were César Manrique's first major architectural project on the island, and possibly his best. Inspired by the natural splendour of the Malpaís de la Corona – the perfect setting, he thought, for "the most beautiful nightclub in the world" – he turned a series of volcanic caverns and open-roofed hollows into a performance centre and meeting place. As well as the bar-nightclub of his dreams, the centre includes a restaurant, an auditorium and an ornamental pool.

This subterranean marvel comprises two *jameos* (roofless caves formed when the rock covering a volcanic tube collapses) connected by a tunnel containing an underground lagoon. The tunnel is part of the same five-thousand-year-old volcanic tube as the Cueva de los Verdes (see below). The site is visually dramatic from the start. You descend by way of a steeply zigzagging hewn staircase, with livid green foliage contrasting starkly with the black volcanic rock. Passing the first bar-restaurant, you come to the lagoon, dark and glassy under the natural vaulting of the tunnel. Dimly lit by a volcanic blow-hole in the rock above and fed by the distant sea, it's home to a highly unusual population of blind, albino crustaceans known as *jameitos*, which look a bit like miniscule white lobsters, and were the inspiration for Manrique's stylized logo for the site. The lagoon is particularly beautiful around midday, when shafts of sunlight beam down through the blow-hole onto the surface.

Further on, you come blinking out into the bright oasis of the ornamental pool area, open to the sky, and overlooked by terraces. To its side is a perfect little bar, an essay in sixties-style minimalist chic. Come here at night to appreciate the after-dark change in atmosphere (see p.146). Beyond the pool is the auditorium, with rugged, hacked-away rock for a ceiling, and surprisingly fine acoustics. Concerts are held here from time to time: the island's tourist offices can usually provide details. In the upper section of the complex is **La Casa de los Volcanes**, a large vulcanology research centre and exhibition, in which you can take a look at instruments that monitor earth movements and measure subterranean temperatures; adorning one wall is a mural made from ancient fishing-boat timbers – another of Manrique's evocative and satisfying works.

Cueva de los Verdes

Malpaís de la Corona, 4.5km northeast of Arrieta ☎928 84 84 84, ⊛www.cabildodelanzarote.com/cact. Daily 10am–6pm, last entry 5pm. €8. The grotto-like cave system of the Cueva de los Verdes is billed as one of the island's most fascinating attractions. Unless you're a cave-mad geologist you probably won't find it as mind-blowing as the hype might suggest, but it's certainly atmospheric and impressive in scale.

The subterranean system comprises a two-kilometre section of volcanic tube that leads all the way to the Atlantic seabed. This tube, which measures 7km, was formed by a lava flow from the mighty Volcán de la Corona, when it erupted 5000 or so years ago. As the lava ran downhill towards the sea, the top layer solidified, and a subterranean build-up of gases created the tube under this basalt crust.

The resulting caves were once used as a hiding place for *Majos* desperate to evade slave-hunters and pirates – they're currently named after their more recent owners, a family of herders called Verde. In the 1960s, the island government's cultural department set about developing it as a visitor attraction, building stairways and walkways and lighting the spaces in suitably artful fashion. César Manrique was chief designer, working closely with fellow artist Jesús Soto, who also designed the Parque Nacional de Timanfaya's Ruta de los Volcanes (see p.104).

The guided walk through the Cueva de los Verdes takes around fifty minutes, plenty of time to admire the colours,

PLACES Haría and the north

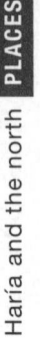

textures and proportions as you stoop your way through the labyrinthine tunnels and crane your neck to admire the cathedral-like scale of the caverns, before ending the tour with a couple of surprising optical illusions. The cave at the deepest point of the tour has been converted into a concert hall – musical events are held here just two or three times a year, as transporting instruments and equipment through the tunnels is a serious undertaking.

Yé

Huddled at the foot of Monte Corona, this pretty hamlet bears a *Majo* name that roughly translates as "the end of the world". Once a centre of lichen-dye production, these days the sense of being miles from anywhere is palpable, and it's worth dropping in at the village socio-cultural centre to soak up the atmosphere over a leisurely drink, local-style.

Playa del Risco

Stretching along the foot of the swaggering El Risco cliffs to the west of Yé, breezy Playa del Risco is a fine but hard-to-get-to beach, much favoured by kiteboarders, hang-gliders and paragliders (see p.172). To make your way there you need to scramble down a track that leads off the road to the Mirador del Río, 500m beyond the hamlet of Las Rositas. After a steep, gravelly four-hundred-metre

descent, turn right; the beach is another kilometre away.

Guinate Parque Tropical

Guinate ℡ 928 83 55 00. Daily 10am–5pm. €10, children €4. With waterfalls, pools and planted borders spread over a series of terraces at the foot of Monte Corona, Guinate's gardens are a relaxing place in which to spend an hour or two. There are also aviaries and pens with over three hundred captive bird species, including some exotics, and regular repeats of a tacky bird show in which trained parrots perform tricks. The mammalian residents are mostly small, furry and cute: lemurs, meerkats and wallabies all make an appearance.

Mirador del Río

About 2.5km north of Yé ℡ 928 52 65 48, ꮃ www.cabildodelanzarote .com/cact. Daily 10am–6.45pm. €4.70 including a drink. The views from the 479-metre-high El Risco cliffs are so spectacular

▼ MIRADOR DEL RÍO

that César Manrique decided to frame them in glass and stone and give them back, gift-wrapped, to the island and its visitors by creating the Mirador del Río, a café-bar with panoramic windows and observation platforms, at one of the most inspirational spots.

To experience the views as he intended, you need to pass through the Mirador's bastion-like entrance and continue along a curvy passageway designed to heighten the anticipation. The windows of the café-bar do, indeed, showcase the scene superbly, particularly in the bright light of midday. Designed by Manrique in the early 1970s, it's an airy vaulted space, with the artist's dynamic metal sculptures hanging from the ceiling.

As you look out over the Archipiélago de Chinijo – La Graciosa in the foreground, with Montaña Clara, Roque del Este, Roque del Oeste and Alegranza beyond – you have the glorious feeling of soaring above the channel, El Río. Head outside to the viewing balconies and take a look down, if you can bear it, for a dizzying sheer-drop sensation.

If you're here outside opening hours, you can catch oblique glimpses of the same view from the cliff-top road to Las Rositas, or the parallel vista from the Mirador de Guinate, slightly further south.

Orzola

The primary reason for coming to Orzola, a tiny fishing village clinging to the northeast coastline, is to make the ferry crossing to Isla de la Graciosa (see p.142). The glass-bottom boats that double as ferries loop around Punta Fariones,

Lanzarote's craggy northernmost point, on their way to the island's main town, Caleta de Sebo.

Orzola itself has the kind of workaday grubbiness common to ferry ports everywhere. It's famous for its fish restaurants – though you'll get fish that's just as good, but in more atmospheric surroundings, elsewhere on the coast (such as El Golfo, Punta Mujeres and Caleta de Famara).

Northeastern beaches

There's an impressive, undeveloped beach northwest of Orzola, **Playa de Cantería**, but currents make it unsafe for swimming – you're better off heading in the opposite direction if you want to take a dip. A kilometre or two southeast of Orzola, on the fabulously scenic coastal route to Arrieta, are a series of stopping points on either side of the road, any of which are worth parking in: the beaches here, particularly **Caleta del Mojón Blanco**, are ravishingly

▼ CALETA DEL MOJÓN BLANCO

beautiful in an unconventional way – black rocks, white sand, shallow rock pools, and, when the tide is out, distant water.

Parque Natural de Recreo Las Pardelas

Orzola, 1km outside the village on the road to Yé ☎928 84 25 45. Daily 10am–6pm (till 7pm in summer). €3, children under-12 €2.40. The main attraction at Las Pardelas is the amenable population of farmyard animals, including previously abandoned or maltreated animals that the owners have rescued. Visitors receive a bowl of vegetables and bread on arrival, to offer the animals titbits – a big hit with children. Other diversions include donkey rides, a pottery studio (where kids can join in) and craft shop, and a fairly traditional Canarian restaurant.

Isla de la Graciosa

Most visitors' first sighting of Isla de la Graciosa is from the Mirador del Río – gazing down from this elevated vantage point, the island looks as if it's floating offshore like a speckled rag, but in fact it's firmly attached to Lanzarote just beneath the surface. The largest island in the Archipiélago de Chinijo – an area so abundant in marine life that in 1986 it was declared a protected area – La Graciosa appeals to those who enjoy peace and calm.

The island's main settlement, **Caleta del Sebo**, is a fishing village of low, whitewashed houses, where the air smells salty and the locals pad barefoot along sandy streets, or bump around in dusty Land Rovers. The views across the narrow strait from here, with the El Risco cliffs draping like curtains into the sparkling water, are stunning. If you're only staying for a few hours and would like to explore, it's probably best to skip a seafood restaurant lunch (which can take some time) in favour of grabbing something from the surprisingly well-stocked village supermarket and setting off right away (Caleta del Sebo has La Graciosa's only shops and eating-places).

All the island's **beaches** have fine, pale sand, and, apart from La Laja in Caleta del Sebo, are entirely undeveloped. From La Laja, take the track that continues southwest along the shore and

▼ ISLA DE LA GRACIOSA, FROM THE MIRADOR DEL RÍO

you'll reach more beaches – most visitors only stroll as far as Playa Francesca, the bay about 2.5km southwest of Caleta del Sebo (a 30-min walk), but if you carry on another 2km you'll reach Playa de las Cocinas (50min from Caleta del Sebo), which lies beneath the extinct volcano of Montaña Amarilla, and is even more peaceful than Francesca.

Continuing around La Graciosa's southwestern point, you reach the wild southwest coast, a stretch that's favoured by in-the-know surfers: its challenging conditions and relative inaccessibility mean it's never busy. The island's most dramatic beach is Playa de las Conchas, on the northwest coast, about 6km along sandy tracks from

Visiting Isla de la Graciosa

To get to La Graciosa, take the **passenger ferry** from Orzola across El Río to Caleta del Sebo. Líneas Marítimas Romero (C/García Escámez 11, La Graciosa ☏928 84 20 55, ☞www.geocities.com/lineas_romero; €13 return, children €7) sail from Orzola at 10am, noon and 5pm, and from La Graciosa at 8am, 11am and 4pm, with an extra crossing at 6.30pm (from Orzola) and 6pm (from Graciosa) in the summer. The twenty-minute journey can be choppy. Most people choose to cross in the morning and return the same day, but there are a few simple places to stay on the island if you're so taken with its gentle ways that you decide to miss the afternoon boat home. The southeast beaches can be reached **on foot** from Caleta del Sebo, but for trips further afield it's worth renting a **bike** (€7/day) from one of the hire places near the waterfront: hacking along sandy trails, you could cover most of the island in four to five hours. If you'd rather take a lift, ask around in the village for a local with a Land Rover – they will **drive** you to the north and back for €8–10.

Caleta del Sebo, and reachable by mountain bike, or by boat with Líneas Marítimas Romero (see p.143). This remote strand is particularly long, with dark rocks, luminous sand and great views across to the neighbouring islet of Montaña Clara. The currents here can be strong, though, so swimming is not recommended.

Hotels

Villa Lola y Juan

C/Fajardo 16, Haría ☎928 83 50 70. Just east of Haría's centre, this small hotel has six self-contained guestrooms with a country-house atmosphere, plus a shared pool and an attractive orchard. €95.

Guesthouses

Pensión Enriqueta

C/Mar de Barlovento 6, Caleta del Sebo, Isla de la Graciosa ☎928 84 20 51. Not quite as good as the *Girasol*, and a block back from the beach, but still good value. €20.

Pensión Girasol

Avda Virgen del Mar, Caleta del Sebo, Isla de la Graciosa ☎928 84 21 18, ☜www.graciosaonline.com. Spotless little family-run bar-restaurant on the village beach with a row of tidy rooms to rent. €20.

Apartments and villas

Apartamentos El Sombreríto

Caleta del Sebo, Isla de la Graciosa ☎928 84 21 06 or 696 94 28 74, ☜www.elsombrerito.com. A choice of seven simple but decent apartments in Caleta del Sebo,

kitted out with all the basics. If they're full, look out for adverts for other apartments to rent posted up around the village, or try the owners of *El Marinero* restaurant, who can sometimes arrange accommodation. €45.

Casitas del Mar

C/Anzuelo 17, Punta Mujeres ☎928 84 82 88, ☜www.cachet-travel.co.uk. Right on the coast but well off the beaten track, a collection of 21 simple two-bed bungalows, with terraces or balconies over-looking the rocky shore. They also share a small freshwater swimming pool. €65.

Finca La Corona

C/Las Rositas 8, Yé ☎928 52 80 19 or 902 36 33 18, ☜www.rural-villas .com. Six apartments (sleeping 2–4 each) in a converted farm near the rural hamlet of Yé, sharing a twelve-metre pool. Attractively furnished, each apartment has its own indi-vidual character – the bedroom in one is in a cave-like former water store. One-bed apartment €100, two-bed apartments from €138.

Finca La Crucita

C/San Juan 63, Haría ☎928 81 05 65 or 696 28 17 91, ☜www.villasdelanzarote .com. In a palm-shaded plot on the eastern edge of Haría, these eight attractive, traditional-style houses are well equipped, and beautifully furnished in rustic style. Two-bed villas €120, three-bed villas €150.

Residencial Vistamar

C/Cortijo 2, Arrieta ☎928 84 82 03 or 616 44 19 36, ☜vistamar@lanzarote .com. Bright two-bed apart-ments with simple modern furnishings. It's near the sea in an untouristy part of the island, but within easy reach of two of its principal attractions, the Jameos del Agua and Cueva de Los Verdes. €60.

Restaurants and tapas bars

Amanecer
C/Garita 46, Arrieta ☎ 928 84 82 66. Closed Thurs. Arrieta's most popular restaurant, with a warm, old-fashioned atmosphere, a small terrace with sea views, and, as you'd expect on this stretch of coast, great fish. Reasonable prices; very busy on Sunday lunchtimes.

Anduriña
Punta Mujeres ☎ 928 51 55 60. A little hard to find – it's sign-posted from C/Quemades after the turn-off from the LZ-1 – but well worth the effort, this oceanside restaurant has amazing fresh fish at moderate prices, a comfortable terrace and a very friendly welcome. A perfect stop-off on the way to or from the Cueva de Los Verdes or the northeastern beaches.

El Charcón
Muelle de Arrieta, Arrieta ☎ 928 84 81 10. Closed Wed. Situated right on the wharf and strung with nets and floats, this place feels very nautical, and serves decent fresh fish, with most main courses under €15.

El Cortijo de Haría
C/Palmeral 4, Haría ☎ 928 83 52 65. Farmhouse restaurant that trades heavily on its Manrique connections, with memorabilia of the artist in the entrance hall. It has an ambitious – but overpriced – local-style menu with some good grilled meat dishes and, though a little tired, a convivial atmosphere.

El Italiano
Avda Virgen del Mar, Caleta del Sebo, Isla de la Graciosa. Close to the ferry, this tiny, informal bar-restaurant serves good pasta and great salads.

El Marinero
C/García Escámez 14, Caleta del Sebo, Isla de la Graciosa ☎ 928 84 21 69. Established fish restaurant with moderate prices, a street back from the harbour.

▼ CALETA DEL SEBO

PLACES Haría and the north

El Varadero

Avda Virgen del Mar 125, Caleta del Sebo, Isla de la Graciosa ☎928 84 21 75. Tourist-friendly restaurant right opposite the ferry, popular with day-trippers, serving huge plates of fish priced around €15. There's a large terrace at the front from which to enjoy views of the harbour.

Jameos del Agua

Malpaís de la Corona, 4.5km northeast of Arrieta ☎928 84 80 24. Restaurant Tues, Fri & Sat 7.30–11.30pm. Café-bars daily 10am–6.30pm; evening Tues, Fri & Sat 7pm–2am. €8 (day), €9 (eve). Settling down over a drink or sandwich during a visit to the *jameos* is a pleasant way to enjoy the cool ambience and admire the natural architecture. It's worth returning for an evening session, too, when a well-heeled crowd shows up to enjoy sophisticated Canarian cuisine and dance to local folkloric musicians.

La Caletilla

C/Candelaria, Caleta del Sebo, Isla de la Graciosa. Tiny, tiled tapas bar that's mainly a locals' hangout; basic and inexpensive, it's set back from the harbour, with good sea views but no terrace.

Mesón de la Frontera

C/Casa Atrás 4, Haría ☎928 83 53 10. Mon & Wed–Sat noon–9.30pm, Sun noon–5pm. Booking recommended. By far the best restaurant in Haría, this superb rustic eatery on the northern edge of town has great views of farmland and palm groves to enjoy while your hand-picked steak charcoal-grills to perfection. Other choices include traditional *potaje*, super-fresh salads, and prawns – and the portions are huge, and

good value at around €14 for a main course. Excellent to the last detail.

Ney-Ha

C/Cilla, Haría. This bar-restaurant in the middle of Haría serves no-nonsense light meals and is something of a macho locals' hangout.

Perla del Atlántico

Avda Caletón 3, Orzola ☎928 81 11 15. Daily 10am–8pm. The best located of Orzola's rustic seafood restaurants, on the harbour, with good sea views. The fish here isn't cheap but the menu's impressive, with local-style *postres* to finish.

Restaurante Girasol

Avda Virgen del Mar, Caleta del Sebo, Isla de la Graciosa ☎928 84 21 18. Despite being right on the village beach, this bar-restaurant is a peaceful place with a simple menu, decently priced.

Restaurante Los Helechos

On the LZ-10, 5km south of Haría ☎928 83 50 89. Daily 10am–6pm. A large, echoing canteen-style country restaurant that's a popular coach-party stop, serving sandwiches, simple meals (main courses around €10) and a surprisingly good selection of fruit flans. There are great views of the Haría valley from the tables by the windows, and from the breezy *mirador* outside.

Volcán de la Corona

C/Malpaís, Yé (just off the Yé-Máguez road) ☎928 51 07 82. Mon–Sat 10am–6pm. A large country-style village restaurant that's a good place to try *gofio*, goat's cheese or Canarian soup; they have a very reasonable *menú del día*.

▲ MIRADOR DEL RÍO

Cafés and bars

Dos Hermanos & Papa Loca
Pl León y Castillo, Haría. While the cooking here is mediocre, it's an appealing place for a drink or snack, with pleasant outdoor tables on a tree-lined pedestrian street.

Heladería La Graciosa
On the track to Playa Francesca, Caleta del Sebo, Isla de la Graciosa. Unexpected gem of a café near the southern edge of the village, selling amazing confectionery, ice cream and hand-made chocolates.

Mirador del Río
About 2.5km north of Yé ☎928 52 65 48, ⊛www.cabildodelanzarote .com/cact. Daily 10am–6.45pm; €4.70 including a drink. The café-bar at this exquisite Manrique-designed lookout serves drinks and snacks, and has elegant *banquettes* from which to enjoy the view.

Fuerteventura

To many holidaymakers, the trademark long, white, windswept beaches of Fuerteventura are enough to make the island a destination in its own right. But those who have based themselves on Lanzarote needn't miss out: the quick and easy catamaran connection from Playa Blanca makes visiting a doddle. A day trip gives you just enough time to get a taste of Corralejo, the island's main town, and the nearby attractions of the Parque Natural de las Dunas de Corralejo and Isla de los Lobos, to the north. With three or more days, you could also explore Fuerteventura's rugged interior, an area of winding mountain passes and valleys dotted with windmills, goat farms and pretty little villages such as Pájara and Betancuria, or head south for the dazzling beaches of the Peninsula de Jandía.

Development on Fuerteventura is proceeding at a rapid pace, particularly along the eastern coast, but head for the wild, gusty western shores and you'll find they're almost completely untouched: for surfers, windsurfers and kiteboarders, the reliably windy climate here makes the island a world-class destination.

Corralejo

Corralejo is developing at the breakneck speed typical of Fuerteventura's tourist resorts, but, in the **Old Town**, a lively pedestrian area of characterful restaurants and bars, it manages to retain some of the atmosphere of the simple fishing village it used to be. The nearby streets, though scruffy, are good

places to find the kind of shops, delis and cafés you'd find in any provincial Spanish town.

Stretching away to the south is the town's main commercial strip, **Avenida General Franco**, also known as Main Street (English-speaking tourists are Corralejo's most frequent visitors), with plenty of shops selling summer clothing and

Visiting Fuerteventura

International **flights** to Fuerteventura arrive at El Matorral airport (see p.165), 4km south of Puerto del Rosario. At the time of writing, there were no internal flights from Lanzarote to Fuerteventura. The daily **catamaran ferries** from Playa Blanca to Corralejo (see p.84) docks at the ferry terminal on the north side of town, a few minutes' walk from the bars and restaurants of Old Corralejo. There's a **tourist office** in Plaza Patricio Calero (☎928 86 62 35; Mon–Fri 8.30am–2.30pm, Sat 9am–noon). For maximum flexibility, the best way to explore the rest of the island is by **renting a car** (see p.167), but it's also possible to book **coach tours** with local operators; all Fuerteventura's major hotels can supply details.

Island neighbours

Fuerteventura may have beaches that easily outclass Lanzarote's for sheer size and splendour, but compared to the natural drama and tidy aesthetics of its northern neighbour, you may find much of the island disappointing. Where Lanzarote has wild open spaces and neat little villages of whitewashed houses, Fuerteventura, the larger and far more sparsely populated of the two, has rugged desert criss-crossed by overhead power cables, and blighted by ugly coastal developments. Where Lanzarote has strict planning controls, Fuerteventura has shady planning deals that put areas of scientific interest and natural beauty at risk. Despite Fuerteventura's president, Mario Cabrera González, expressing his concern for the environment, a great deal of damage has already been done: to some visitors the island presents a stark reminder of what could have happened to Lanzarote if César Manrique and other like-minded champions of sympathetic development hadn't set clear conservation guidelines back in the early days of island tourism.

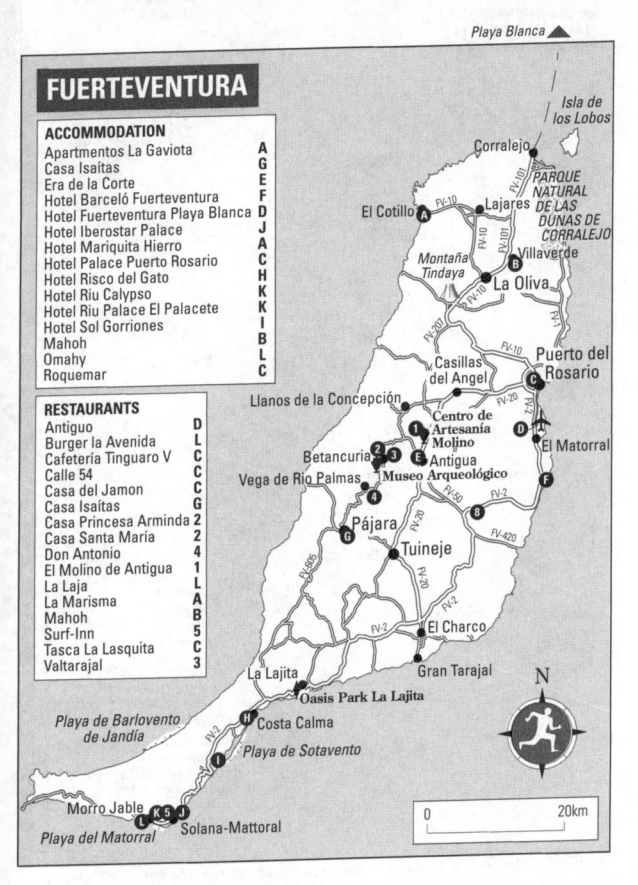

FUERTEVENTURA

ACCOMMODATION

Apartmentos La Gaviota	A
Casa Isaítas	G
Era de la Corte	E
Hotel Barceló Fuerteventura	F
Hotel Fuerteventura Playa Blanca	D
Hotel Iberostar Palace	J
Hotel Mariquita Hierro	A
Hotel Palace Puerto Rosario	C
Hotel Risco del Gato	H
Hotel Riu Calypso	K
Hotel Riu Palace El Palacete	K
Hotel Sol Gorriones	I
Mahoh	B
Omahy	L
Roquemar	C

RESTAURANTS

Antiguo	D
Burger la Avenida	L
Cafetería Tinguaro V	C
Calle 54	C
Casa del Jamon	C
Casa Isaítas	G
Casa Princesa Arminda	2
Casa Santa María	2
Don Antonio	4
El Molino de Antigua	1
La Laja	L
La Marisma	A
Mahoh	B
Surf-Inn	5
Tasca La Lasquita	C
Valtarajal	3

surf gear, mainstream restaurants, and bars open well into the early hours. The town spreads way beyond this commercial centre, encompassing housing estates for local inhabitants on the inland side, and row upon row of holiday villas and apartment blocks in a belt along the coast. Most of the buildings are low-rise, and the developers have made token nods towards Canarian style here and there, but the sheer volume of housing stock is rather overwhelming.

The **Baku Water Park** on Avenida Nuestra Señora del Carmen, the main road at the southern end of town (☎928 86 72 27, ⊛www.bakufuerteventura.com; €19.50, children under-12 €12.50), is a big hit with kids – and fun for adults, too – with plenty of slides, tubes and whirlpools. Watch out in winter: the water can be cold.

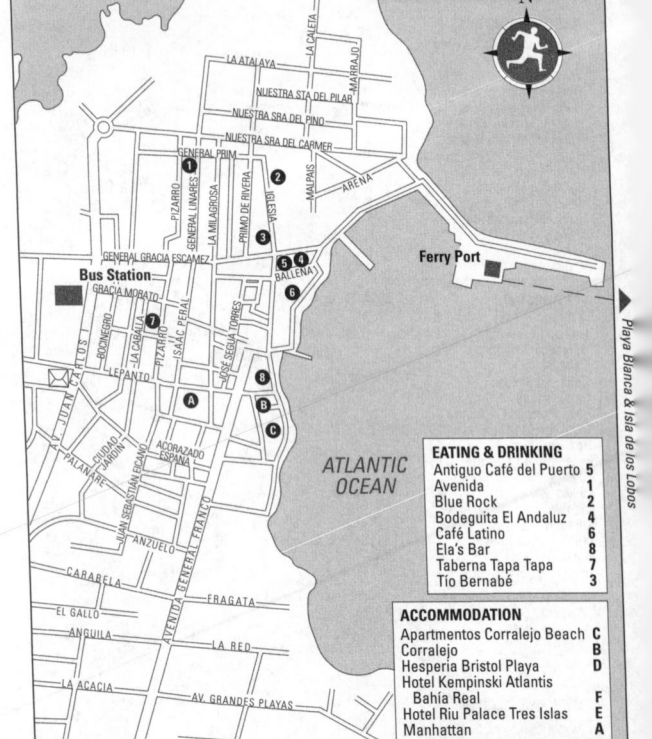

CORRALEJO

0   250 m

N

ATLANTIC OCEAN

Bus Station

Ferry Port

Playa Blanca & Isla de los Lobos

EATING & DRINKING
Antiguo Café del Puerto   5
Avenida   1
Blue Rock   2
Bodeguita El Andaluz   4
Café Latino   6
Ela's Bar   8
Taberna Tapa Tapa   7
Tío Bernabé   3

ACCOMMODATION
Apartmentos Corralejo Beach   C
Corralejo   B
Hesperia Bristol Playa   D
Hotel Kempinski Atlantis
  Bahía Real   F
Hotel Riu Palace Tres Islas   E
Manhattan   A

La Oliva & Baku Waterpark ▼   Parque Natural de las Dunas de Corralejo, ▼   Puerto del Rosario, **D**, **E** & **F**

▲ PARQUE NATURAL DE LAS DUNAS DE CORRALEJO

Parque Natural de las Dunas de Corralejo

South of Corralejo's mushrooming resort area, this protected area is a spectacular ten-kilometre stretch of bleached duneland, pretty beaches and rocky coves. Fuerteventura is well known for its unusually high incidence of endemic flora and fauna, and the rippled dunes that drift up to 3km from the shore in this part of the island are home to rare *euphorbias* (desert-loving succulent plants) and the only known breeding pairs of obarras, the bird that is the symbol of the park.

It was once thought that the park's pale, powdery sands were blown across from the Sahara, but it's far more likely that they are marine deposits, pushed up from the seabed or washed ashore by ocean currents.

You can get to Las Dunas by walking or cycling from Corralejo (the park's northern limit is about 3km from the Old Town), or by catching the *línea* #6 bus bound for Puerto del Rosario, which runs from Corralejo harbour to the dunes approximately every half hour; entry to the park is free.

For drivers, there's plenty of room to park beside the FV-1 highway, which slices right through the dunes, and amble down to the water. Some of the beaches have sunloungers and parasols (which, crucially, double as windbreaks when the breeze picks up), and the more secluded areas of tufted dunes are favoured by nudists. There are a couple of huge hotels in the park – the *Riu Palace Tres Islas* (see p.157) and its neighbour, the *Oliva Beach* – built in the 1970s before the area was fully protected. There's also a windsurfing and kiteboarding school here (see p.174).

Isla de los Lobos

Separated from northern Fuerteventura by the El Río strait, the protected volcanic island of Isla de los Lobos offers some enjoyable hiking, with great views of both northern Fuerteventura and southern Lanzarote – and plenty of peace and quiet (it's practically uninhabited). If you take the 10am ferry across to Los Lobos from the wharf at Corralejo (20min), you'll have time to

▲ ILSA DE LOS LOBOS, FROM LAS DUNAS DE CORRALEJO

climb up the volcano (now extinct) before the return trip at 4pm. Alternatively, you could just enjoy **Playa de la Calera**, the sheltered beach near the harbour of Casas El Puertito, where there's a very simple bar-restaurant.

The volcanic reefs and submerged lava caves around Los Lobos make this a fascinating area in which to **scuba dive**: diving outfits in Corralejo and on Lanzarote (see p.173) make trips over here when conditions are favourable.

El Cotillo

The best reason to visit the once-significant Mahorata stronghold of El Cotillo is to try one of the rough and ready harbourside fish restaurants, or simply to sample the flavour of the west coast. The fresh, breezy beaches under the dark cliffs south of town are good for swimming in summer, although in winter the waves are often too rough. Standing sentinel over this stretch of coast is an eighteenth-century fort, the **Castillo del Tostón**, once used as a refuge from pirates and now restored and opened to the public as an art gallery.

Lajares

Around 8km inland from El Cotillo, the village of Lajares is famous for its lace-making tradition. Fuerteventuran lace, embroidery and cutwork are typically of fine white cotton, worked with windmill-sail motifs. You can see artisans in action, and buy finished pieces, at Artesanía Lajares, in the centre of the village.

Montaña Tindaya

Dominating the landscape in the north of the island is Montaña Tindaya, sacred mountain of the Mahos. A recent project to excavate caves as a visitor attraction has foundered on controversy, not least because the project was endangering Tindaya's Mahorata podomorphs – a style of footprint-shaped rock-art unique to Fuerteventura's prehistoric cave dwellers.

Centro de Artesanía Molino de Antigua

South of the glowering Montaña Quemada, the landscape broadens into a valley dotted with traditional timber and canvas-sailed *molinos* (two-storey

The FV-30 from Pájara to Betancuria

The roads heading out of Pájara pass through some of Fuerteventura's most ruggedly impressive wilderness. The most dramatic route is the **FV-30 from Pájara to Betancuria**, an exhilarating ride that winds north up through Vega del Río de Palmas and over mountain passes so picturesque they could have been custom-made for car adverts (an aesthetic not lost on the film crews themselves, who drop in on a regular basis).

windmills) and *molinas* (one-storey windmills), used to grind *gofio*. You can take a close look at a restored two-hundred-year-old *molino* at the Centro de Artesanía Molino de Antigua, on the main road 1km north of the small town of Antigua (Tues–Fri & Sun 9.30am–5.30pm, Mon & Sat closed; €1.80). This beautifully kept centre has a cactus garden, which includes endemic species, and a small ethnology collection with displays of locally excavated bone and pottery fragments. Its excellent craft shop sells traditional lace, lovely rough pottery, and silver jewellery inspired by *Maho* rock art. There's also a bar-restaurant in a fine stone building with a lofty domed ceiling, formerly used as a grain store.

Pájara

Pájara is a quiet, attractive village with an unusual church, the Iglesia de Nuestra Señora de la Regla, named after a town in Cuba – Fuerteventura has strong cultural ties with the Americas, since many islanders have emigrated there over the years, particularly in the drought years of the mid-1800s. Outside the church is an impressive arch with Aztec-style carving, and inside there's a richly dressed and adorned statue of the Virgin thought to have been brought over from Cuba. The church has two naves, and twin altars – it's

likely that, for symmetry, a third had originally been planned.

Betancuria

Founded in the early fifteenth century, the small village of Betancuria is Fuerteventura's prettiest, and, along with Teguise on Lanzarote, the Canary Islands' oldest settlement. Capital of Fuerteventura for five centuries, the village is home to a striking triple-naved church – called, rather grandiosely, the Cathedral-Church of Santa Maria of Betancuria, even though Betancuria doesn't actually have a bishop. There's also a small archeology and ethnology museum (C/Roberto Roldan; Tues–Sat 10am–5pm, Sun 11am–2pm; free) and, deep in the valley, an atmospheric ruined Franciscan monastery that's overgrown with wild flowers in spring.

▼ THE FV-30 FROM PÁJARA TO BETANCURIA

The romería to Vega del Río de Palmas

The tiny village of **Vega del Río de Palmas**, 10km north of Pájara, is the focus of Fuerteventura's biggest and most devout annual **romería**, or holy pilgrimage. On the third Saturday in September, Catholics arrive on foot from all over the island to pay their respects to the tiny ivory statue of the Virgen de la Peña, housed in the village's small but exquisite church (Tues–Sun 11am–1pm & 5–7pm). The village is taken over by stalls and stages and the revelry continues long into the night.

Puerto del Rosario

The primary focus of Puerto del Rosario, Fuerteventura's capital, is the port after which it is named, and there's a concentration of bars and restaurants around the harbour, most of them the sort of rough-edged joints you'd find in any port town. The fact that the town makes no concessions to tourism is enough to make it appealing to some, but for most visitors, the attraction can seem rather more obscure.

Softening the scene somewhat is a liberal scattering of public art, including the large sculptures of sea shells that perch on the foreshore in the city centre. Inland, the Casa de la Cultura and the Sala de Juan Ismael host regular art, photography and sculpture exhibitions.

Caleta de Fuste

Caleta de Fuste (also known as El Castillo) is a modern resort popular with families on package holidays. A tidy but nondescript conglomeration of hotel, bungalow and apartment complexes that have grown around a decent, sheltered, child-friendly beach, this small, attractive marina is distinguished

by an eighteenth-century fort, El Castillo de Fuste (a *fuste* was a type of ship). The main drag leading towards the sea has plenty of resort-style shops, bars and restaurants, and there's a golf course, Fuerteventura's first (see p.172) nearby.

Oasis Park La Lajita

Crta Jandía, La Lajita ☎ 928 16 11 35. Daily 9am–6pm. Park €17, children 3–11yrs €8.50. Camel rides €7.50, children 3–11yrs €3.75. Part zoo, part botanical gardens, this beautifully designed (but slightly pricey) park is extremely popular with kids, and well

▼ JARDÍN BOTÁNICO

worth a half-day visit. The overall impression is of luxuriant leafiness – very welcome on this tree-deprived island – as the entire park has been lushly planted, and the gardens have had twenty years to mature. A definite highlight is the bird collection, with large walk-in aviaries allowing you to get close to exotic tropical species such as violet turacos and glossy starlings. There are also caged reptiles and primates (including marmosets and lemurs), plus hyperactive coatis (large, racoon-like animals from South America) and a few African savannah animals such as giraffes, antelopes and zebras.

Scheduled throughout the day are various shows and demonstrations, from the predictably tacky (like the parrot show) to the awesome (if you'd like to hug a crocodile, this is the place), via the downright hilarious – the performing Patagonian sea lions are the park's real stars.

The **Jardín Botánico** is largely devoted to cacti, succulents and palms, with an amazing range of mature specimens spread attractively over steep slopes at the far end of the park. With more than 2500 varieties represented, it makes the Jardín del Cactus on Lanzarote look rather meagre by comparison. If you're here while the cacti are in flower you're definitely in for a treat.

Península de Jandía

At the southern tip of Fuerteventura, the Península de Jandía is a largely protected area of dunes, hills and beaches. Fringing its slimmest part is the windsurfing hotspot of **Playa de Sotavento**, a remarkable 27-kilometre stretch of fine,

pale sand that's one of the best places in the world to jump the waves – it hosts the Windsurfing and Kiteboarding World Cup every summer (see p.174). What makes it so good is the fact that the winds on this side of the island (*sotavento* means leeward) are so consistent. It's perfect for beginners as well as pros – there's plenty of space and, at high tide, a sand bar creates a shallow lagoon that makes an ideal platform for anyone who finds themselves in the water more often than on it. You can improve your technique with help from the Rene Egli Pro Center (see p.174), the best windsurfing school on Fuerteventura.

To the northwest, and set in a pleasant tree-shaded valley, **Costa Calma** is a compact purpose-built resort with its own beach, rocky at its northeast end but golden, sheltered and safe towards the

▼ PLAYA DE COSTA CALMA

PLACES Fuerteventura

southwest. South of Sotavento, and once isolated at the heel of the island, **Morro Jable** started out as an insignificant fishing village, but with a beach as spectacular as the long and lovely **Playa del Mattoral** on its doorstep, the place has grown into a major resort. The centre of the original village, for all its prosperity, is disappointingly shabby and seedy, its saving grace the dramatic situation of its tiny seafront, sandwiched between dark cliffs and pale dunes. From the village, a wide and pleasant coastal path leads all the way along the marvellous beach to the far end of the resort. As well as sunbathing (clothed or otherwise) and swimming, Playa del Mattoral is good for sailing, and there are a few dive sites nearby.

City and resort hotels

Hotel Barceló Fuerteventura

Caleta de Fuste ☎928 16 31 01, ⓦwww.barcelo.com. Large, family beach-hotel with a spa, a sauna and a huge, attractive pool area, within easy reach of the Caleta de Fuste golf course. €98.

Hotel Fuerteventura Playa Blanca

C/Playa Blanca 45, Puerto del Rosario ☎928 85 11 50, ⓦwww.cabildofuer .es. The location of this three-star former *parador* isn't immediately appealing – it's on the edge of the city, on the road to the airport – but it's still the best hotel in Puerto del Rosario, competitively priced and right on the city's only decent beach. The rooms are a decent size, with a measure of old-fashioned elegance, and the restaurant is one of the capital's most upmarket options (see p.159). €84.

Hotel Iberostar Palace

Urb Las Gaviotas, Morro Jable ☎928 54 04 44, ⓦwww.iberostar.com. Concrete abounds in this large, modern four-star complex, but you can't fault the sea views (it fronts onto Playa del Mattoral) and the sense of space – the rooms are bright and a decent size, and there's a large pool terrace. The catering is well above average, and it's particularly popular with German holidaymakers on half-board or full-board packages. €114.

Hotel Kempinski Atlantis Bahía Real

Avda Grandes Playas, Corralejo ☎928 53 64 44, ⓦwww.bahia-real.com.

▼ HOTEL IBEROSTAR PALACE, MORRO JABLE

▲ HOLIDAY APARTMENTS, MORRO JABLE

This spacious and elegant five-star luxury hotel is in a class of its own, styled like an enormous Andalucían palace, with good facilities, a lovely courtyard pool garden, attentive service and a very well-to-do atmosphere. Set on a narrow beach of rocks and creamy sand, it has stunning views of Isla de los Lobos and Lanzarote, but it's rather marooned, as Corralejo has little else to offer people with luxury tastes. €251 (inland view) or €271 (sea view).

Hotel Mariquita Hierro

C/Maria Hierro, El Cotillo ☎928 53 85 98. Modest hotel with well-kept, spacious rooms, and a great rooftop swimming pool. €45.

Hotel Palace Puerto Rosario

C/Ruperto González Negrín 9, Puerto del Rosario ☎928 85 94 64, ⊛www .jmhoteles.com. This medium-sized three-star hotel near the capital's container port has a business-like atmosphere. It's unremarkable, and there's no pool, but it's the most comfortable option in the city centre. €70.

Hotel Riu Calypso

Morro Jable ☎928 54 00 26, ⊛www .riu.com. In a great location on the edge of Morro Jable

village, with direct access to a very attractive stretch of beach, this four-star hotel is smarter than most in the area. Looking straight out to sea, the rooms, their balconies softened with trailing flowers, are arranged in a terrace that cascades down the cliff to a pleasant pool and lush lawn. €143 (inland view) or €184 (sea view).

Hotel Riu Palace El Palacete

C/Acantilado, Morro Jable ☎928 54 20 70, ⊛www.riu.com. Smaller and cosier than the other Jandía hotels, and on the edge of the village, this is a good choice if you're looking for a beach hotel with four-star comfort and the mega-resorts aren't your style. Most rooms have balconies with perfect sea views, and there's a small pool overlooking the beach. €246.

Hotel Riu Palace Tres Islas

Avda Grandes Playas, Corralejo ☎928 53 57 00, ⊛www.riu.com. Built in the 1970s, and showing its age, this is nonetheless a popular resort hotel, serving a regular, middle-aged clientele. In a vast cliff-like block, with a prime out-of-town beachfront location in the Corralejo dunes it's quite a landmark. There are two large, attractive pools, and plenty of other facilities including a buffet restaurant that provides gargantuan spreads for breakfast and dinner. €200 (inland view) or €248 (sea view).

Hotel Risco del Gato

Costa Calma ☎928 54 71 75. Favoured by well-to-do Germans, this luxury five-star hotel set up on a seafront escarpment is strikingly modern, with comfortable single-storey villas, a gym, a spa and a highly regarded restaurant. €130.

Hotel Sol Gorriones

Playa de Sotavento ☎928 54 70 25, ⊛www.solmelia.com. This four-star hotel, recently re-opened after extensive renovations, is windsurf central, with an unrivalled, isolated position right above Sotavento beach. Jumping the waves is the main attraction, but there are also pools and gardens to enjoy. €110.

Rural hotels

Casa Isaítas

C/Guize 7, Pájara ☎928 16 14 02, ⊛www.casaisaitas.com. The pleasant, rustic rooms, pretty courtyard and warm welcome make this beautifully restored farm a delightful village retreat. What's more, there's an excellent little bar-restaurant on site (see p.159). €84.

Hotel Rural Era de la Corte

C/Corte 1, Antigua ☎928 87 87 05, ⊛www.eradelacorte.com. With a charming, family-house feel and friendly owners (who may persuade you into the kitchen to try your hand at a few Canarian recipes), this excellent place was Fuerteventura's first rural hotel. The rooms are good-sized and characterful, and are cool in hot

weather. There are also books to read, sofas to relax on and space to sunbathe, plus a flower-filled patio and a small, attractive swimming pool. €90.

Hotel Rural Mahoh

Sitio de Juan Bello, Villaverde ☎928 86 80 50, ⊛www.mahoh.com. This gorgeous country hotel, founded by an ardent conservationist, has individually designed stone-walled bedrooms, some with four-posters, a small but enticing pool, and a restaurant (see p.160). From €72.

Apartments

Apartamentos Corralejo Beach

Avda Nuestra Señora del Carmen 3, Corralejo ☎928 86 63 15, ⊛www.corralejobeach.com. Brilliantly positioned close to the centre of town and next to a good beach, this three-storey complex has roomy studios and apartments arranged around a huge central pool terrace. €50.

Apartamentos La Gaviota

El Cotillo ☎928 53 85 67. Interesting apartments, close to the sea in the laid-back coastal village of El Cotillo. €64.

Hesperia Bristol Plaza

Urb Lago de Bristol 1, Corralejo ☎928 86 70 20, ⊛www.hesperia-bristolplaya.com. Modern seafront complex of studio apartments, stylish and good value, with three pools and a tennis court. €53.

Guesthouses

Hotel Corralejo

C/Delfín 1, Corralejo ☎928 53 78 27. Old fashioned, and with luridly decorated hallways, the *Corralejo* nonetheless has decent sized rooms and is very close to the action of the Old Town. Popular with bargain hunters. €35.

Hostal Manhattan

C/Gravina 22, Corralejo ☎928 86 66 43. Worth considering if you're on a tight budget, this urban *hostal* has tiny rooms that are clean and tidy, though a little tired. Discounts are available for stays of a week or more. €30.

Pensión Omahy

C/Maxorata 47, Morro Jable ☎928 54 12 54. Simple guesthouse in Morro Jable village itself – one of the few budget options within reach of the incredible Jandía beaches. €24.

Hotel Roquemar

C/Ruperto González Negrín 1, Puerto del Rosario ☎928 85 03 59. This diminutive, friendly seafront guesthouse has spotless rooms, each with a small shower room, and some with a balcony. There's no cafeteria or restaurant, but it's close to a number of local *tascas*. €37.

Restaurants and tapas bars

Antiguo

Hotel Fuerteventura Playa Blanca, C/Playa Blanca 45, Puerto del Rosario ☎928 85 11 50. Daily 1–3.30pm & 8.30–10.30pm. Open to non-residents, this former *parador* restaurant has a pleasant, traditional atmosphere and serves fairly authentic Canarian dishes; it's also a reliable choice for Spanish and international cooking.

Avenida

C/General Prim 11 (corner of C/Pizarro), Corralejo. Tues–Sun 1–4pm & 6–10.30pm. A short walk away from the port, this local-style place serves up hefty piles of reasonably priced Spanish and Canarian dishes, and is very popular with a cheerful local crowd.

Bodeguita El Andaluz

C/Ballena 5, Corralejo ☎676 70 58 78. Evenings only, 7–10.30pm. Closed Wed. Booking recommended. This tiny restaurant on a side street near the port is one of the most upmarket and appealing places in Corralejo, with a menu full of tempting meat and fish dishes from southern Spain, such as pork with paprika, and sizzling shrimps.

Casa Isaítas

C/Guize 7, Pájara ☎928 16 14 02, ⊛www.casaisaitas.com. Mon–Thurs noon–6pm, Fri–Sun noon–10pm. Charming traditional farmhouse bar-restaurant with a

▼ CASA ISAÍTAS, PÁJARA

pretty patio, serving imaginative tapas such as cured tuna with pomegranate seeds, and excellent, simple dishes such as rocket salad, sausages in wine, and *bizcochón* cake with prickly pear and *gofio*. The owners make a point of sourcing top-quality organic ingredients, most of them locally produced.

Casa Santa María

Pl Santa María, Betancuria ☎928 87 82 82. Daily 11am–6pm (summer noon–7pm). Although a little pricey, this German-run restaurant, close to Betancuria's attractive church, is popular for its delightfully creaky, historic atmosphere and excellent traditional cooking – oven-baked leg of kid and roast lamb are specialities. It also has a *cafetería* with good ice cream, coffee and cakes, and there's a craft centre (Mon–Sat 11am–4pm) with a very well-produced audiovisual show attached.

Don Antonio

Pl Peña, Vega del Río de Palmas ☎928 87 87 57. Tues–Thurs & Sun 11am–5pm, Fri & Sat 11am–10pm. A beautiful little rustic-style restaurant that's worth a special trip. It's German-run but the cooking is Canarian, with a sophisticated twist – on an ever-changing menu, you can expect delicacies such as carpaccio of veal fillet and king prawns with Noilly Prat vanilla vinaigrette. The wine list is first-rate, too. Higher than average prices, but worth it.

El Molino de Antigua

1km north of Antigua, on the main road. Tues–Fri & Sun 9.30am–5.30pm, museum entry €1.80. Canarian coffee and beer, plus a full lunchtime menu of local dishes in an attractive old stone building, part of the pleasant Centro de Artesanía Molino.

La Casa del Jamón

C/La Asomada 27, Puerto del Rosario ☎928 53 00 64. Thurs–Sat. Closed Sun–Wed evenings. Family-run, traditional-style restaurant a little out of town, specializing in Basque, Canarian and Spanish cooking (at above-average prices), with particularly good roasted kid, local cheeses and, as the name suggests, excellent ham.

La Laja

Paseo Marítima 1, Morro Jable ☎928 54 20 54. The best of the seafront eateries in Morro Jable village, with waves crashing onto the rocks below, *La Laja* dishes up huge plates of fresh fish for around €15.

La Marisma

C/Pedro Cabrera Saavedra, El Cotillo ☎928 53 85 43. Daily 12.30–11pm. Excellent rustic seafood restaurant in a backstreet of El Cotillo. Generous portions of very good fresh fish.

Mahoh

Sitio de Juan Bello, Villaverde ☎928 86 80 50, ⊛www.mahoh.com. Open to non-residents, this classic rural restaurant has a good reputation for fine Canarian cuisine, and a weekday set menu that's excellent value. While some dishes can disappoint, it's worth trying out their specialities such as pepper stuffed with parrot fish and prawns, or one of the special roasts served on Sundays.

Taberna Tapa Tapa

C/Mirlo 7, off C/Pizarro, Corralejo. Mon–Sat 9am–11pm. Town-centre tapas bar with the authentic flavour of urban Spain. Plates of tapas start at just €1.50, and main meals are good value, too.

PLACES Fuerteventura

Tasca La Lasquita

C/Almirante Lallermand 66, Puerto del Rosario ☎928 85 91 26. With contemporary art on the walls and a warm atmosphere throughout, this grillhouse is one of Puerto del Rosario's better eating-places.

Tío Bernabé

C/Iglesia 17, Corralejo ☎928 53 58 95. Daily noon–midnight. Good for Canarian cuisine, with excellent tapas, and delicious steaks, cooked over eucalyptus wood.

Valtarajal

C/Roberto Roldan, Betancuria. Closed Mon. Typical Canarian cuisine served at roadside tables, close to the centre of this pretty village.

Cafés and bars

Antiguo Café del Puerto

C/Ballena 10, Corralejo. Daily 10am–midnight. Near the harbour, this is much more of a bar than a café; it's a civilized choice for drinks, with a short menu of tapas from €4.

Blue Rock

C/Iglesia 28, Corralejo. Daily 1pm–2am. A popular spot with tourists, locals and expats alike, this bar is best known for its evening sessions of live rock and blues.

Burger la Avenida

C/San Miguel, Morro Jable. Just off Morro Jable's scrap of beach, this café has a bright, young Spanish-urban feel, and is a good place for Canarian coffee or tapas.

Café Latino

Avda Marítima 11, Corralejo. Daily 9.30am–10.30pm, bar open till midnight. With cool, young staff and a lovely little garden terrace overlooking the rocky beach near the port, this is a great place to stop for ice cream or a drink. They also serve salads, tortilla and other light meals at very reasonable prices.

Cafetería Tinguaro V

Pl España, Puerto del Rosario. This busy city-centre rendezvous has views over the port; a good place for *chocolate con churros* in the morning or a drink at any time.

Calle 54

C/Cruz, Puerto del Rosario. On a street that's busy with eating and drinking venues, this attractive little Canarian late-night bar gives wall space to local artists.

Casa Princess Arminda

C/Juan de Bethencourt 2, Betancuria ☎928 87 89 79. Traditional village bar run by a Canarian-Canadian family, a few steps uphill from Betancuria's central square. Beer, wine and tapas in a friendly local atmosphere, with occasional live music.

Ela's Bar

Avda Marítima, Corralejo. Chirpy, British-run harbourside café serving sensibly priced toasties, burgers and English breakfasts.

Surf-Inn

Jandía Playa Beach Center 128, Morro Jable ☎928 54 22 72. With surfing and snowboarding videos, darts, backgammon, cocktails and shakes, this upbeat café-bar attracts a lively young crowd.

Essentials

Arrival

Most visitors to Lanzarote and Fuerteventura arrive **by air**: both islands are served by direct scheduled and charter flights from Europe. A fast and efficient ferry service connects Lanzarote's southern port, Playa Blanca, with Fuerteventura's northern port, Corralejo.

Lanzarote

Arrecife's **Guacimeta Airport** (ACE; ☎ 928 84 60 00, ⊕ www.aena.es) is compact, and arrival procedures are straightforward. Visitors on package holidays are met by their rep in the arrivals hall, which has several ATMs, a bureau de change, a tourist-information point and a row of car-rental desks.
The airport is just off the LZ-2 highway, 5km west of central Arrecife. Approximate taxi fares and journey times from the airport are: Arrecife €8, 10min; Puerto del Carmen €11, 10–15min; Puerto Calero €13, 15–20min; Teguise €15, 20–25min; La Santa €23, 25–30min; Playa Blanca €31, 30–40min; Orzola €37, 40–50min. Buses (*guagua* routes #22 and #23) run from the airport to central Arrecife via Playa Honda roughly every thirty minutes; the fifteen-to twenty-minute trip costs €0.90.

Fuerteventura

Fuerteventura's **El Matorral** airport (FUE; ☎ 928 86 06 00, ⊕ www.aena.es) lies 5km south of Puerto del Rosario and has similar facilities to Guacimeta. Approximate taxi fares and journey times from the airport are: Puerto del Rosario €3, 10min; Corralejo €35, 35min; Morro Jable €75, 50min. Buses from the airport run to Puerto del Rosario and Caleta de Fuste (*guagua* route #3; roughly every 30min; €1.15) and Morro Jable (*guagua* route #10; 3 daily except Sun; €7.70).

Information

Tourist offices in Lanzarote and Fuerteventura (see the box at the beginning of each relevant "Places" chapter for location details) can provide information on accommodation and attractions and have decent free maps of the islands and their resorts. The main branch in **Lanzarote** is in Arrecife (C/Blas Cabrera Felipe ☎ 928 81 17 62, ✉ info@turismolanzarote.com; Mon–Fri 8am–2pm, till 3pm in winter); in

Fuerteventura, the main tourist office is in Corralejo's Plaza Patricio Calero (☎928 86 62 35; daily 8am–2pm in summer, 8am–3pm in winter).

The *Lanzarote Gazette*, a free monthly magazine stocked by some hotels and cafés, is good for listings and articles about upcoming events (☻www.gazettelive.com).

Accommodation

While the majority of visitors to Lanzarote and Fuerteventura book a package with resort accommodation included, most of the coastal **hotels** and **apartment complexes**, including all those listed in this guide, will also accept bookings from independent travellers. Standards on the islands are generally high; there's a growing number of luxury hotels, apartments and villas, and even the cheap package hotels that cater for thousands of visitors each year tend to be reasonably well maintained. In the mid-range hotels, double rooms typically cost €60 to €120 per night; luxury hotels charge between €120 and €200.

For freedom, flexibility and the ability to spread out, **self-catering** is a great option. You'll have much more space than you would in a hotel room and you can set your own timetable. Most apartments and villas have a shared or private pool; some complexes can provide childcare and other services. While some places can be booked for just a night or two, a seven-night minimum stay is often required. Costs tend to be significantly lower than the hotels, particularly if more than two people share one property.

Away from the resorts, both Lanzarote and Fuerteventura have embryonic **rural tourism** movements aimed at visitors who'd like to try something utterly unlike the package-holiday experience. The best of the islands' *casas rurales* and *hoteles rurales* – which may be anything from a converted *finca* in a quiet country village to a rustic cottage with spectacular sea views – are, without exception, original and characterful places to stay, and are covered in the listings at the end of each chapter (for more information on rustic places to stay on Fuerteventura, see ☻ www.ecoturismocanarias.com). To enjoy your stay in the rural areas to the full, you'll almost certainly need to hire a car.

The simple urban **guesthouse** (*pensión* or *hostal*) is far rarer on the islands than in mainland Spain; you'll find a handful in the major towns, with rooms priced around €20–40.

Accommodation rates

The accommodation rates quoted throughout this guide are for two people sharing a standard double room, apartment or villa for one night in high season. Hotel rates quoted include breakfast. A surcharge may apply at peak times such as Easter, Christmas and New Year.

Transport

By far the best way to explore Lanzarote and Fuerteventura is to **rent a car**: public transport on both islands is limited to a skeletal bus service, and while taxis are convenient for short hops in the urban areas they're much more expensive than self-drive over long distances. Another popular option, particularly for those based in the resort complexes, is to take a guided coach **tour** of the major sights.

Buses

Known locally as *guaguas*, Lanzarote and Fuerteventura's **buses** are a cheap way to get around, but their basic network and limited frequency outside the main urban areas means that you'll have to plan carefully if you intend to rely on them for extensive explorations.

On **Lanzarote**, Arrecife's bus station, on Vía Medular (☏ 928 81 15 22), is the hub; the most frequent services cover the routes to Costa Teguise (€0.95), Puerto del Carmen (€1.30) and the airport (€0.90). Most other towns and villages are served by just a few buses a day. A complete timetable is published online at ⓦ www.arrecifebus.com, and also on the "Agenda" page of the Spanish-language daily newspaper *La Voz*.

On **Fuerteventura**, the principal stops for the Tiadhe buses (ⓦ www.tiadhe.com) in Puerto del Rosario are near the junction of Avda Juan de Bethencourt and Avda de la Constitución (☏ 928 85 21 66). The most frequent services run to Corralejo, Caleta del Fuste and the airport.

Taxis

Taxis are easy enough to find in the urban areas: you can phone to book, hire one at a rank or hail one in the street when its green light is illuminated. In the rural areas, booking by phone is the best option. Fares are metered; the minimum charge is €2.54 (6am–10pm) or €3.08 (by night), and there's a supplement of €1.65 for airport trips. Waiting time is charged at an hourly rate. Example fares

are: Puerto del Carmen to Playa Blanca €39; Costa Teguise to Arrecife €9.

Taxi companies

Lanzarote
Airport ☏ 928 52 06 67
Arrecife ☏ 928 81 70 90
Costa Teguise ☏ 928 52 42 23
Haría ☏ 928 83 53 68
Puerto del Carmen ☏ 928 52 42 20
San Bartolomé ☏ 928 52 06 67
Tías ☏ 928 52 42 20
Tinajo ☏ 928 84 00 49
Yaiza ☏ 928 52 42 22 or ☏ 928 83 01 63

Fuerteventura
Airport ☏ 928 85 54 32
Corralejo ☏ 928 86 61 08
Morro Jable ☏ 928 54 12 57
Puerto del Rosario ☏ 928 85 02 16

Cars

Renting a car is the best way to get around the islands, and unless you're on the tightest of budgets, a worthwhile investment.

Most companies offer unlimited mileage, collision damage waver, theft protection and tax as standard, but it's worth checking the details when booking. Prices start at around €120–140 per week for a small car; there's an additional charge for a second driver and for delivery if needed. The majority of companies will rent cars to drivers aged 21 or above but some require drivers to be 25 or older; some also require you to have held your licence for over a year. When driving, you should carry your passport, driving licence and rental agreeement with you.

Traffic drives on the right, and the speed limit is 60km/h in urban areas (unless otherwise indicated), 90km/h elsewhere. Lanzarote and Fuerteventura's **signposts and junctions** can be very confusing (look out for entry and exit ramps to and from the fast lane, and left-hand turns that require you to turn into a right-hand sliproad and stop before crossing the traffic), but the roads are generally well maintained. **Parking** is rarely problematic except in the busiest areas of Arrecife and Puerto del Carmen – zigzags on the road or solid, yellow kerb markings mean parking is prohibited; blue markings mean parking is restricted to short-term pay-and-display; and broken white kerb markings or no markings at all mean free parking.

Petrol stations on the islands are not self-service, so you'll need to wait for the attendant – unleaded petrol (*sin plomo*) costs around €0.80 per litre.

Car-rental companies

The following car-rental agencies have desks at **Arrecife airport**. If you're crossing to Fuerteventura, you can take your car with you (let the company know in advance for insurance purposes). There are also local outfits in all of Lanzarote and Fuerteventura's main urban centres.

Avis ☎928 84 62 45; ⊕www.avis.com
Betacar ☎928 84 62 60; ⊕www.betacar.biz
Cabrera Medina ☎928 84 62 76; ⊕www.cabreramedina.com
Cicar ☎928 84 62 66; ⊕www.cicar.com
Hertz ☎928 84 61 90; ⊕www.hertz.com

Tours

A number of local tour companies run coach **tours** that take in the major sights. Details are posted in all the major resort hotels and, if you're based in one of these, you can book through your holiday rep. The most popular itineraries include trips to Parque Nacional de Timanfaya, Jameos del Agua, Cueva de los Verdes and the La Geria winelands, all of which are just as easy to visit independently if you've hired a car. To really cram it all in, there are various Grand Island Tours on offer: these tend to be pricey at around €60 per person for a half day or up to €110 for a full day.

Inter-island transport

Inter-island **ferry** services transport vehicles and foot passengers between Playa Blanca on Lanzarote and Corralejo on Fuerteventura; there are also ferries serving the smaller islands of La Graciosa (from Orzola) and Los Lobos (from Corralejo), which carry foot passengers only. Details are given in the relevant chapters. It's not normally necessary to pre-book but it's a good idea to turn up at the port 45 minutes or so before departure to buy tickets and get in the embarkation queue.

Food and drink

Few of Lanzarote's resort restaurants specialize in Canarian cooking, preferring to offer impressive renditions of gourmet classics or crowd-pleasing menus of international favourites such as grills, pizza and pasta. That said, most places will include at least a dish or two that could be described as genuinely Canarian, and a few offer an entire menu of *cocina conejera* – the real thing.

Hotel **breakfasts** generally include, at the very least, a continental-style spread; many resort hotels also lay on specialities such as *chocolate con churros* (fingers of batter to dip in hot chocolate), bacon and eggs, or *würst* and cheese to please the palates of Spanish, British and German guests. In a café, the standard morning fare is coffee, fruit juice and pastries or bread. For **lunch**, served from around noon, some restaurants offer a *menú del día* (set menu). More common in Arrecife and the rural areas, this is often excellent value, from as little as €10 for three courses. Restaurants serve **evening meals** from around 7pm. In the resort areas, most close around 11pm, while elsewhere (or wherever the clientele is mainly Spanish) they stay open later.

As you'd expect, **fish and seafood** are often excellent. In a restaurant that has multiple varieties of fish on the menu, it's always best to check out the catch of the day – that way you'll be guaranteed something fresh, rather than frozen.

Fish is generally served grilled or in a stew such as *sancocho* (made with salt fish, potatoes, *mojo* and chickpeas). Favourite **meat** dishes centre around roast kid, goat, rabbit or pork but many restaurants also serve imported beef: if steak is your thing, you should seek out the speciality grills for the best cuts.

Vegetarians should know that traditional vegetable dishes often contain meat – or are made with meat stock. Examples include *garbanzos*, chick peas, often served with spicy sausage, and *puchero canario* – a vegetable casserole with spare ribs, served with oil and vinegar. A safe option is the perennial side

order, *papas arrugadas con mojo*: small, sweet and delicious local potatoes boiled in their skins with sea salt, and served with a garlic dip that's either *rojo* (red, with chili and red pepper) or *verde* (green, with parsley and coriander). An ingredient that crops up in many traditional dishes is *gofio*, sweet ground maize, wheat or barley that's often toasted and mixed into soups, stews and desserts. Canarian goat's cheese, which is very good quality, is sometimes coated in *gofio*.

Traditional **puddings** include *frangollo*, a kind of custard with almonds, raisins and honey, and *bienmesabe*, a pudding made with eggs, coconut and, sometimes, sweet potato or pumpkin. Local **fruit** is available all year round.

Lanzarote's best known **wine** is *vino de malvasía*, a crisp white from La Geria (see p.97). In general, the island's whites are very drinkable, but the reds aren't highly rated, so many restaurants prefer to serve red wine from mainland Spain. Another favourite local tipple is *ron miel* – a syrupy dark **rum** made with honey. Look out for Artemi Oro, made in Gran Canaria, a golden, buttery rum with a strong molasses flavour and a powerful kick. Artemi also make a good three-year-old rum, Artemi Tres Años, aged in oak.

Festivals and public holidays

Every town and village in Lanzarote has an annual **fiesta** to honour its patron saint. This is marked with religious processions bearing effigies of the saint and, sometimes, a *romería* or pilgrimage in traditional costume. It's also an excuse for music, drinking and general revelry. Some important fiestas are celebrated all over the islands.

January
Nuevo Año Jan 1. Public holiday.

Cabalgata de los Reyes Magos Jan 6. Epiphany Parade of the Kings, commemorating the arrival of the Three Wise Men in Bethlehem: three men dressed in cloaks, beards and crowns ride camels through the streets of all the major towns, throwing sweets to the crowd.

February
Nuestra Señora de la Candelaria Feb 2. Candlemas *romería* and fiesta in La Oliva. **Carnaval** Fortnight leading up to Shrove Tuesday. Celebrated everywhere, especially

ESSENTIALS

Sports and activities

Arrecife and Corralejo, with *cabalgatas* (parades of floats and dance groups), *murgas* (satirical singers), pageants, drag shows, fireworks and much drinking of rum. Special events include the Parranda de los Buches or Sailors' Parade, in which costumed participants charge about trying to bop bystanders on the head with inflatable objects (traditionally inflated fish stomachs were used), and the Entierro de la Sardina or Funeral of the Sardine, in which a giant paper fish is paraded through the streets and then set on fire.

March/April
Semana Santa Easter week. Marked by traditional parades.

May
Fiesta del Trabajo May 1. Public holiday.

June
Corpus Christi Date varies. Spanish Catholics all over the world celebrate the feast of the Eucharist by decorating church squares with carpets of petals; in Arrecife and Teguise, where flowers are scarce, coloured salt or sand is used instead.
Fiesta de San Juan June 24. Midsummer bonfires are lit in Haría.

July
Nuestra Señora del Carmen July 16. Patronal fiesta in Teguise, with traditional music, costumes, dancing, wrestling matches and other public events. In Puerto del Carmen, local sailors honour the Virgen del Carmen, patron saint of fishermen, with a maritime parade. Also celebrated in Playa Blanca and Caleta del Sebo.

August
Fiestas del Carmen Aug 1–15. A fortnight of events including parades, musical performances and funfairs marks Puerto del Carmen's patronal fiestas.
Fiestas de San Ginés Aug 1–31 (particularly Aug 25). Lanzarote's patronal fiesta, celebrated all over the island – especially in Arrecife – with processions, dancing and funfairs.
La Asunción de la Virgen Aug 15. Public holiday.

September
Nuestra Señora de los Remedios Sept 8. *Romería* in Yaiza.
Virgen de los Volcanes (Nuestra Señora de los Dolores) Sept 15. Major *romería* to Mancha Blanca followed by a four-day fiesta and craft fair.
Nuestra Señora de la Peña Third Sat in Sept. Fuerteventura's patronal fiesta, with a *romería* to Vega del Río de Palma, and big celebrations.

October
Día de la Hispanidad Oct 12. Public holiday.

November
Todos Santos Nov 1. Public holiday.

December
Christmas Eve (Dec 24) and **Christmas Day** (Dec 25). Towns are decked out with decorations, nativity plays and processions.

Sports and activities

Boat trips and yacht charters

The islands offer plenty of opportunties to mess around in **boats**, from pleasure boat trips and underwater adventures to skippered yacht charters. Puerto del Carmen, Puerto Calero, Marina Rubicón and Corralejo harbours are the best starting points.

Boat-trip companies

Blue Delfin Catamaran C/Teide 30, Puerto del Carmen ☎928 51 23 23, ⊛www .bluedelfin.com. Mini cruises along the coast and to Punta de Papagayo, Fuerteventura and Isla de los Lobos in a pleasure boat with underwater viewing compartments and a sun deck.

Extreme athletics

Held on a Saturday in May, the **Lanzarote Ironman** is the biggest fixture in the island's sporting calendar. Organized by *Club La Santa*, it's one of the toughest triathlons in the world, and you'll see competitors training on the island throughout the year. A full day of gruelling physical punishment kicks off at 7am with a 3.8-kilometre swim in the sea near Puerto del Carmen. Immediately after comes a 180-kilometre bike race that covers the whole island. Then it's time to run a marathon: 42.2km along the south coast. Of the 795 super-fit souls who entered in 2005, 130 failed to complete the challenge. Ain-Alar Juhanson, from Estonia, won the men's race in just under nine hours, while the fastest woman, Virginia Berestegui Luna, of Spain, made it home in just over ten, but the stragglers were still running long after dark. You can register online for the next event at ⊛www.ironmanlanzarote.com.

Just as spectacular an athletic challenge is the **Tres Islas Quadrathlon**, a one-day event held in May by Youths United (⊛www.youthsunited.com). Competitors swim 2km from Isla de la Graciosa to Lanzarote's Playa del Risco, where they run up a 2-kilometre cliff track that climbs to an altitude of 650m, then cycle a 72-kilometre course to Playa Blanca before finally windsurfing, kiteboarding or kayaking their way across to Fuerteventura, 10km away.

Lanzarote's annual **marathon** (⊛www.lanzarotemarathon.com) – tame in comparison at a mere 42.2km on a course that's more or less flat – takes place each December in Costa Teguise. The all-day programme includes shorter events and fun-runs for kids, too.

Canarias Yacht Charter Puerto Calero ☎620 61 55 50, ⊛www.canariasyachtcharter.com. Skippered yachts available to rent for three- or six-hour trips, or for private charter.

Catamarán Catlanza Local 1, Puerto Calero ☎928 51 30 22, ⊛www.catlanza.com. Catamaran cruises from Puerto Calero to Papagayo, lunch and jet-skiing included, for €61 (€35 for kids). A bus collects passengers from Costa Teguise, Playa Blanca and Puerto del Carmen.

Líneas Marítimas Romero C/García Escámez 11, Isla de la Graciosa ☎928 84 20 55. As well as routine ferry trips from Orzola to Caleta del Sebo on La Graciosa, this line runs leisurely cruises from Orzola to Playa de la Francesca.

El Majorero Muelle de Corralejo ☎928 86 62 38. Offers return trips from Corralejo to Los Lobos, and three-hour mini-cruises including a stopover on the islet.

Submarine Safaris Local 2, Puerto Calero ☎928 51 28 98, ⊛www.submarinesafaris.com. Dive to depths of 30m in a 44-seater sub for a spot of underwater sightseeing. Around €45 for adults, €26 for kids.

Yachtaholic Local 1, Puerto Calero ☎690 07 60 16, ⊛www.yachtaholic.com. Offers five-hour cruises in a fifty-foot skippered yacht for €75 per person, plus charters for €500 per yacht.

Cycling

Lanzarote and Fuerteventura's volcanic inclines and high winds can present quite a challenge to **cyclists** – you'll need to carry as much water as you can if you're going on a long ride. It's also important to be extremely traffic-aware, as accidents are not uncommon on the islands' narrow roads and blind corners. While you may

▼ LANZAROTE IRONMAN

see plenty of cyclists in racing gear on the main roads, hiring a mountain bike and riding along minor roads and tracks is a much safer option. La Graciosa is particularly good for its easy-going, traffic-free routes. Lanzarote's best **bike shop** (Cíclomania, C/Almirante Boado Endeiza 9, Arrecife ☎928 81 75 35) rents bikes for €10 per day; you'll also find rental places in Caleta del Sebo, Puerto del Carmen, Costa Teguise and Corralejo.

Golf

Lanzarote's well-established 18-hole golf course is green and pleasant – quite an achievement on this arid island – and its popularity has inspired developers to start work on a new course just outside Tías, plus another in Playa Blanca, due for completion in 2007. **Fuerteventura's** golfing facilities are also expanding rapidly with new courses being built near Pajara, El Cotillo, Puerto del Rosario and Morro Jable.

Golf clubs

Golf Costa Teguise Avda del Golf, Costa Teguise ☎928 59 05 12, ⊛www.lanzarote-golf.com. See p.114.
Fuerteventura Golf Club Ctra de Jandía, Km 11, Caleta de Fuste ☎928 16 00 34. Quality 18-hole, par-70 course, with practice facilities including a driving range and a large putting green.

Hang-gliding and paragliding

The cliffs of El Risco de Famara on Lanzarote offer exciting **hang-gliding** conditions for experienced pilots who have the skills to tackle the unusually strong winds. On calmer days, it's also possible to **paraglide**. The British Hang-gliding and Paragliding Association (⊛www.bhpa.co.uk) sells a map showing the best sites (€7). Lanzarote's principal hang-gliding and paragliding club, Delta Club Zonzamas (☎928 81 52 03, ⊛www.zonzamas.com) offers hang-gliding tuition in two-person gliders with qualified instructors; an introductory tandem flight costs €60.

Helicopter tours and scenic flights

On clear days, a tour by **helicopter** or **light aircraft** offers a thrilling new perspective on Lanzarote's dramatic landscapes.

Tour companies

Heli TourService Canaria ☎690 68 04 77 or 676 70 16 93, ⊛www.helitourservice.com. Runs thirty-minute sightseeing trips by helicopter for €166 and fifty-minute trips for €266 on Fri, Sat and Mon.
Lanza Air CC Charcos 20, Costa Teguise ☎928 59 05 33, ⊛www.lanzaair.com. Scenic flights in a four-seater plane, from €66 per person for just over an hour.

Jeep safaris, quad-biking and go-karting

A novel way to explore the islands' backroads and tracks is to set off cross-country on a **jeep** or **quad-bike** tour; just as much fun, and not quite as dusty, are Lanzarote's **go-karting** tracks.

Tour companies and go-kart tracks

Tamarán Jeep Safaris CC Hoya 18, Puerto del Carmen ☎928 51 24 75, ⊛www.tamaran.com. Discover Lanzarote's lesser-known tracks and back roads in a convoy of 4x4 vehicles.
Mega Fun CC Costa Mar, Pocillos, Puerto del Carmen ☎928 51 28 93, ⊛www.megafun-lanzarote.com. Rents quad bikes and organizes guided quad-bike safaris along scenic backroads and over sand dunes.
Go-Karting San Bartolomé San Bartolomé, ☎928 52 00 22. Smaller than the Tías centre, but well equipped.
Gran Karting Club Lanzarote La Rinconada, Tías, off the LZ-2 near the airport ☎619 75 99 46, ⊛www.grankarting.com. Competition-standard tracks, plus a small one for young children.

Scuba diving and snorkelling

Lanzarote and Fuerteventura's underwater world is not going to knock you out, but it's worth a look, and conditions are generally favourable all year round. The best **scuba diving** sites are around Puerto Calero, Isla de la Graciosa and Isla de los Lobos, where the visibility is surprisingly good, and you're likely to see moray, barracuda and angel sharks, plus plenty of algae, sponges and interesting rocks. Boat trips tend to be short, as the water gets deep quickly once you're offshore. There are a few shore diving sites, too. Lanzarote has over a dozen diving centres and schools, most of which offer try-dives and PADI courses; to qualify as an Open Water Diver costs around €400 for a three days of tuition including four ocean dives. Costs for qualified divers are typically €30 per dive, or €40 with full gear; divers also need a local permit, which the dive shops can supply. Most dive shops are open Monday to Saturday.

Playa Chica, Playa de la Barrilla and the beach at Charco del Palo in Lanzarote are all good for **snorkelling**. You can expect to see parrot fish, groupers and maybe, hidden in the rocks, moray eels.

Scuba-diving companies

Calipso Diving Avda Islas Canarias, Costa Teguise ☏928 59 08 79, ✆www .calipso-diving.com. Long-established outfit covering the coast from Mala to Puerto del Carmen and running BSAC and PADI training courses.
Dive Center Corralejo C/Nuestra Señora del Piño, Corralejo ☏928 53 50 96, ✆www.divecentercorralejo.com. A good centre from which to head out to the waters around Isla de los Lobos.
Island Watersports Dive Centre Local 4, Puerto Calero ☏928 51 18 80, ✆www .divelanzarote.com. Efficient, British-run outfit with a good dive shop, which runs trips around Puerto Calero, southern Lanzarote and Los Lobos.
MA Diving C/Juan Carlos I 35, Puerto del Carmen ☏928 51 69 15, ✆www.madiving .com. Makes regular visits to the best local sites such as the Cathedral, a huge, clear underwater cave.
Marina Rubicón Diving Center Marina Rubicón 77B, Playa Blanca ☏928 34 93 46, ✆www.rubicondiving.com. Well-equipped and highly professional dive school. Nitrox and rebreather training available, plus courses for kids. Daily trips by rib plus weekly outings to Los Lobos.

Safari Diving Playa de la Barilla 4, Puerto Carmen ☏928 51 19 92, ✆www .safaridiving.com. Well-established Dutch-run outfit offering a comprehensive schedule of training courses at reasonable prices; qualified divers can rent equipment and dive independently or with a guide, either from the shore or from a boat.

Swimming

All the major resort hotels and apartment complexes, and many of the smaller ones, have swimming **pools** for their guests. Some of the best include the *Gran Meliá Salinas* (Costa Teguise), the *Los Jameos Playa* (Puerto del Carmen), the *Princesa Yaiza* (Playa Blanca) and the *Iberostar Palace* (Morro Jable) – all of which grant access to non-guests, too.

The best **beaches** for swimming are Playa Grande and Playa Blanca in Lanzarote and, in Fuerteventura, Playa Costa Calma and Playa del Mattoral.

Costa Teguise has a **water park**, Aquapark (see p.114), and there's a newer, better one in Corralejo (Baku; see p.150).

Walking and hiking

Setting out on foot is an excellent way to appreciate Lanzarote and Fuerteventura's unusual terrain and delicate flora and fauna. The most rewarding **routes** take you to spectacular viewpoints that are impossible to reach by car, such as the Risco de Famara cliffs, the Atalaya de Femés and the Tremesana lava fields (only accessible on guided hikes; see p.104). It's even possible to scale dormant volcanoes and climb into their calderas. All you need is a little planning, a good map, a generous supply of water and a sense of adventure.

Windsurfing, kiteboarding and surfing

Strong winds and reliable conditions make both Lanzarote and Fuerteventura world-class **windsurfing** and **kiteboarding** destinations. On Lanzarote, while beginners can get to grips with the basics in the safe waters off Playa de las Cucharas in Costa Teguise, the open water offers plenty of challenges for the more experienced: the **Professional Windsurfers Association Championships** (@ www .pwaworldtour.com) are held here in July. In Fuerteventura, the Peninsula de Jandía is windsurfing and kiteboarding central: Playa de Sotavento hosts the **Windsurfing and Kiteboarding World Cup** (@ www.fuerteventura-worldcup.org) over a fortnight in July and August, shallow tidal lagoon on the beach is a good training ground.

For **surfers**, Lanzarote's biggest waves are found near La Santa, Playa de San Juan, Playa de Famara and Risco de Famara. The **La Santa Surf Pro Surfing Championship** is held in this area each October (see p.128). For information on breaks and tides, check out @ www.lanzarote.com/surf. The UK-based company Pure Vacations (@ www .purevacations.com/surf) run **surfing trips** to Lanzarote and Fuerteventura.

Schools and rental companies

Calima Surf C/Achique, Caleta de Famara ☎626 91 33 69, @ www .calimasurf.com. Runs surfing and kiteboarding classes from beginners up, including seven-day packages; can also provide local accommodation.
Club Nathalie Simon C/Olas 18, Costa Teguise ☎928 59 07 31, @ www .sportaway-lanzarote.com. Rents out windsurfing gear, and runs classes for various levels of proficiency.

Costa N-Oeste C/Montaña Clara 9, Caleta de Famara ☎928 52 85 97, @ www.costanoroeste.com. Runs surfing and kitesurfing courses and holidays.
Famara Surf Avda Marinero 39, Caleta de Famara ☎928 52 86 76, @ www .famarasurf.com. Surf classes, a surf shop and very reasonably priced apartments to rent in Caleta de Famara.
Flag Beach Windsurf & Kitesurf School C/General Linares 31, Corralejo ☎928 86 63 89, @ www.flagbeach.com. Strong on tuition, offering beginners three-day windsurfing courses for €120 and two-day kiteboarding courses for €220, plus improver sessions and hourly private tuition for the more experienced.
René Egli Pro Center Hotel Sol Gorriones, Sotavento ☎928 54 74 93, @ www .rene-egli.com. Fuerteventura's leading centre for windsurfing and kiteboarding, with training from beginner to championship level, plus kids' courses. World Cup events take place here in July and August. The shop is one of the best places in the world to pick up equipment, including used sails at bargain prices.

Wrestling

Generally a spectator sport, and often an integral part of the islands' patronal fiestas, wrestling (or *lucha Canaria*) as a test of machismo is a popular feature of traditional fiestas. Adversaries offer each other a formal greeting and the two then grapple; no punching or kicking is allowed. The aim is to force your opponent to let any part of his body other than the soles of the feet touch the ground – so, one finger down, and you're out.

Directory

Addresses Common abbreviations (used throughout this book) include: C/ for Calle (street), Ctra for Carretera (highway), Avda for Avenida (Avenue), CC for Centro Commercial (shopping centre), Pl for Plaza (square), Urb for Urbanización (housing development).
Banks and exchange The currency in the Canary Islands is the euro (€), which, at the time of writing, was selling at approximately

€1.46 for £1, €0.84 for $1. Banks are open Mon–Fri 9am–2pm & Sat 9am–1pm.
Consulates British Consulate Edifico Cataluña, Luis Morote 6, 35007 Las Palmas de Gran Canaria ☎928 26 25 08; **Irish Consulate** C/León y Castillo 195–1ºdcha, 35004 Las Palmas ☎928 29 77 28; **American Embassy** C/Serrano 75, 28006 Madrid ☎91 587 2200
Credit cards For lost or stolen cards, con-

tact VISA/Mastercard ☎915 19 60 00 or American Express ☎902 37 56 37.

Customs For customs purposes the Canary Islands do not count as part of the EU. The current limits on what you can import to the UK without paying duty are 2 litres of still wine, 1 litre of spirits or liqueur over 22 percent volume or 2 litres of fortified wine; 200 cigarettes or 250g of tobacco or 50 cigars, and 60cc of perfume or 250cc of cologne. You can also bring back £132 of all other goods including gifts and souvenirs, but no more than 50 litres of beer or 50 lighters.

Dialling codes International dialling code (+34) then the nine-digit number to dial the islands from abroad; +00 to dial abroad from the islands.

Electricity 220/240 volts AC, with standard European two-round-pin plugs.

Emergency services For police, ambulance and fire brigade, call ☎112.

Hospitals and medical services Lanzarote: Hospital General, Ctra Arrecife-Tinajo km 1.3, Arrecife ☎928 59 50 00, Hospital Insular de Lanzarote, C/Juan de Quesada s/n, Arrecife ☎928 81 05 00, Clínica Lanzarote ☎900 10 04 50, Hospiten Lanzarote, C/Lomo Gordo s/n, Puerto del Carmen ☎900 70 77 77. **Fuerteventura**: Hospital General de Fuerteventura Ctra Aeropuerto km 1, Puerto del Rosario, Puerto del Rosario ☎928 86 20 00. British visitors are entitled to free medical treatment under the Spanish Health Service; private treatment can be extremely expensive. There are pharmacies (faramacías) in all urban centres; several are open 24hr on a rota published in the local press. They sell antibiotics over the counter as well as painkillers and other standard medicines.

Internet Many hotels offer coin-operated Internet access to their guests, and a few rent out modems or allow access to their wireless network for a daily charge, but it's generally more economical to use an Internet café: there are a small number of these in the major towns.

Mail Lanzarote's main post offices are in Arrecife, on the seafront (Mon–Fri 9am–2pm) and in Puerto del Carmen, next to the Biosfera shopping centre (Mon–Fri 8.30am–2.30pm & Sat 9.30am–1pm). Public post boxes are yellow; some hotel receptions have their own collection box. Deliveries outside Spain and the Canaries can be quite slow – it can take up to ten days for a postcard to reach the UK.

Maps The free maps available from tourist offices are useful but if you're planning to do much exploring by car, by bike or on foot you'll need something more detailed. By far the best maps of Lanzarote are David and Ros Brawn's *Lanzarote 1:75,000 Indestructible Map* (The Indestructible Map Company) and *Lanzarote 1:40,000 Tour and Trail Map* (Discovery Walking Guides). A clear road map showing both islands is published by Michelin (no.221, *Lanzarote 1:150,000 & Fuerteventura 1:175,000*).

Markets Weekly markets selling a variety of crafts, clothing, jewellery and gifts take place in Parque Ramírez Cerdá on the Arrecife seafront (Wed 9am–3pm), Marina Rubicón in Playa Blanca (Wed 9am–2pm), Pueblo Marinero in Costa Teguise (Fri 6–9pm), Terraza Concorde in Playa Honda (Sat 9.30am–2pm), and, most famously, Teguise (Sun 10am–2pm).

Newspapers The Lanzarotean Spanish language daily is *La Voz*. British newspapers are sold at resort shops and supermarkets.

Nude sunbathing Head for the Papagayo beaches near Playa Blanca or the coves at Charco del Palo. If you're discreet, nude sunbathing is also tolerated in the more secluded areas of the Playa de Famara, the Orzola beaches, Playa de Quemada, Isla de La Graciosa, the Corralejo dunes, the El Cotillo beaches and Playa del Mattoral. Hotels that have areas set aside for nude sunbathing include the *Los Jameos Playa* (Puerto del Carmen) and the *Timanfaya Palace* (Playa Blanca).

Shopping hours Shops are typically open from 9am or 10am to 8pm or 9pm and may close in the afternoon between 1pm and 4pm or 5pm.

Police Arrecife ☎928 81 13 17, San Bartolomé ☎928 52 07 12, Teguise ☎928 84 52 52, Tías ☎928 83 41 01, Yaiza ☎928 83 01 07. In an emergency, call ☎112.

Radio Stations broadcasting in English include: Power FM (91.5 & 91.7FM), with chart music and local news from Lanzarote plus BBC World Service progammes; QFM (98.0FM), based in Corralejo and covering Lanzarote and Fuerteventura; and Holiday FM (98.2 & 105.5 FM), which has no local content but broadcasts hit music from the UK to resorts all over Europe. Popular local Spanish-language commercial stations include: Radio Cristal (92FM) and Radio Lanzarote (90.7FM). Stations from Radio Nacional de España include Radio 1 (92.5FM), for news and interviews; Radio Clásica (94.9FM), for classical and avant-garde contemporary music; Radio 3 (102.8FM), for popular music and culture; and Radio 5 (100.2), for news.

Tax IGIC (the Canary Islands' VAT) of 5 percent is added to bills for purchases and services including hotel and restaurant bills. The IGIC on car rental is 13 percent.

Time Lanzarote and Fuerteventura are in the same time zone as the UK and Ireland (GMT), making them five hours ahead of the US east coast and eleven hours behind east-coast Australia.

Tipping In restaurants, bars, cafés and taxis it's normal to round up to the nearest euro (for small sums), or add five to ten percent.

TV Lanzarote receives five terrestrial channels from mainland Spain plus local stations TV Canaria and LTV (Lanzarote Television).

Most hotels and many self-catering villas and apartments have satellite TV.

Visas As a Spanish territory, the Canary Islands belong to the EU, meaning that EU citizens do not require a visa, and that citizens of Australia, Canadia, New Zealand and the US do not require a visa for stays of up to ninety days.

Water The islands' tap water is desalinated and, though safe to drink, varies considerably in flavour from area to area. The locals drink bottled water: plain (*agua sin gas*) or mineral (*agua con gas*). Natural water supplies are very limited, so it's important to conserve water wherever possible.

Language

Spanish

For beginners, **Spanish** is the easiest language there is, and even in Lanzarote and Fuerteventura, where English is widely spoken, you'll get a lot more out of your encounters with the Canarians if you try to communicate in their own tongue. For more than a brief introduction to the language, pick up a copy of the Rough Guide **Spanish Dictionary Phrasebook**; be aware, however, that Canarian pronunciation is slightly different to that of mainland Spain.

Pronunciation

The penultimate syllable of each word is **stressed**, unless there's an acute accent to denote otherwise – hence *América* is pronounced as in English.

When a word **ends in S**, this is often dropped – so *buenas noches* is pronounced "BWE-na NO-che".

Word endings of *-fe*, *-se* and *-te* are pronounced as a syllable, hence "Tenerife" is "te-ne-RI-feh", "Teguise" is "te-GHEE-seh" and "Lanzarote" is, of course, "lan-za-RO-teh".

A somewhere between the A sound of "back" and that of "father".

E as in "get".

I as in "police".

O as in "hot".

U as in "rule".

C is spoken like an S before E and I, hard otherwise: *gracias* is pronounced "GRA-see-ass".

CH is pronounced as in English.

G is a guttural sound (like the "ch" in loch) before E or I, a hard G elsewhere – *gigante* becomes "hi-GAN-te".

H is always silent.

J is the same as a guttural G: *jamón* is "ha-MON".

LL sounds like an English Y: *tortilla* is pronounced "tor-TEE-ya".

N is as in English unless it has a tilde (accent) over it, when it is pronounced like the "ni" in "onion", so *mañana* is "ma-NYA-na".

QU is pronounced like an English K, so *queso* is "KE-sso".

R is rolled, RR doubly so.

V sounds more like B, *vino* becoming "BEA-no".

X has an S sound before consonants, but is the same as a guttural G before a vowel: *maxorata* to "maho-RA-ta".

Z is pronounced like an S, so *cerveza* is pronounced "ser-VE-ssa".

Words and phrases

Basics

si, no, vale	yes, no, OK
por favor, gracias	please, thank you
de nada	you're welcome
¿dónde? ¿cuando?	where? when?
¿qué? ¿cuánto?	what? how much?
¿cuánto es?	how much is it?
aquí, allí	here, there
esto/a, eso/a	this, that
abierto/a, cerrado/a	open, closed

Words and phrases

con, sin	with, without
bueno/a, malo/a	good, bad
gran/grande, pequeño/a	big, small
barato, caro	cheap, pricey
caliente, frío	hot, cold
más, menos	more, less
precioso/a, bonito/a	lovely, pretty
exacto, incorrecto	correct, incorrect

Greetings and responses

¡hola!	hello!
buenos días	good morning
buenas tardes	good afternoon/ evening
buenas noches	good night
¿como está?	how are you?
¿qué tal?	how's it going?
bien, gracias	fine thanks
muy bien	very well
adiós, hasta luego	goodbye, see you later
lo siento / disculpe	sorry
perdón	excuse me
no entiendo	I don't understand
no hablo español	I don't speak Spanish
¿habla inglés?	do you speak English?
¿como te llamas?	what's your name?
me llamo…	my name is…
soy inglés/a / escocés/a / galés /a / irlandés/a / australiano/a / canadiense/a / americano/a / neozelandés/a	I'm English / Scottish / Welsh Irish / Australian /Canadian / American / New Zealander

Transport and directions

llegadas	arrivals
salidas	departures
avión	plane
barco	boat
guagua	bus
bicicleta	bicycle
coche	car
gasolinera	petrol station
lleno, por favor	fill it up, please
¿sabe…?	do you know…?
no sé	I don't know
¿dónde está…?	where is…?
¿por dónde se va a…?	how do I get to…?

izquierda, derecha	left, right
todo recto	straight on
el banco más cercano	the nearest bank
la playa	the beach
el mercado	the market
la tienda	the shop
el mar	the sea
la estación de guaguas	the bus station
¿de dónde sale la guagua para… ?	where does the bus to… leave from?
quisiera un billete para…	I'd like a ticket to…
ida y vuelta	return
¿a qué hora sale?	what time does it leave?
aquí, por favor	here, please

Numbers

1	un / uno / una
2	dos
3	tres
4	cuatro
5	cinco
6	seis
7	siete
8	ocho
9	nueve
10	diez
11	once
12	doce
13	trece
14	catorce
15	quince
16	dieciséis
17	diecisiete
18	dieciocho
19	diecinueve
20	veinte
21	veintiuno
30	treinta
40	cuarenta
50	cincuenta
60	sesenta
70	setenta
80	ochenta
90	noventa
100	cien
101	ciento uno
200	doscientos
500	quinientos
1000	mil

Time and dates

a las seis da la mañana	at six in the morning
a las nueve de la tarde	at nine in the evening
ahora, más tarde	now, later
ahora mismo	right now
hoy, mañana	today, tomorrow
ayer	yesterday
el año pasado	last year
temprano, tarde	early, late
lunes	Monday
martes	Tuesday
miércoles	Wednesday
jueves	Thursday
viernes	Friday
sábado	Saturday
domingo	Sunday
enero	January
febrero	February
marzo	March
abril	April
mayo	May
junio	June
julio	July
agosto	August
setiembre	September
octubre	October
noviembre	November
diciembre	December

Hotels, restaurants and bars

quiero	I want
quiesiera	I'd like
¿hay… ?	is there…
no hay	there isn't
por favor, deme (uno así)	please give me (one like that)
tiene… ?	do you have… ?
tengo…	I have…
una habitación	a room
con dos camas /cama matrimonial	with two beds/ double bed
con ducha, con baño	with a shower/ bath
con vista del mar	with a sea view

balcón, terraza	balcony, terrace
piscina	swimming pool
cocina	kitchen
junto al / a la…	next to the…
cerca del / de la…	near the…
es para una persona	it's for one person
para dos personas	for two people
para una noche	for one night
una semana	one week
¿se puede ver?	can I take a look?
¿se puede probarlo?	can I try it?
una mesa para dos	a table for two
reservación	reservation
a comer	to eat
a beber	to drink
desayuno	breakfast
almuerzo	lunch
cena	dinner
menú del día	set lunch menu
vegetariano/a	vegetarian
alergia	allergy
ración pequeña	small portion
por favor, un poco más	a little more please
para niños	for children
cuchillo	knife
tenedor	fork
cuchara	spoon
delicioso/a, muy rico/a	delicious
¡que rico!	how delicious!
terminado/a	finished
servicios / baños	loos
señoras / damas	ladies
señores / caballeros	gentlemen
me gusta mucho	I like it very much
no me gusta	I don't like it
la cuenta	the bill
IGIC incluido	VAT included
servicio no incluido	service not included
aquí tiene	here you are
por favor, firma aquí	sign here, please

Food and drink

Cooking terms

a la marinera	with seafood, garlic, onions, wine
a la parilla	grilled over charcoal
a la plancha	grilled on a hot plate
a la romana	fried in batter
al ajillo	with olive oil and garlic
al horno	baked or roasted
asado	roast
picante	spicy

Meat and fish

ahumados	smoked fish
albóndigas	meatballs
almejas	clams
anchoas	anchovies
atún	tuna
bacalao	salt cod
beicon	bacon
bistec	steak
boquerones	pickled anchovies
burgados	winkles
caballa	mackerel
cabrito	kid
calamares	squid
cangrejo	crab
carne	meat
cerdo	pork
cherne	sea bass
chipirónes	baby squid
chorizo	spicy sausage
conejo	rabbit
congrio	eel
cordero	lamb
empanada	savoury pie
espada	sword fish
estofado	stew
filete	steak
gambas	prawns
higado	liver
jamón de york	roasted ham
jamón serrano	cured ham
jareados	sundried fish
lapas	limpets
lenguado	sole
mariscos	seafood
mejillones	mussels
merluza	hake
mero	grouper
ostra	oyster
morena	moray eel
pescado	fish
pollo	chicken
potaje canario	thick soup of fish stock, meat and vegetables
puchero canario	stewed meat and vegetables
pulpo	octopus
ropa vieja de pescado	chickpea stew with chunks of white fish
salchicha	sausage
sama	local white fish
sancocho	salt-fish stew
sardinas	sardines
ternera	veal
tocino	bacon
tollas	Canarian dried fish
vieja	parrot fish
zarzuela	fish stew

Vegetables and accompaniments

aceite	oil
aceitunas	olives
aliño	dressing
alioli	garlic mayonnaise
arroz	rice
berenjena	aubergine
bocadillo	sandwich
especial	spice
cebolla	onion
champiñones	mushrooms
croquetas	croquettes
ensalada	salad
garbanzos	chick peas
gofio	sweet toasted corn
huevo	egg
lechuga	lettuce
mantequilla	butter
mojo	garlic dip
pan	bread
papas arrugadas	potatoes boiled in their skins
patatas fritas	chips
pimienta/os	pepper/s
queso	cheese
queso de cabrito	goat's cheese
revueltos	scrambled eggs
sal	salt
salsa	sauce
sopa	soup
tomate	tomato

tortilla potato omelette
verdures vegetables
vinagre vinegar

Desserts

azúcar sugar
bienmesabe egg and coconut pudding
flan crème caramel
frangollo custard with almonds, raisins, honey
fresa strawberry
fruta fruit
frutos secos dried fruit and nuts
helado ice-cream
higo fig
manzana apple
melón melon
melocotón peach
mermelada de tunera cactus jam
miel honey
naranja orange
nata cream

nueces nuts
pastel, tarta cake or flan
postre dessert
piña pineapple
plátano banana
sandía watermelon

Drinks

agua con gas fizzy water
agua sin gas still water
bebidas drinks
una botella de… a bottle of…
café con leche white coffee
café cortado espresso with a shot of milk
café solo black coffee
caña small glass of beer
cerveza beer
copa de tinto glass of red wine
leche milk
ron miel honey rum
té tea
vino (blanco/ rosado/tinto) (white/rosé/red) wine
zumo de naranja orange juice

Glossary

ahumedería smokery
avenida avenue
ayuntamiento town hall
barranco gorge, or small valley
bodega winery; can also be a wine-bar
cabalgata Carnival parade of floats
calle (usually abbreviated to C/) street or road
casa rural country guesthouse
CC (centro comercial) shopping and entertainment mall
Conejeros native Lanzaroteans
dragos type of tree, sacred to the aboriginal islanders
ermita hermitage or chapel
guagua local name for buses
iglesia church
jable local name for the flat, sandy, fertile terrain found in central Lanzarote

jameito blind crustacean that inhabits subterranean lakes
jameo volcanic bubble
juguete del viento wind mobile (literally, "wind toy")
línea bus route
lucha Canaria Canarian wrestling
mahos/majos aboriginal islanders (Lanzarote/ Fuerteventura)
majo an island dialect
malpaís badlands
menú del dia daily menu in a restaurant
mercadillo craft market
mirador view point
molino/molina (one-storeyed/two-storeyed) windmills
paseo a stroll, often in the late afternoon
picón volcanic gravel used in vineyards to catch water

pinchos	Basque-style tapas dishes	terraza	outdoor bar
playa	beach	timple	Canarian instrument, similar to the guitar
plaza	square		
rascadero	traditional musical instrument made of bones	veleta	weather vane
romería	a holy pilgrimage	zocos	dry-stone walls that protect vines from the wind
tasca	local-style café-bar		

Travel store

ROUGH
GU

For more information go to www.roughguides.com

Visit us online
www.roughguides.com
nformation on over 25,000 destinations around the world

- **Read** Rough Guides' trusted travel info
- **Access** exclusive articles from Rough Guides authors
- **Update** yourself on new books, maps, CDs and other products
- **Enter** our competitions and win travel prizes
- **Share** ideas, journals, photos & travel advice with other users
- **Earn** points every time you contribute to the Rough Guide
  community and get rewards

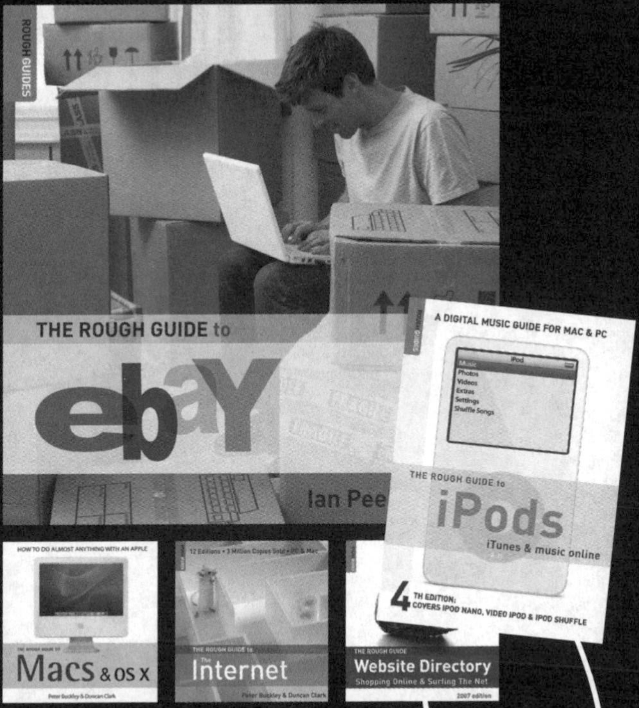

WHEREVER YOU ARE,

WHEREVER YOU'RE GOING

WE'VE GOT YOU COVERED!

Rough Guides Travel Insurance

Visit our website at www.roughguides.com/insurance or call:

🕾 UK: 0800 083 9507

🕾 Spain: 900 997 149

🕾 Australia: 1300 669 999

🕾 New Zealand: 0800 55 99 11

🕾 Worldwide: +44 870 890 2843

🕾 USA, call toll free on: 1 800 749 4922

Please quote our ref: **Rough Guides books**

Cover for over 46 different nationalities and available in 4 different languages.

SMALL PRINT Notes

small print & Index

SMALL PRINT

A Rough Guide to Rough Guides

In 1981, Mark Ellingham, a recent graduate in English from Bristol University, was travelling in Greece on a tiny budget and couldn't find the right guidebook. With a group of friends he wrote his own guide, combining a contemporary, journalistic style with a practical approach to travellers' needs. That first Rough Guide was a student scheme that became a publishing phenomenon. Today, Rough Guides include recommendations from shoestring to luxury and cover hundreds of destinations around the globe, including almost every country in the Americas and Europe, more than half of Africa and most of Asia and Australasia. Millions of readers relish Rough Guides' wit and inquisitiveness as much as their enthusiastic, critical approach and value-for-money ethos. The guides' ever-growing team of authors and photographers is spread all over the world.

In the early 1990s, Rough Guides branched out of travel, with the publication of Rough Guides to World Music, Classical Music and the Internet. All three have become benchmark titles in their fields, spearheading the publication of a range of more than 350 titles under the Rough Guide name, including phrasebooks, waterproof maps, music guides from Opera to Heavy Metal, reference works as diverse as Conspiracy Theories and Shakespeare, and popular culture books from iPods to Poker. Rough Guides also produce a series of more than 120 World Music CDs in partnership with World Music Network.

Visit www.roughguides.com to see our latest publications.

Rough Guide travel images are available for commercial licensing at www.roughguidespictures.com

Publishing information

This first edition published **September** 2006 by Rough Guides Ltd, 80 Strand, London WC2R 0RL. 345 Hudson St, 4th Floor, New York, NY 10014, USA.

Distributed by the Penguin Group
Penguin Books Ltd, 80 Strand, London WC2R 0RL
Penguin Group (USA), 375 Hudson Street, NY 10014, USA
14 Local Shopping Centre, Panchsheel Park, New Delhi 110017, India
Penguin Group (Australia), 250 Camberwell Road, Camberwell, Victoria 3124, Australia
Penguin Group (Canada), 10 Alcorn Avenue, Toronto, ON M4V 1E4, Canada
Penguin Group (New Zealand), Cnr Rosedale and Airborne Roads, Albany, Auckland, New Zealand
Typeset in Bembo and Helvetica to an original design by Henry Iles.
Printed and bound in China

Rough Guide credits

Text editor: Keith Drew
Layout: Ankur Guha
Photography: Emma Gregg
Cartography: Animesh Pathak
Picture editor: Jj Luck

Proofreader: Helen Castell
Production: Katherine Owers
Design: Henry Iles
Cover design: Diana Jarvis

SMALL PRINT

The author

Emma Gregg, a regular visitor both to the Spanish mainland and islands and to Africa, loves the eastern Canaries for their windy days, warm nights and thought-provoking landscapes. Based in the UK, she contributes travel writing and photography to numerous publications and is the editor of *Travel Africa* magazine. She is also the co-author of *The Rough Guide to The Gambia*.

Acknowledgements

The author would like to thank everyone who assisted her in researching and writing this first edition, including: Almudena Castro of the Spanish Tourist Office, Rita Martín and Enrique Alvarado of the Patronato de Turismo de Lanzarote, Michael Müggler of *Heredad Kamezí*, Damian Hidalgo of *Casa Tomarén*, Gonzalo Bethencourt of *Caserío de Mozaga*, Mercedes Fernández of *Casa Isaítas*, Pedro Perello of Sol Meliá, Daniela Moser of Las Casas Canarias, Tatiana Polonkova of the *Casona de Yaiza*, Alan and Gill Nugent of *Cabreras Sol*, Alba Mingo of Iberostar, Claudia Schunk of Riu, Blanca Pérez of *Casa Tegoyo*, Iñaki Fuentes of the *Hotel Lancelot*, Stefanie Basner of the *Arrecife Gran Hotel*, Lyng Dyrup of *Bungalows Playa Famara*, Caroll Hartington of Villa Holidays, Brigg Ford of the *Lanzarote Gazette*, Willem de Meerleer, Cathy Visser of the Fundación César Manrique, Christian Niehoff of Helitours and Helen Atkinson of Rubicón Diving. Grateful thanks also go to all the team at Rough Guides, especially Keith Drew, Claire Saunders, Simon Bracken and Jj Luck. Finally, extra special thanks go to Nathan Pope for support and encouragement and for sharing his enthusiastic appreciation of Lanzarote's finest beaches and restaurants.

Photo credits

All images © Rough Guides except the following:

Front cover picture: Jameos del Agua © Alamy/Cesar Manrique
Back cover picture: Man leading pack of camels © Bob Krist/CORBIS
p.11 Helitour © Willem de Meerleer/Helitours
p.11 Cueva de los Verdes © Alan Copson City Pictures/Alamy
p.15 Apartamentos Lanzarote Park © Iberostar
p.23 Hotel Palace Jandia, Morro Jable, Fuerteventura © Riu
p.26 Biking © mediacolor's/Alamy
p.27 Helicopter flying along the coast of Isla de los Lobos © Willem de Meerleer/Helitours
p.27 Hang-gliding near Famara © Delta Club Zonzamas
p.27 Scuba diver diving with Rubicon Divers, Lanzarote © Helen Atkinson
p.27 Ironman © Asiphoto
p.29 Baku Water Park © Baku Water Park

p.29 Kikoland kids' club, Playa Blanca © Kikoland/Princesa Yaiza
p.32 Carnival band, Arrecife © Lanzarote Gazette
p.32 Wrestling © Lanzarote Gazette
p.33 Festival © Pat Behnke/Alamy
p.33 Entierro de la Sardina, Arrecife © Lanzarote Gazette
p.33 Cabalgata de los Reyes Magos © Lanzarote Gazette
p.33 Virgen de los Volcanes, Ermita de los Dolores © Willem De Meer
p.42 Hotel Gran Melia Volcan © Sol Melia
p.73 Cesar Manrique © Pablo Neudstadt/Fundacion Cesar Manrique
p.105 Hotel Costa Calero, Puerto Calero © Iberostar
p.156 Hotel Palace Fuerteventura, Morro Jable © Iberostar
p.171 Ironman © Asiphoto

Index

Maps are marked in colour

INDEX

INDEX